THE
MAN WHO
INVENTED FICTION

THE
MAN WHO
INVENTED
FICTION

*How Cervantes Ushered in the Modern
World*

WILLIAM EGGINTON

B L O O M S B U R Y
NEW YORK · LONDON · OXFORD · NEW DELHI · SYDNEY

Bloomsbury USA
An imprint of Bloomsbury Publishing Plc

1385 Broadway	50 Bedford Square
New York	London
NY 10018	WC1B 3DP
USA	UK

www.bloomsbury.com

ISBN: HB: 978-1-62040-175-0
       ePub: 978-1-62040-176-7

LIBRARY OF CONGRESS CATALOGING-IN-PUBLICATION DATA HAS BEEN APPLIED FOR.

2 4 6 8 10 9 7 5 3 1

Typeset by RefineCatch Limited, Bungay, Suffolk
Printed and bound in USA by Berryville Graphics Inc., Berryville, Virginia

To find out more about our authors and books visit www.bloomsbury.com. Here you will find extracts, author interviews, details of forthcoming events and the option to sign up for our newsletters.

Bloomsbury books may be purchased for business or promotional use. For information on bulk purchases please contact Macmillan Corporate and Premium Sales Department at specialmarkets@macmillan.com.

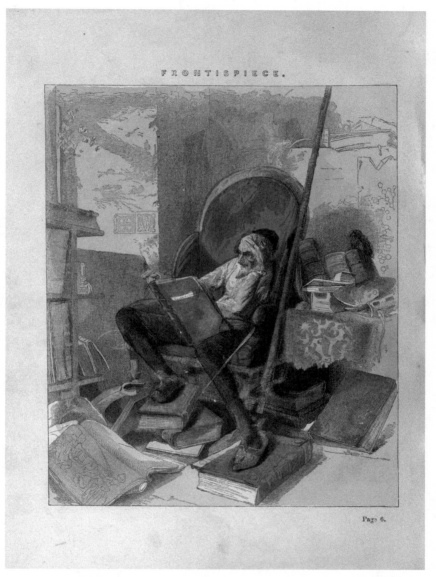

FRONTISPIECE.

Page 6.

Sir Marvellous Crackjoke, with illustrations by Kenny Meadows and John Gilbert, *The Wonderful Adventures of Don Quixote and Sancho Panza Adapted for Youthful Readers*. London: Dean & Son, 1872. George Peabody Library, the Sheridan Libraries, Johns Hopkins University

For my wife, Bernadette, and our children, Alexander, Charlotte, and Sebastian—readers every one.

CONTENTS

Introduction: Within and Without   xi

1. Poetry and History   1
2. Open and Closed   23
3. Soldier of Misfortune   47
4. A Captive Imagination   71
5. All the World's a Stage   93
6. Of Shepherds, Knights, and Ladies   117
7. A Rogue's Gallery   141
8. The Fictional World   163

Acknowledgments   185
A Note on the Sources   187
Notes   189
Bibliography   213
Index   227

INTRODUCTION

Within and Without

Something strange happened in the winter of 1605. At the heart of the world's most powerful empire, in a time of economic decline and political stagnation, word started spreading about, of all things, a book. The dealers quickly sold out; those who could read passed increasingly threadbare copies from hand to hand; and those who could not read began to congregate in inns, village squares, and taverns to hear the pages read aloud.

Packed in tightly around worn wooden tables, clutching goblets of acrid wine and warmed by a smoky hearth, those fortunate enough to be in attendance when a literate benefactor declaimed the opening words were not treated to an epic rendering of heroic deeds, a lyrical paean to a shepherd's love, or a pious reflection on the martyrdom of a beloved saint. Instead, as they washed back their dregs and squeezed in closer to get a better seat, they were among the first to hear these now immortal opening words: "Somewhere in La Mancha, in a place whose name I do not care to remember, a gentleman lived not long ago . . ."[1]

It would not be long until the tipsy crowd was cackling in delight over the misadventures of what would become world literature's most recognizable protagonist: a rickety, geriatric member of the lower gentry who, foolish enough to have traded in much of his land for countless books of chivalry, "became so caught up in reading that he spent his nights reading from dusk till dawn and his days reading from sunrise to sunset, and so with too little sleep and too much reading his brains dried up, causing him to lose his mind."[2] In this state the pitiful gentleman has the strangest thought any lunatic in the world ever had, which was that it seemed reasonable and necessary for him, both for the sake of his honor and as a service to the nation, to become a knight errant and travel the world with his armor and his horse to seek adventures and engage in everything he had heard that knights errant engaged in, righting all manner of wrong and, by seizing the opportunity and placing himself in danger and righting those wrongs, winning eternal renown and everlasting fame.[3]

How they howled with laughter as they heard for the first time the exploits of this ridiculous geezer wandering a countryside they recognized as their own, and coming face-to-face with the kinds of people they spent their days with, the kinds of people they were likely rubbing shoulders with as they listened to his tale: mule drivers and scullery maids, farmers and prostitutes, barbers and innkeepers.

For the first half hour our tavern crowd is treated to the circus it came for: the aging madman mistakes a shabby inn for a castle, its owner for a noble knight, and two common wenches for exquisite ladies. He requests the boon of an official dubbing from the wily innkeeper, who knows his tales of chivalry enough to keep in character even as the hapless hero wreaks havoc on the innkeeper's guests and provokes giggles in the ladies of easy virtue. And he chastises a farmer for beating his servant, but then trusts in his chivalry enough to send them off again together with a mere promise of recompense, to the farmer's sly delight and the servant's enduring agony. The story that our tavern crowd is hearing is pure and bawdy satire, an unbridled ribbing of an impoverished and degenerate gentry anaesthetized by the clichéd literature of a previous century.

Well into their second or third round of libations, our tavern goers hear how the aged gentleman comes to realize he is missing something, and resolves "to return to his house and outfit himself with everything, including a squire, thinking he would take on a neighbor of his, a peasant who was poor and had children but was very well suited to the chivalric occupation of a squire."[4] At home for two weeks, the delusional knight convinces his peasant neighbor to join him, promising him upon completion of their quest an island—which he insists on calling, in proper epic form, by its Latinate name, an *insula*—insouciant to the geographically inconvenient fact that they are wandering around the arid plains of central Spain, many days' travel from any significant body of water.

The introduction of this stout, simple neighbor changes everything—for the listeners in the tavern and for us, their literary descendants. Until Don Quixote seeks out Sancho Panza (for these, of course, are the characters I have been describing), he is but a foil, a rube—a brilliantly crafted one, for sure, but nonetheless an object of derision that our tavern fellows would feel comfortable ridiculing. At the time, the mentally ill were protected from prosecution from certain crimes, but they were not protected from abuse, marginalization, or being used as the butt of the joke for a populace starved for entertainment. Having found Sancho Panza, though, Quixote suddenly becomes something quite different.

Within a page or two of setting off together, the two companions encounter their most iconic adventure:

> "Good fortune is guiding our affairs better than we could have desired, for there you see, friend Sancho Panza, thirty or more enormous giants with whom I intend to do battle and whose lives I intend to take, and with the spoils we shall begin to grow rich, for this is righteous warfare, and it is a great service to God to remove so evil a breed from the face of the earth."
>
> "What giants?" said Sancho Panza.
>
> "Those over there," replies his master, "with the long arms; sometimes they are almost two leagues long."
>
> "Look, your grace," Sancho responded, "those things that appear over there aren't giants but windmills, and what looks like their arms are the sails that are turned by the wind and make the grindstone move."[5]

Predictably, famously, Don Quixote does not heed his good squire's commonsense admonitions, but instead charges ahead, spearing the enormous sail of a windmill's arm with his lance and being lifted, horse and all, off the ground and smashed back down in a miserable, aching heap. Sancho's reaction to his mishap, though, is different from those that greeted all Quixote's previous antics. Where the others treated Quixote as a spectacle, entertainment, or a nuisance, Sancho responds with compassion. Seeing his master lying next to his fallen horse and shattered lance, Sancho

> hurried to help him as fast as his donkey could carry him, and when he reached them he discovered that Don Quixote could not move because he had taken so hard a fall with Rocinante.
>
> "God save me!" said Sancho. "Didn't I tell your grace to watch what you were doing, that these were nothing but windmills, and only somebody whose head was full of them wouldn't know that?"[6]

From the limited outlook of his own simplicity, Sancho sees his master fail, sees the calamitous consequences of his delusions, and yet decides to accept him despite them: "'It's in God's hand,' said Sancho. 'I believe everything your grace says, but sit a little straighter, it looks like you're tilting, it must be from the battering you took when you fell.'"[7]

In the space of a few pages, what started as an exercise in comic ridicule and, as the narrator insists on several occasions, a satirical send-up of the tales of chivalry, has taken on an entirely different dimension; it has begun to transform itself into the story of a relationship between two characters whose incompatible takes on the world are bridged by friendship, loyalty, and eventually love. When deep in the second part (published ten years after the first) a mischievous duchess elicits Sancho's confession that he does indeed know that Quixote is mad, and then accuses him of being "more of a madman and dimwit than his master" for following him, Sancho replies:

> "If I were a clever man, I would have left my master days ago. But this is my fate and this is my misfortune; I can't help it; I have to follow him: we're from the same village, I've eaten his bread, I love him dearly, he's a grateful man, he gave me his donkeys, and more than anything else, I'm faithful; and so it's impossible for anything to separate us except the man with his pick and shovel."[8]

As the great German scholar Erich Auerbach wrote of Sancho's attachment to Quixote, the former "learns from him and refuses to part with him. In Don Quijote's company he becomes cleverer and better than he was before."[9]

The firelight flickering across the faces of our eager listeners registers no pall cast by this change; the raucous tavern crowd continues to laugh as before. Yet as the innkeeper shouts for last call and starts to close up shop, as the stragglers put their empty cups down and make for the door, chattering about the tale and making plans to return the next evening so as not to miss what happens next, something imperceptible to them has happened. The crowd that arrived that first evening was used to ridicule; they were fluent in the language of satire. With *Don Quixote* they were learning a new language. Today we call that language fiction.

Most of us if asked would probably define fiction as an untrue story we read for entertainment, in full knowledge that it's not true. And certainly that much is accurate. But think about what actually happens to us when our eyes start reading the words on the page or the characters in our favorite show start to interact with one other. In a memorable scene from F. Scott Fitzgerald's *The Great Gatsby*, Nick Carraway's mind drifts out of the apartment where he is entangled in some debauchery and imagines how "high over the city our line of yellow windows must have contributed their share of human secrecy to the casual watcher in the darkening streets, and I saw him too, looking up and wondering. I was within and without, simultaneously enchanted and repelled by the inexhaustible variety of life."[10]

Like Nick, when we engage with fiction we are both within and without the story we are reading or watching; we are simultaneously ourselves, locked into our own particular view on the world, and someone else, maybe even someone very different from us, feeling how he or she inhabits a very different world from ours. And like Nick we can, on the pages of our book or the screen before our eyes, be simultaneously enchanted and repelled by the inexhaustible variety of life. That ability to experience different and at times even contradictory realities without rejecting one or the other is one of the main reasons we are so drawn to fiction, in all its forms.

This is no simple feat. It took our culture millennia of technological and intellectual developments to refine the practice of fiction into the forms it has taken on today; and that process will surely continue. The essence of fiction, though—in which we experience different worlds and perspectives and the emotions they generate as if they were our own, without ever giving up the knowledge that we are, in fact, elsewhere—assumed its present form roughly four hundred years ago. And while he benefitted from centuries of wisdom and techniques passed down by the writers and thinkers who came before him, the man who, more than any other, innovated and combined the techniques used to make fiction today was not a scholar in the Renaissance mode, protected and financed by princes and free to dedicate himself to a life of learning. Rather, he was a soldier, an adventurer, a prisoner, and a debtor who, after countless attempts and as many failures, toward the end of his life penned the book that would provide the model for all fiction to come.

That man was Miguel de Cervantes Saavedra. The book he published in 1605 was called *The Ingenious Gentleman Don Quixote of La Mancha*. As much to his surprise as to anyone else's, Cervantes's book became an international bestseller, bringing him fame, if not fortune, until his death eleven years later. His renown continued to spread after his death, until *Don Quixote* became what it is today: widely acknowledged as the first modern novel and one of the most important and influential works of literature of all time.

When Cervantes published his book he didn't think of it as fiction in the same way we understand the word today. In his time the term was used almost exclusively to denigrate or dismiss an account as false or invented. Literary theorists had learned from commentaries on the ancient Greek philosopher Aristotle to distinguish between *history*, what did happen, and *poetry*, what could have happened but didn't. Poetry could *delight* the reader; but in the words of the Roman rhetorician Horace, another classical favorite of the day, for it to be deemed worthwhile, it would have to *instruct* as well—that is, poetry should say what is *both* pleasurable and morally good.[11]

What we call fiction today is different from either the history or poetry known to readers before Cervantes's time. For a prose narrative to be fictional it must be written for a reader who knows it is untrue and yet treats it for a time as if it were true. The reader knows not to apply the traditional measure of truthfulness for judging a narrative; he suspends that judgment for a time, in a move that the poet Samuel Taylor Coleridge popularized as "the willing suspension of disbelief," or "poetic faith."[12] He must be able to occupy two opposed identities simultaneously: a naïve reader who believes what he is being told, and a savvy one who knows it is untrue.[13] In order to achieve this

effect, the author needs to pull off a complex trick. At every step of the way a fictional narrative seems to know both more and less than it is telling us. It speaks always with at least two voices, at times representing the limited perspective of its characters, at times revealing to the reader elements of the story unknown to some of or all those characters.

This ability of the fictional perspective to be simultaneously within and without is what permits an author to create *characters* in the sense we understand the word today.[14] For modern readers, fictional characters need to seem "real" even when we know they are not. We admire authors who create characters that are "three-dimensional," or who seem to "step off the page," just as we are critical or indifferent to "flat" or "one-dimensional" characters. And while they are clichés, these metaphors say a lot about what we expect in a character and how the author achieves it.

A character comes alive in this way when the point of view of the narrative is able to shift from describing the character externally to portraying how he perceives and emotionally inhabits the world, as if the reader were stepping into a molded hollow in the book's world and looking out through its eyeholes. That point of view, of course, is defined as much by what the characters cannot see as by what they do see, as much by their misperceptions as by their knowledge. Characters begin to stand out by virtue of the contrasts between how they experience the world and how their fellow characters do. Furthermore, characters that are drawn this way ignite our emotions and invite us to empathize with them, because they seem similar to us even if they come from worlds that are impossibly far away.[15] Their very blindness convinces us of their existence, even while we fully grasp they are constructs on a page. Like us, they are bewildered by the intentions of others, strive and often fail to grasp the world around them, and yearn for greatness while often settling for a laugh and a good meal.

Cervantes's brilliance at creating characters that feel real depended in part on his rich descriptions and his attentiveness to their voices; but underlying all his characters was his fascination with how differently people might experience the same situation, and how real emotions, from laughter to despair, can flow from that experience. Don Quixote's passionate attachment to the ideals he has learned in his books clouds his ability to distinguish fantasy from reality; in a similar way, what makes all Cervantes's characters stand out are the idiosyncrasies and differences in how each inhabits his or her world, the passions that bind them to those perceived worlds, and the feelings produced by characters' successes or failures at crossing those divides.

HOW DID HE DO IT? How did this adventurer and soldier; crippled in the service of his king and country; kidnapped and held in slavery in the dungeons of Algiers for five long years; who returned to his country hoping in vain to be granted a post worthy of his name and sacrifices; who was reduced to collecting taxes for an unpopular government; who was sued and sent to prison on multiple occasions— how did this man invent a way of writing that would be so different from what came before it and have such a profound impact on what would follow?

Born in 1547 in Alcalá de Henares, a university town at the heart of the world's most powerful empire, Cervantes lived, until his death in 1616, at a time of enormous changes that profoundly influenced how European societies and their colonial descendants evolved. Where Europe's political landscape had been organized into feudal fiefdoms, principalities, and city-states, the sixteenth century saw the emergence of powerful nation-states covering vast areas and exerting control through complex and wide-reaching bureaucracies. Where medieval political power mostly took the form of a direct relation of respect and coercion between vassals and their lord, modern political power would depend on large populations being mobilized to believe in the legitimate authority of men whom they seldom if ever encountered.[16] In order to inspire such mass devotion, leaders began to use new media like the printing press and the public theaters to guide popular opinion. In doing so, they learned that symbols—by inspiring feelings of pride and of belonging to the state and also hatred and fear of outsiders—could be more effective even than coercive force for controlling a populace.

These changes paralleled transformations in other spheres of life. In the arts the development of perspective since the fourteenth century gradually allowed for more lifelike portrayals of people and places. A modern theatrical industry was evolving in which actors could portray characters from far-off worlds as if they were right there on

the stage. Great scientists such as Copernicus, Kepler, and Galileo forged a new understanding of the universe that was no longer enclosed and centered on the earth, along with new methods for objectively and more accurately measuring and understanding it. Finally, it was during this time that the European powers sought to expand their influence across a globe that had recently become accessible to them, and the new avenues of trade and the monetary systems that emerged helped generate the global economy that still thrives today, for both good and ill.

Despite the particularities of these transformations, they had certain basic aspects in common. Like cartographers drawing a map of a land they themselves inhabited, people were learning to experience the world from two perspectives simultaneously: an internal, subjective one, in which they encountered others like themselves, face-to-face, on a daily basis; and an abstract, externalized one, an objective *reality* in which they could imagine themselves as pieces in a much larger picture. In such a world, people could both look out at the cosmos from the earth under their feet and, at the same time, begin to conceptualize that world objectively, as if from some imagined, external point. Or they could sit in the audience of a theater looking at a stage and simultaneously imagine themselves as a character in the world being portrayed. One could be a villager, an innkeeper, a courtier, or a king and still feel with pride one's identity as citizen of a powerful global empire. People, in other words, were learning to experience the world simultaneously from within and without.[17]

During that same period, Spain's sense of identity and worth as a people and a geopolitical power had achieved unprecedented heights and then fallen precipitously to shatter on the hard rocks of economic and political reality. So prevalent was the sense of lost promise in the culture at large that the age became identified with the concept of *desengaño*, which means disillusionment or disappointment. As the great historian J. H. Elliott once noted, "The crisis of the late sixteenth century cuts through the life of Cervantes as it cuts through the life of Spain, separating the days of heroism from the days of *desengaño*."[18] And indeed it does seem as though Cervantes's life, from the impetuous glories of his youth to the disappointments of his old age and the extraordinary creativity that accompanied it, dovetailed to a curious degree with Spain's own destiny.

A student and intellectual, Cervantes was forced to flee his homeland as a young man after wounding another man in a duel. Joining the forces of the Catholic League in Italy, he experienced firsthand the Spanish state's violent confrontations with Islam in the Mediterranean. En route back to Spain as a decorated hero, he was captured by Barbary pirates and held in squalid captivity for five years, during which time he experienced both the depravities and the humanity of an enemy culture. Ransomed at last, he regained a homeland that seemed to have forgotten his sacrifices and that was intent on covering the patent failures of its domestic and foreign policy with a patchwork of religious fanaticism and ethnic scapegoating. Rebuffed and humiliated repeatedly in his quest for reward and recognition for his service, the aging warrior returned to his first love, writing, eventually producing *Don Quixote* along with a trove of other great works.

Strangely, it seems that Cervantes's unparalleled literary success was forged by a life of almost continuous failure, for the relentless frustration of his youthful aspirations, and the disillusionment he felt at seeing his beliefs deflated by the reality of his experience, became the engine of his invention of fiction. In focusing his attention on how we perceive and inevitably misperceive our reality, he was prompted by his own disillusion to imagine how the fellow humans in all their inexhaustible variety whom he encountered in his adventurous life perceived and misperceived theirs.

His own disappointments in turn seemed to prime him to be unusually attuned to the suffering and misfortune of others. In a time and a culture when xenophobia was the national religion, when the poor were assumed to have deserved their lot, and when women were thought to be naturally subservient to men, Cervantes regularly used his writing to explore the feelings and experiences of religious and ethnic minorities, social outcasts, and women. He not only depicted those fellow humans from his own perspective, but he also learned how to describe what they might be feeling and thinking from what he imagined to be their perspectives. He encountered people, but he turned them into characters.

In turning people into characters, far from objectifying them, Cervantes was learning how to inhabit their worlds. After a youth colored by nationalism, honor, and war, his life of defeat and humiliation wrought not hatred and resentment but understanding, sympathy, and kindness. Recent generations of scholars have labeled as hagiographic the earlier great biographies of Cervantes that glorify his genius and heroics while glossing over any potential flaws. While I have no wish to turn the man into a saint, reading his work in light of his life, one cannot escape the sense, above all, of Cervantes's deep and pervasive goodness, of a love for his fellow humans that transcends their differences—all the more striking in a time and culture besotted with hatred and violence toward others. Many geniuses have built their legacy on condescension toward their fellow humans; Cervantes was not one of them.

While writers and intellectuals of the time recognized the widespread *desengaño* and commented on it, merely experiencing frustration in his own life and recognizing it in the social circumstances around him were not enough to make Cervantes the inventor of a new mode of writing. What makes Cervantes's writing unique is how he drew on his disillusionment to shape not only *what* he was writing about, but also *how* he wrote. A great lover and patron of the nascent theater and an experienced playwright, Cervantes was drawn to the form of the spectacle itself, to the distance between an actor and the role he is playing, and the sort of commitments made by the public that allow the magic of the theater to take place at all. One way Cervantes achieved his innovation was thus by importing into his writing an idea he learned from the theater: that we can play roles without believing in them; and that this difference between what a person seems to be on the outside and what he or she feels or thinks on the inside is essential when creating a character and making it come to life.

Like a playwright including a play within a play, who divides his characters into actors playing other characters and audience members on the stage, Cervantes made his books be about books, and the characters in his books into readers and interpreters of other characters in those books. He was realizing in his writing what Shakespeare had his character Jaques famously proclaim in his play *As You Like It*: "All the world's a stage, and all the men and women, merely players."[19] In Cervantes's version of this famous metaphor, we men and women are players because our selves are divided into the characters we portray for the benefit of others and the actors who don those roles. We are performing for our fellow men and women all the while striving to understand what motivates their performances. We are all wearing our own masks while trying to see the truth behind each other's masks.

It's hard not to see in his two greatest characters, Don Quixote and Sancho Panza, an extension of Cervantes's own struggles with belief and idealism, loss and disappointment. As his moribund state wrapped itself in a mantel of religion and blood purity, Cervantes at first, like any young man at the time, devoted himself to Spanish identity and its touchstone, honor. Like Don Quixote, he dreamed of "righting all manner of wrong and, by seizing the opportunity and placing himself in danger and righting those wrongs, winning eternal renown and everlasting fame."

But loss and failure, captivity and abandonment, and his experience of the empty label that honor had become in his time eroded that youthful zeal. Although he easily could have fallen back on a jaded cynicism like many of his compatriots, Cervantes maintained a love for that ideal, even as he recognized and derided his own naïveté in loving it. Don Quixote and Sancho embody those tangled sentiments of love and derision. In the one we see Cervantes's own passionate attachment to ideals he knew his society had abandoned; in the other we see his refusal of the false ideals that had taken their place. For where Don Quixote remains devoted to a real honor that no longer exists, Sancho could not care less about the fake one that took its place. Cervantes must have seen something of himself in both of them.

Cervantes's work incorporated, reacted to, and was shaped by the myriad changes taking place around him and that led to the modern world. The style he invented was the expression of a world in flux, and he helped give that flux a literary shape. And since he went on to become arguably the most widely read author of all time,[20] his way of writing had enormous influence on how subsequent generations wrote stories, made arguments, and in general perceived themselves and others. In addition to the more obvious impact he had in literature and the arts, his work even influenced thinkers whose writings would later lay the foundations for developments in politics, economics, and science. Adrift in a time of tumultuous change, Cervantes invented fiction to help him digest and understand his world; and that fiction in turn helped give birth to ours.

With the publication of *Don Quixote*, Cervantes created one of the world's first runaway, international bestsellers.[21] From its publication in the early days of 1605 to the present, *Don Quixote* has become the most published work of literature in history.[22] More than that, its influence on writers who have followed has been unparalleled. In the words of the critic Harold Bloom, *Don Quixote* is a novel that "contains within itself all the novels that have followed in its sublime wake."[23] When the Norwegian Nobel Institute polled one hundred leading fiction writers to name the single most important work of literature in history, more than half of them named *Don Quixote*; no other author's work came close. In 1997, *Life* magazine declared the book's publication one of the hundred most important events of the millennium.[24]

The popularity of *Don Quixote* at the time of its publication, while impressive in itself, pales in comparison with the book's impact over the centuries since then. Not only would it become the template for all novels to come, but it also became a keystone of Western intellectual culture, read and appreciated by thinkers from David Hume and Baruch Spinoza to Hegel and the German Romantics, who went so far as to call it the first sign of a truly modern consciousness. While this co-optation has irked some literary scholars who believe it to stem from a misreading of Cervantes's intention, there can be no doubt that these thinkers saw something essential and new at work in Cervantes's prose, regardless of what he intended. When he handed his manuscript over to his publisher in Valladolid more than four hundred years ago, the aging, impoverished, and crippled veteran of the world's most powerful empire did something no one at the time could have foreseen: he encoded in a new form of writing the emerging modern world.

This book explores Cervantes's life and his world in order to show how he was able to achieve the innovation he did. It describes both how the works he wrote—especially his immortal *Don Quixote*—emerged from his life and influences, and how they have changed the course of literary and intellectual history since then. Many years ago the great Spanish literary scholar Américo Castro wrote that Spain, for all its prominence in world history, had produced not a single innovation of importance.[25] To my mind, Castro was blinded by his proximity to one of the greatest innovations in human history. With this book, I hope to cast a new light on what fiction is and to show how it was that Miguel de Cervantes came to invent it.

1.

Poetry and History

A few other details were worthy of notice, but they are of little relevance and importance to the true account of this history, for no history is bad if it is true.

If any objections can be raised regarding the truth of this one, it can only be that its author was Arabic, since the people of that nation are very prone to telling falsehoods, but because they are such great enemies of ours, it can be assumed that he has given us too little rather than too much. So it appears to me, for when he could and should have wielded his pen to praise the virtues of so good a knight, it seems he intentionally passed over them in silence; this is something badly done and poorly thought out, since historians must and ought to be exact, truthful, and absolutely free of passions, for neither interest, fear, rancor, or affection, should make them deviate from the path of the truth, whose mother is history, the rival of time, repository of great deeds, witness to the past, example and adviser to the present, and forewarning to the future.

O n a hot August day in 1604, a man walked through the dusty streets of Valladolid, Spain, clutching in his right hand a heavy package. In the absence of any authentic portraits, we must trust his own words to know that he was brown-haired and silver-bearded, with an aquiline (but well-proportioned, he adds) nose and cheerful eyes partly hidden behind a pair of smeared spectacles resembling, in the words of one of his literary rivals, badly fried eggs.[1]

Of medium build, and missing most of his teeth, which was common enough in those times for a man just shy of sixty years, he

CERVANTES.

Nineteenth-century rendition of Cervantes, from Cervantes, *El Ingenioso Hidalgo Don Quixote De La Mancha*. Nueva ed., London: Lackington, Allen, y Co., 1814. George Peabody Library, the Sheridan Libraries, Johns Hopkins University

had lost the use of his left hand many years earlier, when he was hit by a harquebus shot while boarding a Turkish galleon at the Battle of Lepanto. His clothes, from the wide ruff collar around his neck to the woolen stockings exposing the hardened muscles of his calves, would have broadcast to his fellow pedestrians his status as a member of the gentry, just as their ragged state would have advertised his precarious financial straits.

Even though just recently arrived, the man was hardly a stranger to his neighbors in Valladolid's meatpacking quarter, the *rastro de carneros*, where he and his wife, two sisters, a niece, and his illegitimate daughter by another woman occupied the floor above a raucous tavern. The *rastro* was on the outskirts of a town that, in 1604, could not keep pace with its exploding population. The rush of newcomers driven by the transfer of King Philip III's court from Madrid three years earlier had brought new life and glamour to Valladolid, but it had also imposed a severe housing crisis. While the government tried to control growth and crowding by issuing zoning laws limiting the city's brightly colored buildings to two stories, the city's savvy landlords responded by constructing houses with hidden stories in the back. Thus the man's motley clan was not alone in the landlord Juan de Navas's house; all told, there were some twenty tenants living in its thirteen rooms, almost all of them friends or relations of Miguel de Cervantes Saavedra.[2]

As the aging soldier stepped gingerly over the rivulets of blood and offal that cut through the district's dirt-and-stone streets, his one good arm hugged that heavy package tightly to his chest. In it were hundreds of sheets of paper, each sheet packed to the margins with the neat, slanted hand of a professional scribe. Cervantes's own more rounded, slightly meandering script, which overflowed the many more hundreds of pages of his blotted, scratched, and corrected manuscripts, can be seen today on few precious remnants: a signed document from his 1597 stay in Seville's municipal jail, where it is thought that he first dreamt up *Don Quixote*; a letter to the Archbishop of Toledo; and some itemized accounts.

None of his original manuscripts survive. In fact, very few manuscripts from that period do. At the time, the very idea of saving manuscripts would have seemed most unusual. An original manuscript, which by the nineteenth century would be endowed with an almost mystical connection to the genius of the author, was more likely to be seen as an imperfect starting point, a draft to be jettisoned once a more reliable source for the printers was available. No, Cervantes would have followed the practice of the time (especially for such a large book) of handing the original pages over to a professional scribe who would have compiled them into a *copia en limpio*, or "clean copy," and, in the process, added spacing and punctuation that could easily have been missing from the author's manuscript.[3]

For this was the heyday of a burgeoning, modern print industry, and Cervantes was hoping desperately to reap a share of its growing profits. Literacy rates had exploded during the previous century, and for the first time in history large chunks of the population could read, including, astoundingly, a growing number of people outside the

Facsimile of Letter from Cervantes to the Archbishop of Toledo, from Henry Edward Watts, *Miguel de Cervantes, His Life and Works*. London: Adam and Charles Black, 1895. George Peabody Library, the Sheridan Libraries, Johns Hopkins University

clergy and nobility: commoners and townspeople, merchants and farmers.[4] We see the presence and influence of books in the very first pages of Cervantes's great novel, where he describes the aging gentleman who will become Don Quixote as being so consumed with books that "in his rash curiosity and folly he went so far as to sell acres of arable land in order to buy books of chivalry to read."[5] And while these books are the ostensible cause of Quixote's madness, they also quickly become the subject of commentary by and heated exchange among the novel's legions of characters, no matter their station in life. As Quixote is escorted home after his first ill-fated outing, his household is in an uproar, with his housekeeper lambasting his books at the top of her voice, crying, "Woe is me! Now I know, and it's true as the death I owe God, that those accursed books of chivalry he's always reading have driven him crazy."[6] The housekeeper's complaints are seconded by Quixote's niece and his friends the village priest and barber, as the group proceeds to rifle through his library, tossing the books they find there out the window and into the corral below to be burned.

But their enthusiastic foray into book burning, a task usually reserved for the Inquisition, soon founders on the mixed opinions some of them have formed of the books themselves. Thus, after a long series of comments on the relative merits and flaws of books he is clearly very familiar with, Quixote's friend and neighbor the village priest suggests that two be spared and the rest thrown away, at which point Master Nicolás, the barber, pulls out another book that ought to be saved, and the whole process reignites, until the group again becomes distracted and thus never gets around to burning anything. Books, it is clear, have become ubiquitous objects, things not only to read, but also to buy, exchange, argue about, despise, and fall in love with. As the priest says upon seeing in the barber's hands the title *The Tears of Angelica*, a book published in 1586 by Luis Barahona de Soto, "I would have shed [tears] myself if I had sent such a book to be burned."[7]

The sale of books to a burgeoning mass market was an outgrowth of a technological innovation born about one hundred fifty years earlier, itself one of the very first examples of the mass production that would become the signature of the industrial age. A mechanical printing press using moveable letters molded into quadrangular bits of metal was the brainchild of Johannes Gutenberg, a financially strapped goldsmith with a luxuriant beard and piercing eyes who was living in the city of Mainz when the first of his almost two hundred Bibles rolled off the press. The ability of a printer to set the type for one page, spread an oil-based ink onto its metal surface, and proceed to press out any number of virtually identical copies of that page before resetting the type and starting on the next page—this was an innovation that perhaps more than any other helped usher in the modern world.[8]

Prior to 1450 most knowledge had to be maintained and communicated by memory, oral tradition, or books painstakingly copied by hand, word for word. Now any tome considered worthwhile reading had no other upper limit on the number of copies it engendered than its printer's reckoning of potential demand against the costs of his materials and labor. The works of theology, literature, and history that had previously found multiple readers had been disseminated through the extraordinary efforts of rooms full of patient monks slowly losing their eyesight through countless hours of tediously copying and often illuminating manuscripts for the wealthy and powerful to own, perhaps to read, but more frequently to put on display as emblems of their taste and learning. Now all that was needed to propagate hundreds of copies of a political treatise, a national history, a religious tract, or a raucous satire was a press, a printer, and the money to fund them.

Well, not exactly *all*. As Cervantes was keenly aware, one also needed the blessings of the state and, specifically, of the royal censor, in this case one Antonio de Herrera y Tordesillas, an official historian in the pay of the crown. He was a "one-man think tank" who had scrupulously read each and every line of Cervantes's manuscript, crossing a good number out and demanding that others be rewritten, before finally granting his approval, the famous "license and privilege" of publication.[9] Herrera y Tordesillas's decision had the imprimatur of the king himself, whose approval in the form of a statement ending with the words "I, the King" would grace the front matter of each book published in his realm.

For the monarchy had begun to realize both the advantages and potential dangers of the new information economy, and assiduously controlled the form and content of what could be published in or imported into its borders, just as its religious wing, the Inquisition, imposed strict guidelines on the moral and religious contents of published works. The Inquisition's *Index Librorum Prohibitorum*, first published in 1559, ballooned larger and larger with each edition. The 1667 *Index* includes, along with its many thousands of specifically banned titles, a series of general rules prohibiting "all books in vulgate dealing with disputes and controversies having to do with religion, between Catholics, and Heretics of our time," while explicitly condoning "books dealing with ways of living well, contemplating, confessing, and such arguments, in vulgate."[10]

If there were no room for corruption, graft, or at least a little bending of the rules between friends, however, it wouldn't have been Spain at the turn of the seventeenth century. The government's censors were all literary men themselves who frequented the same academies and taverns and passed around one another's work, contributing poems of praise when they approved of a new book or sending barbs and pasquinades when they did not. When the second volume of *Don Quixote* came out in 1615, for instance, it seems that Cervantes managed to convince the royal censor assigned to that tome, a man named Francisco Márquez Torres, to allow him to pen his own official approbation and pass it off as the censor's words.

That text, which has all the signs of Cervantes's love for playing with the boundaries of reality and fiction, recounts Márquez Torres's meeting with some visiting dignitaries in the company of the French ambassador. We can imagine Márquez Torres and Cervantes sharing a good laugh as the former reads the latter's version of the conversation that ensues. For when the supposed Frenchmen learn that Márquez Torres is reading a new book by Miguel de Cervantes, they begin to sing his praises and to ask about his social standing in Spain. When the censor in turn explains to them that Cervantes is "old, a soldier, a gentleman, and poor," one of them ostensibly replies, "If his neediness obligates him to write, then may it please God that he never have abundance, so that he may enrich the whole world with his works, even if he remains poor himself."[11] Cervantes, as always, is winking at us across the ages as he wryly reminds his friend and eventually his reading public that fame and adulation, as welcome as it is, won't pay the bills on their own.

When he inserted that apocryphal encounter into the front matter of the second volume to *Don Quixote*, Cervantes was doing more than just using his newfound influence to mess with his government's system of censorship. He was also continuing to push the boundaries of a technique that he had already mastered in the book's first volume and that was central to its success and influence. To be sure, Cervantes's penchant for letting his stories bleed into the front matter of his books, and the informality with which he treats the border between what is supposed to be fanciful in a book and what we assume to be true, are crucial aspects of what was so new and exciting about his writing.

At that time, it was generally accepted that literature should fall into one of two general categories as defined by Aristotle: poetry and history. Aristotle's views on poetry and history have come down to us in the short work known as *The Poetics*, the fragmentary remains of a larger body of lectures on poetic theory that were available to medieval and Renaissance culture only through Arabic translations and commentaries. In those lectures, Aristotle stipulates that "the poet and the historian differ not by writing in verse or in prose . . . The true difference is that one relates what has happened, the other what may happen. Poetry, therefore, is a more philosophical and a higher thing than history: for poetry tends to express the universal, history the particular."[12] Today we tend to think that what Aristotle had in mind with his concept of *poeisis* was something like fiction. The problem with that assumption is that it imposes on Aristotle our own aesthetic and literary prejudices, which mainly revolve around our idea of what Aristotle meant by tragedy being about a hero who is undone by his "tragic flaw."[13] While this notion is taught to almost every student who reads Sophocles's *Oedipus the King* in school, none of it is representative of what Aristotle actually taught.

To begin with, Aristotle does not speak of a hero. He even insists, on several occasions, that tragedy is an imitation of an action, not of a human being.[14] He speaks of a change of fortune as being essential, but is ambiguous about whether that change need be for the better or the worse; and while we usually understand the infamous tragic flaw to refer to something wrong with the hero's character—most famously the hubris we associate with Oedipus—the Greek term *hamartia* means something more like an error in judgment.[15] All in all, where we tend to understand Aristotle's theory of tragedy as being about character, it is really about situations.[16]

In order to attain general truths, then, poetry could not be concerned with the particularities of specific characters, their perspectives, the depths of their unique emotions, the interiority of their states of mind—precisely those aspects we value most in fiction today. While Aristotle does speak of a kind of emotional connection with what's going on in the tragedy (the *catharsis* or purgation of fear and pity that the spectator experiences), it would be wrong to think that Aristotle envisions this as taking place through what we would call identification with a character. Rather, the most important aspect of tragedy is, as he writes, "the structure of the incidents. For Tragedy is an imitation, not of men, but of an action and of life"; character, he insists, is "subsidiary to the actions."[17]

Today, in contrast, we think of catharsis as having everything to do with character, with entering into a character's world, experiencing his values and choices, and suffering or finding pleasure vicariously through them. As the great critic Northrop Frye once wrote, the essential difference between novel and romance lies in the conception of characterization. The romancer does not attempt to create "real people" so much as stylized figures which expand into psychological archetypes. It is in the romance that we find Jung's libido, anima, and shadow reflected in the hero, heroine, and villain respectively . . . The novelist deals with personality, with characters wearing their *personae* or social masks.[18]

For us, then, what Aristotle called poetry would most properly be an imitation of character, and the action or events that occur to that character would be secondary. That is because we assume as natural a category that didn't exist for Aristotle: fiction.

Well versed in Aristotelian thought through his familiarity with a widely circulated commentary published by the Spanish philosopher Alonso López Pinciano in 1595, Cervantes makes frequent allusions to the problem of poetry and history in the many debates about literature he stages in his books. One of his funniest statements on the subject occurs early in *Don Quixote* when, without warning, the narrator breaks the flow of the story and claims that "the author of the history" has left it pending, apologizing for having "found nothing else written about the feats of Don Quixote other than what he has already recounted."[19] At this moment the narrator's voice suddenly divides into two: the "author of the history" and a "second author" who then goes on to recount in first person how, desperate to find out more about Don Quixote, he discovered some notebooks written in Arabic in a Toledo market and had them translated by a Morisco. (Moriscos were the descendants of the Moors living in Spain who had converted to Christianity or were forced to practice Islam in secret.) This second author then tells us that the story we have been and will continue to be reading was, in fact, written by an Arab historian named Cide Hamete Benengeli, before launching into the harangue on truth and history from which I took the epigraph to this chapter.

"No history is bad if it is true," he writes, and then immediately adds that "if any objection can be raised regarding the truth of this one, it can only be that its author was Arabic."[20] In this passage, Cervantes is having a great deal of fun at the expense of the literary critics. On the one hand, he is claiming for his story the status of history and hence truth; on the other hand, he is questioning the veracity of its source as an Arab historian; and he is doing both within the margins of a story that is patently untrue. Historians, the fictive text reads, "must and ought to be exact, truthful, and absolutely free of passions, for neither interest, fear, rancor, or affection, should make them deviate from the path of the truth."[21] Of course, were we to take him at his word, it would follow that history can never attain the truth that the critics claim for it because, told as it is by humans, it will never be free of passions, interest, fear, rancor, or affection. Indeed, Cervantes is telling us, such a truth would be an impoverishment, for it is precisely our passions, interests, fear, rancor, and affections that make our versions of the world worth telling in the first place.

It is no coincidence that one of the greatest writers of the twentieth century, the Argentine Jorge Luis Borges, chose exactly this passage when he created his fantastic parody of what he termed "the art of erroneous attribution" around two chapters of *Don Quixote* that had supposedly been penned anew, verbatim, by an early twentieth-century French author named Pierre Menard. In Borges's version, Cervantes's invocation of history as the "mother of truth" is shown to be the stale, conventional rhetoric of a sixteenth-century man of letters when juxtaposed with the same language as written by a modern, avant-garde French writer. Borges's faux comparison perfectly grasps the brilliant irony of an ode to history coming from the hand of an untrustworthy narrator in the midst of undermining the veracity of the very story he is telling. Here's how he ends that so-often-quoted story of quotations:

> Menard (almost without intending to) has enriched the idle and rudimentary art of reading by way of a new technique: the technique of deliberate anachronism and erroneous attributions. That technique of infinite applications induces us to peruse the *Odyssey* as if it were posterior to the *Aeneid* and the book *Le Jardin du Centaure* by Madame Henri Bachelier as if it were by Madame Henri Bachelier.[22]

In the patent absurdity of having to read a book *as if* it had been written by the author who in fact wrote it, Borges reveals the startling redundancy of promoting erroneous attribution when it comes to fiction. For fiction, which is not concerned one whit with "truth, whose mother is history," but instead with how different people judge something to be true in the first place, is the mode of writing that induces us to attribute motives to the text itself, by treating its characters as if they were human beings like us.

While critics have often been divided on the extent to which Cervantes's innovations were intentional, in the preface he penned for the 1613 publication of his collection of twelve *Exemplary Novellas*, he makes it clear that he is conscious of how his fiction upsets the prevailing wisdom of his times. To begin with, he boasts of his stories' originality, claiming that, unlike "the many novellas that are in print in that language [and which] are all translated from foreign languages . . . these are my own, neither imitated nor stolen; engendered by my wit, born of my pen, and now being raised by the printing press."[23] In asserting their originality, Cervantes is placing them squarely on the side of poetry in Aristotelian circles and hence depriving them of the attribute of historical truth. To pass the scrutiny of the censors, though, he would have to make a claim to some other kind of truth for them, namely moral truth, which Cervantes then asserts in the form of their exemplarity: "I have given them the name *exemplary*, and if you look at it well, there is not one from which you cannot take some profitable example, and if not to avoid going on at too great length, maybe I would show you the tasty and morally beneficial fruit that could be taken from all together, as well as from each one on its own."[24]

The novellas, Cervantes was claiming, both are entirely fantastic, in that they were born exclusively of his own imagination and have real pertinence for his readers' lives. They have, he says, a "mystery hidden in them that raises them up,"[25] and the key to unlocking that mystery is how one reads the stories. For, "while my mouth may stutter, that won't impede it telling truths."[26] These completely original fruits of his imagination contain truths that discerning readers will know how to decipher if they read them with care, with an eye to their own "passions, interests, fear, rancor, and affections," applying them as examples to their own lives. In order to see what lessons they can glean from them, his readers would have to approach the stories as if they themselves were the protagonists, dividing themselves into a reader who judges and a character who enters the story on their behalf.[27]

In the autobiographical poem he published around the same time, *The Journey to Parnassus*, Cervantes described his innovation this way: "I opened with my *Novellas* the path through which the Castilian tongue can show with naturalness a piece of fantasy."[28] *Natural fantasy.*

With these two words Cervantes shows that, contrary to the arguments of generations of critics, he did grasp the nature of his innovation.[29] Fiction presents the untrue in the form of truth, poetry in the form of history, and in doing so, allows access to a different kind of truth—not Aristotle's more general truth, divorced from the specificity of character, but rather its very opposite: subjective truth, a truth so internal, so specific to how individuals inhabit their world, that it would pass forever unnoticed by a history confined to grasping human actions from the outside.

THE PREVIOUS NOVELLAS translated from foreign languages that Cervantes alludes to in his preface were, for the most part, those written by the great Italian author Giovanni Boccaccio in the fourteenth century, along with his many imitators. While he inherited its basic shape from a prior tradition of prose narratives, Boccaccio—the son of a Florentine banker, who first studied law before embracing his calling as a poet[30]—created the form of the novella as an extended narrative relating, for entertainment's sake, a series of events focused on a particular theme or example, endowing those events with an unprecedented degree of attention to atmospheric detail.[31] Nevertheless, Cervantes's take on the genre more than two hundred years later would revolutionize it.

Boccaccio's most lasting and influential work was the *Decameron*, a collection of one hundred stories exchanged over ten days by a group of gentry who have retired to the countryside to escape the bubonic plague then decimating the urban populations. In a typical tale of seduction and deception, cunning and simplicity, one of Boccaccio's storytellers describes how a philandering friar connives his way into a married woman's bed. To her objection that lying with a man who is not her husband would be a sin, Fra Rinaldo replies,

> "If you forego pleasure for such a scruple you are a fool. I do not say that it is not a sin, but only that, if one repents, there is no sin so great that God will not pardon it. Now tell me: who is more truly a father to your son, I who held him at his baptism, or your husband who begot him?"
>
> "My husband," answered the lady.

"And you speak correctly," responded the friar, "and does your husband not sleep with you?"

"Why, yes," said the lady.

"Then," rejoined the friar, "I who am less a relation of your son's than is your husband, should also be allowed to sleep with you, as does your husband." The lady, being no logician, needed little to convince her: she thus believed or pretended to believe that what the friar told her was true. And so, "Who might rise to respond to your words of wisdom?" she said, and proceeded to forget the godfather in the lover and thus complied with his desires.[32]

For all their great charm, comedy, and titillating details, Boccaccio's tales describe the events and characters that populate them from the outside. Even as they deceive one another, and even as their deceptions are revealed to us, Boccaccio's characters remain objects in the world, no matter how rich the pictorial realism of their actions, environments, and behaviors. In contrast, Cervantes's narratives function by constantly leading us to question the intent behind the descriptions, by pointing to the difference between the masks the characters show to one another and the internal feelings and emotions that animate them.[33]

Here is Cervantes's description of Don Quixote's feelings after his all-but-accidental defeat of the "Knight of the Mirrors," in truth, his barely disguised good friend Sansón Carrasco:

Don Quixote was filled with contentment, pride, and vainglory at having achieved victory over so valiant a knight as he imagined the Knight of the Mirrors to be, and from his chivalric promise he hoped to learn if the enchantment of his lady was still in effect, since it was necessary for the conquered knight to return, under pain of no longer being a knight, to tell him what had transpired with her. But Don Quixote thought one thing and the Knight of the Mirror thought another, for his only thought then was to find a place where he could apply a plaster.[34]

Here again he recounts the reaction of the handmaidens ordered by a mischievous duke and duchess to treat Don Quixote as if he were truly a knight errant:

When his armor had been removed, Don Quixote was left in his narrow breeches and chamois doublet—dry, tall, thin, his jaws kissing each other inside his mouth—and if the maidens who were serving him had not been charged with hiding their laughter, for this was one of the precise orders their mistress and master had given them, they could have split their sides laughing.[35]

Here he has Sancho respond to Quixote's insistence that he conduct a test known to seafaring men that will tell them if the boat they have absconded with has passed the equinoctial line:

"I don't believe any of that," responded Sancho, "but even so, I'll do what your grace tells me to, though I don't know why we need to make these tests, since I can see with my own eyes that we haven't gone five rods from shore, and we haven't moved two rods away from the animals because there's Rocinante and the donkey exactly where we left them, and looking carefully, which is what I'm doing now, I swear that we're not even moving or traveling as fast as an ant."[36]

In all these passages, in addition to a vibrantly flavored scene, the reader is confronted by the incompatibility of the perceptions of two or more characters and the emotions that burst from those conflicts. This focus is present throughout Cervantes's writing. His ability to shift fluidly among different points of view and voices was fueled by his obsession with portraying not just the world and the people and events that filled it, but how people perceived and misperceived that world and one another and how they reacted to and at times even bridged the emotional crevices ripped open by their inability to see the same world. Boccaccio's characters end at the limits of what they can see; Cervantes's characters begin there.

Some scholars admonish us not to read too much into *Don Quixote*, insisting that what Cervantes meant to write was a funny book, and that's all. Well, if that was his task, he certainly succeeded. *Don Quixote* is indeed a very funny book; legend has it that King Philip III once exclaimed, upon seeing a student doubled up in raucous laughter one day, "that student is either out of his mind or he is reading the story of Don Quixote!"[37] But just as the tenderness evident in Sancho's confession of his love for Quixote is conjured not in spite of but because of the very incompatibility of the lived worlds it transcends, so is much of the book's famous humor. When the hunchbacked and half-blind scullery maid Maritornes slips into bed with Don Quixote in the dark of night, the hilarity doesn't come just from the fact that she's fat and ugly and he's old and bony, or that her true amorous target, the mule driver, gets angry and beats up Quixote after he's already suffered two or three terrible beatings the same day; rather, here is a bewildered Quixote recounting his latest misadventure to Sancho:

> "I have great confidence in your love and courtesy, and so you must know that tonight I have had one of the strangest adventures one could ever imagine; to make the story brief, I shall tell you that a short while ago the daughter of the lord of this castle came to me, and she is one of the most elegant and beauteous damsels to be found anywhere on earth. What can I say of the grace of her person, the nobility of her understanding, the other hidden things which, in order to keep the faith I owe to my lady Dulcinea of Toboso, I shall keep inviolate and pass over in silence? I wish only to say that heaven, envious of the good that Fortune had placed in my hands, or perhaps, and this is more likely, the castle, as I have said, being enchanted, as I was engaging in sweet and amorous conversation with her, without my seeing or knowing whence it came, a hand attached to the arm of some monstrous giant came down and struck me so hard a blow on the jaws that they were bathed in blood."[38]

What makes the scene so funny and at the same time so strangely moving is that Quixote is convinced that Maritornes is the innkeeper's beautiful daughter and a lady to boot, that when he declaims his devotion and service to her she doesn't have the slightest idea what he's talking about; and that the mule driver thinks his tryst for the night has preferred another man to him, and so hands him the beating that Quixote concludes must have come "from the arm of some monstrous giant."

In composing *Don Quixote*, Cervantes used many of the same tricks and themes that have elicited laughter throughout human history, even stooping to those scatological and coprophilic sensibilities that have clung to the lowest rungs of humor throughout literary history.

Freud identified these excremental eruptions as the cultural symptoms of a natural perversity repressed by modern civilization. But as anyone with small children knows, you don't need much repression to enjoy a good poop joke.

The French humanist François Rabelais, who was born in the century before Cervantes, was one of many sixteenth-century writers who relished a dirty joke; and his enormously influential series of satirical novels about the giants Gargantua and Pantagruel are packed with scatological humor. In fact, the principal character of his books, the giant Pantagruel, is literally born in shit, his mother, the giantess Gargamelle, having overconsumed tripe the night she gives birth. Rabelais, a physician as well as a writer, revels in *not* sparing us the details:

> A little while later she began to groan and wail and shout. Then suddenly swarms of midwives came up from every side, and feeling her underneath found some rather ill-smelling excrescences, which they thought were the child; but it was her fundament slipping out, because of the softening of her right intestine—which you call the bum-gut—owing to her having eaten too much tripe.[39]

Almost a century later, Cervantes would turn to such tried-and-true themes as well in his desire to spur his readers to laugh. But where prior writers focused their efforts on depicting the grotesque, the humor in his version derives almost entirely from the emotional reactions of two characters as they perceive and misperceive what is happening.

Lost in the woods in the dead of night, Sancho becomes frightened by the sound of "strokes falling with a measured beat, and a certain rattling of iron and chains that, together with the furious din of the water, would have struck terror into any heart but Don Quixote's." To prevent his master from heading toward the sound, Sancho secretly ties Quixote's mount's hind legs together and begins distracting him with stories, when he feels "the urge and desire to do what no one else could do for him." Afraid to move away from Quixote, he first tries to relieve himself in secret, but finds he cannot do so without making a noise—one, as Cervantes writes, "quite different from the one that had caused him so much fear."

"What sound is that, Sancho?" Quixote asks. "I don't know, señor," Sancho responds. "It must be something new; adventures and misadventures never begin for no reason." His second attempt is more successful, and silent, but this time it is a sense other than hearing that gives him away, and Quixote remarks, holding his nose, "It seems to me, Sancho, that you are very frightened."[40]

Notice the abyss that divides these two scatological moments in literary history. Where Rabelais achieves his effect by describing the obscenity of basic human functions with an anatomical zeal leavened by his impish disdain for propriety, Cervantes's prose brings into relief his characters' emotions, their embarrassment, their fear, their desire to pull the wool over each other's eyes, and their rueful responses when they fail. Rabelais wrote patently untrue stories that entertained their readers with their bawdy satire; Cervantes wrote fiction.

Fiction, rather than merely referring, in the words of one of today's most important critics, to "a verbal performance in which the events depicted never happened, and which everyone knows they didn't,"[41] can and often does convey the truth, albeit a different kind of truth from that described by either of Aristotle's categories. This is how we should understand the unusual approach the contemporary novelist Javier Cercas takes in depicting a key moment in late twentieth-century history: the coup attempt of February 23, 1981, that very nearly brought Spain's fledgling democracy to an early end.[42] Despite the care Cercas took to ensure that his book stay entirely faithful to historical fact, he wrote it as a novel because, as he put it in a lecture at the Hay Festival in Britain's Black Mountains, in a novel "it is possible to gain access to a truth that would otherwise remain inaccessible."

While the goal of history books is to answer who a protagonist really was, what actually happened, and why it did, Cercas explained in that lecture, that the novelist seeks to explore essentially *moral* questions, and does not attempt to provide definitive answers to them. In the Russian critic Mikhail Bakhtin's famous words, "We ourselves may enter the novel."[43] This ability of fiction to sink into the moment and experience it from the inside of a character's point of view was not the sort of truth Aristotle or his early modern interpreters had in mind when they spoke of poetry as accessing a higher truth than history. And yet not only is it exactly the sort of truth Cercas has in mind, but he also specifically credits Cervantes with giving birth to the tradition from which he, as a novelist, works.

THE MAN WHO WALKED the streets of his nation's capital on that hot August day held high hopes for the package he grasped in his one good hand. He knew that what he had written was new, something the world had not yet seen. There is no way, however, that either he or anyone else could have predicted what would happen starting in January of the following year, when the press of Juan de la Cuesta, the Madrid-based printer whom Francisco de Robles hired to produce the book, would start running off the first of what would be countless editions of *The Ingenious Gentleman Don Quixote of La Mancha*.++

Within a few months of its original publication, Cervantes needed to apply for a new license to have the book distributed throughout the Iberian Peninsula, and Robles and de la Cuesta began work on a second edition, to be released that same summer. Before that edition hit the bookstores, two pirated editions appeared in London, along with two others in Valencia and Zaragoza. Already by April, Robles was spending a good part of his time preparing legal suits against the purveyors of pirated copies. Within few months, stacks of copies were loaded onto the galleons embarking from Seville for the New World, and by June of the same year the book's protagonists, the deluded knight Don Quixote and his squat and simple sidekick, Sancho Panza, had become iconic figures, their effigies carried in parades and imitators popping up in celebrations both royal and plebian.

Cervantes's newfound fame was not limited to the Spanish world. Spain's cultural influence at the time was as widespread as its political and military presence, and Spanish works were regularly disseminated and translated in England, France, and Germany, not to mention in the Netherlands and Italy, which were still under Spanish control. Brussels saw two editions released by 1611; figures dressed as Don Quixote and Sancho Panza appeared at a procession in Heidelberg in 1613; and in England, John Fletcher and Francis Beaumont adopted one of the novel's interpolated stories into their play *The Coxcomb*, written between 1608 and 1610. In 1612, Thomas Shelton published his enormously successful English translation, *The History of the Valorous and Wittie Knight-Errant Don-Quixote of the Mancha* and, although it has been lost, William Shakespeare joined forces with John Fletcher to write a play called *Cardenio*, which was inspired by another episode from the novel.[45]

For all its instant success, as Cervantes's wry prank some ten years later attests, the publication of the world's first modern novel did not significantly improve the living conditions of its author or his family. As had been the case for almost all the prior years of his already long and peripatetic life, Cervantes would continue to be beset by financial and familial woes. The brief time he spent in Valladolid would be marked by the excitement of his greatest literary triumph, but it would also end up being a microcosm of the life and world that fed and nourished that triumph: a life of constant hoping and endless disappointments, a world of false values veiling real bitterness and defeat.

Walking down the Calle del Rastro and away from the stench of the fetid stream carrying slaughterhouse offal past Juan de Navas's house, Cervantes would have passed the Hospital of the Resurrection. There, indigent soldiers lay dying or, if lucky, just barely recovering from their wounds of war or convalescing from syphilis, like the delirious soldiers of his greatest exemplary tale *The Dogs' Colloquy*. Like many of those men, Cervantes had spent years waiting fruitlessly to be rewarded by a government he'd faithfully served, losing limb and almost his life. Passing its lugubrious doors and trying in vain to ignore the screams of pain and despair rising from men having their limbs severed without anesthesia, Cervantes would be reminded each evening of his own long and painful convalescence in Sicily, of the persistent pains of his own aging and crippled body, and of the debt owed to him and never paid. As he approached his squalid home, with its five women who looked to him as their patriarch even as they pragmatically found their own ways to get by, he would be reminded each night of his family's long struggle to fit in among the privileged classes of Spain, and its consistent failure to do so.

Those women—his older, careworn sisters, Andrea and Magdalena; Andrea's daughter, Constanza; and now his own daughter, Isabel—each and every one had been embroiled repeatedly in that all-too-common legalistic scrimmage with men of noble lineage and less-than-noble intentions. The women, infatuated or just too naïvely hopeful for a liaison that might lift them from their poverty, had too quickly exchanged their only capital (the "virtue" so highly touted in the literature of the age) for empty promises of marriage never to be upheld. Now, with his sisters well into or past middle age, Cervantes could only look on in apprehension and regret as the next generation prepared to make the same mistakes.

And that was what remained. His father had died years before; his mother more recently; his brother, loyal Rodrigo, with whom he had survived years of soldiering and brutal captivity, had been killed on another of his king's barren fields of war. Of his friends from the heroic days of Lepanto, Italy, and North Africa, and his closest companions in poetry (such as Pedro Laínez, whose wife was now a neighbor in Juan de Navas's house), many were now dead. The few surviving members of his literary circle, who certainly visited from time to time to catch the gossip of the capital, were living elsewhere. In any event, life in literary circles was far from easy-going camaraderie; it was as cutthroat a world as the mean streets outside the tavern in Juan de Navas's building, and Cervantes was often on the losing side of the verbal knife fights. Even if the fame *Don Quixote* was bringing him was a welcome respite, it didn't necessarily translate into literary respectability, and it certainly wasn't translating into material well-being.

Passing the royal municipal prison on his way to Francisco de Robles's shop that day, Cervantes might have looked up and reflected on the fact that his own grandfather and father had each spent time locked behind those forbidding walls—the former for a legal dispute with a nobleman over a broken promise of marriage, and the latter for failing to pay his debts, but both at least obliquely for the crime of aspiring to a higher station that would never admit them. He certainly would not have guessed that within that very year he, too, would enter its gates under suspicion of murder, his family scrutinized and his honor in question for the number of men visiting a household of women at all hours. He would have thought by then that his days as undeserved victim of his country's corrupt and inefficient legal system would be over. He would have been wrong.

Remarkably, the near-constant failures, the humiliation, the brutal attacks on his person and his freedom, rather than producing a crotchety, resentful cynic—"as old as the Castle of San Cervantes and, because of his years, so malcontent that everything and everyone annoys him,"[46] as one of his detractors wrote in the preface to an anonymous plagiarism of Cervantes's greatest characters—seemed in

Cervantes's case to have had the opposite effect. Like Albert Camus's marvelous reimagining of Sisyphus, the mythical sufferer condemned to push a boulder up a hill for eternity, Cervantes, in a literary gaze cast back over a life of almost unimaginable hardship, can't seem to stop laughing. Or caring. For his humor and his love for other mortals stem from the same source: by reflecting on his own blindness and the failures it engendered, he reaches into the souls of his fellow travelers and shares in their blindness as well. Life is absurd, so laugh—but also feel, because life's travails hurt others as much as they hurt you.

This, finally, is what the soldier, adventurer, gambler, captive, and all-round failure brought to the debates around history and poetry that were raging at the dawn of the modern age. If history must tell the truth of what happened, and poetry is a higher, more philosophical truth—the truth of what could happen—then fiction, Cervantes's new art, would transmit a different truth entirely. The truth of fiction would be a subjective truth, but one not for that reason any less valuable, and perhaps, for the ages that followed, even more so. For by plumbing the depths of character, by being drawn to imagine the lives and feelings of others, not despite his and their inability to experience others' lives but because of it, Cervantes opened the door to a vast and undiscovered country for all those who followed him to explore.

2.

Open and Closed

As for citing in the margins the books and authors that were the source of the sayings and maxims you put into your history, all you have to do is insert some appropriate maxims or phrases in Latin, ones that you know by heart or, at least, that won't cost you too much trouble to look up . . . And with these little Latin phrases and others like them, people will think you a grammarian; being one is no small honor and advantage these days.

Américo Castro had good reasons for his denigration of Spanish contributions to intellectual history. At the crest of that great intellectual ferment known as the Renaissance, just as new ideas and challenges to religious authority were spreading around Europe from hot spots in Italy and the Netherlands, Germany and Switzerland, Spain's empire was coalescing around a rigid combination of state power and religious dogma. Spain's ruler, the emperor Charles V, himself of Flemish birth and open to new ideas, was at first a proponent of the importation and dissemination of new scientific ideas in Spain. But the half-century of his reign leading to the ascension of his son Philip II is a story of gradual closure, and the regrouping of a regime around orthodoxy and fear.[1]

The reception in Spain of the ideas of the great Dutch humanist Desiderius Erasmus of Rotterdam is particularly illustrative of this trend. Erasmus's *Enchiridion militis christiani*, or *Manual of the Christian Knight*, was published in a Spanish translation in 1526 and enjoyed immediate and long-lasting success. Erasmus believed that following the personal model of Christ was far more important than the arcane trivia of academic theology or the sedimented practices of religious institutions. In his *Enchiridion*, he lambastes the monastic life for emphasizing ritual and a show of faith over what he calls interior devotion (*devotio intima*) and good works. His work became known for the dictum *monachatus non est pietas*, or "monasticism is not piety," and became the basis for intellectual criticisms of traditional religious values and practices in Spain.[2] The book circulated widely enough in the few years following its publication for the translator to write back to Erasmus, "At the Court of the Emperor, in the towns, in the churches, in the monasteries, even in the inns and on the roads, everyone now has the *Enchiridion* of Erasmus."[3]

The work that Erasmus is most known for today is his satirical excoriation of learned, elite society called *The Praise of Folly*, which he wrote in 1509, dedicated in a letter to Thomas More in 1510, and first published in Paris in 1511.[4] Although written in Latin, Erasmus rendered the title in Greek as *Morias encomion*, in order to take full advantage of the proximity, as he explains in his dedicatory letter to More, between More's name and the Greek word for folly, *mória*.

With *The Praise of Folly*, Erasmus was building on a tradition of thought that was closely allied with his own while creating a format for criticizing ecclesiastical and secular authorities, whose lack of leadership and slavish devotion to dogma, he felt, were leading the faith toward perdition and the world toward internecine war. Like the German bishop Nicholas of Cusa, who in his *Of Learned Ignorance* had argued that humans must deliberately unlearn much of the muddying nonsense of dogma in order to see the truth of how limited their knowledge actually is, Erasmus believed in a more direct relation between individuals and the truth.[5] But he also believed that those in power tended to use their positions and their knowledge for selfish ends rather than for the good of all.

In *The Praise of Folly*, Erasmus portrays Folly speaking for herself, and her words as revealing more truth than those of the powerful, learned, and influential. Like his good friend Thomas More, whose *Utopia* would hide its sharp criticisms of power and hypocrisy behind the defense of a nonexistent land, Erasmus could claim his book was all in fun and had no obvious referents in the real world,[6] all the while skewering the targets of his disapproval obliquely. As Folly says at one point in the book:

For in this point I have seen fit to imitate the rhetoricians of our times, who are quite confident that they are all but divine if (like the horseleech) they have two tongues. They think they have done a noble deed if they sprinkle some Greek tags in their Latin speech, however inappropriate, like bright bits of mosaic. In fact, if they don't have some esoteric expressions, they scrape together four or five obsolete words from some moldy manuscripts in order to baffle their readers.[7]

While Erasmus's criticisms are pointed, his style, as he himself notes, has many predecessors. Many years later Cervantes would adapt to his own purposes the strategy of having foolishness speak the truth, even going so far as to make a madman the protagonist of his greatest work. But he would add a special twist. Where the worlds created by More and Erasmus remain clearly marked as fantastic and the characters mere parodies, Cervantes has his madman roam through a world that seems in every sense real.

How he makes Erasmus's strategy his own is clear from the very prologue of his great book, where he tells the reader how he would have given up for fear of revealing his ignorance had a friend not given him the advice to make his writing sound better by making up quotations and throwing in little bits of Latin here and there:

if you speak of freedom and captivity, you can say:

Non bene pro toto libertas venditur auro.

And then, in the margin, you cite Horace or whoever it was who said it. If the subject is the power of death you can use:

Pallida mors aequo pulsat pede pauperum tabernas,
Regumque turres.

If it's the friendship and love that God commands us to have for our enemies, you turn right to Holy Scripture, which you can do with a minimum of effort and say the words of God Himself: *Ego autem dico vobis: diligite inimicos vestros.* If you mention evil thoughts, go to the Gospel: *De corde exeunt cogitationes malae.* If the topic is the fickleness of friends, Cato's there, ready with this couplet:

Done eris felix, multos numerabis amicos,
Tempora si fuerint nubila, solus eris.

And with these little Latin phrases and others like them, people will
think you are a grammarian; being one is no small honor and advantage these days.[8]

In this exchange we get a glimpse of the personality behind the
genius, for if Cervantes animated his characters in part by calling on
his vast life experiences and putting himself into their shoes, this is
even more the case when the character in question is Cervantes himself.
In this regard the prologue to *Don Quixote* is enormously revealing.
On the one hand, Cervantes is calling on an ancient rhetorical tradition of *captatio benevolentiae,* or "capturing the reader's goodwill," by
way of feigned self-deprecation. On the other hand, by turning himself
into a character, Cervantes is profoundly convincing in his admissions
of feelings of inadequacy. Instead of the direct yet obviously scripted
confessions of a conventional authorial voice, we are greeted by a man
who speaks to us personally, in the same tone he uses in conversation
with the friend he claims gives him the advice.

"I can tell you," Cervantes writes to us, his readers, about the book
he is introducing,

> that although it cost me some effort to compose, none seemed greater
> than creating the preface you are now reading. I picked up my pen
> many times to write it, and many times I put it down again because I
> did not know what to write; and once, when I was baffled, with the
> paper in front of me, my pen behind my ear, my elbow propped on
> the writing table, and my cheek resting on my hand, pondering what
> to say, a friend of mine, a man who is witty and wise, unexpectedly
> came in and seeing me so perplexed asked the reason.[9]

Not only is Cervantes bucking centuries of convention in passages like
this, by making the conventions he is bucking part of a conversation
that we readers are invited to join. In the case of the character called
Cervantes, we feel we are in his room with him, witnessing this baffle-
ment and uncertainty in a man we are already coming to know, sitting
before us with his pen behind his ear and his cheek resting in his

hand, at a loss for words. We see him from without, but we also experience what he is feeling, from within.

Cervantes penned that prologue shortly before bringing his manuscript to Francisco de Robles's shop. Fifty-seven years old, in fact, he had long since gotten past being short for words, if he ever really was. In the oral skirmishes in the academies and taverns of Seville and Madrid, where the great authors of the day met to read one another's words, his wit had to overcome the challenge of a persistent stutter that must have caused him endless anguish as a child, but on paper he could be free. The prologue to *Don Quixote*, a masterpiece in its own right, stages that liberation, with Cervantes the brilliant ironist turning Cervantes— the hesitant, uncertain, stammering, literary ingénue—into a character of his own design. There is also little doubt as to who was the inspiration for the author's "friend" who comes to save the day with his fool's advice. Of all Cervantes's detractors, it was Lope de Vega, the one who so memorably described Cervantes's spectacles as resembling badly fried eggs, who both threatened Cervantes with his evident talents and productivity and had repeatedly denigrated him as an inferior poet.

In the prologue, we see Cervantes getting even. It would have been obvious to Cervantes's readers at the time that the "friend" who enters and advises him to write his own laudatory poems and to pepper his work with quotations in Latin was a thinly masked Lope de Vega, who regularly packed his own front matter with poems he wrote in praise of his own work and then tacked on names of real authors, or even of his mistress, the actress Micaela de Luxan. The fact that the poems that follow the prologue are patent exercises in ridicule and foolishness— from silly "broken-footed" poems to odes in praise of Quixote's horse, Rocinante, penned, naturally, by other famous steeds—only serves to sharpen the insult. And, finally, no one was better than Lope at packing his works with classical allusions and citations in Latin to make the work seem more erudite. Cervantes's lampoon was spot-on.[10]

Like Erasmus, Cervantes made fun of how the trappings of knowledge are used to create the effect of wisdom. But he was also taking the next step by incorporating this insight into the very way he wrote. Instead of undermining erudite pretention by having a character called Folly speak the truth, Cervantes portrayed himself as a character in the midst of revealing his tricks as a writer. Likewise, rather than merely criticizing hypocrisy and dogma by putting pearls of wisdom in the mouths of fools (which he also did, to be sure), Cervantes created characters who are fooled into believing that showy erudition represents truth, or that their worth depends on how many generations of Christians they can trace their lineage back to, or that what others think about their honor is more important than life itself.

In a short play published toward the end of his life, Cervantes depicts a small town whose leaders decide to hire a team of puppeteers to put on a magical puppet show in honor of the wedding of one of their daughters. The conman who convinces them to invest in his phony scheme tells them that they will see marvels beyond their wildest dreams on the makeshift stage, but also warns them that the magic of the performance is denied to anyone "who has any trace of that other faith, or who was not born and procreated by parents bound in legitimate matrimony." The men of the town naturally begin to bluster and protest. As one of the town elders, Benito, says, "I can tell you that, for my part, I can go safely to the test, because my father was the mayor of this town; and I've got rancid old Christian meat four inches thick on the four flanks of my lineage; you tell me if I'll have any problems seeing the show!"[11]

Once the puppet show begins and, of course, nothing at all appears onstage, the villagers respond to the theater "director's" promptings by acclaiming the wonders they know they should be seeing with ever more feverish enthusiasm. Their imaginary bacchanalia comes crashing down, though, with the arrival of a quartermaster of the king's army, who demands, as would have been his right at the time, that his solders be billeted for the night.

Capacho:	So, you mean to say you don't see Herod's damsel dancing there, Sir quartermaster?
Quartermaster:	What damned damsel should I be seeing?
Capacho:	That's it! He's one of them!
Governor:	He's one of them! He's one of them!
Juan:	He's one of them! The quartermaster is one of them! He's one of them!
Quartermaster:	I'm of the same Christian whore as the rest of you are! And by the living God, if I have to put hand to my sword, you'll be going out by the window and not by the door.[12]

Unlike Erasmus's Folly, and despite the obvious absurdity of their situation, these characters seem three-dimensional, alive. Their reality is due not only to the rich detail of their voices and dialects, which Cervantes mimics with an anthropologist's ear, but also to our seeing them both from without, as fools to be mocked, and from within, as people wanting desperately to belong to something even when they know it to be a hoax. In the case of the hapless governor—who asks in an aside, "Could it be that I'm the sole bastard among so many legitimate men?"[13]—his desperation is caused by his wondering if he belongs at all.

Cervantes doesn't merely mock the foolish; he understands them. And he understands them because he recognizes himself in them. Each of his innumerable characters carries something of Cervantes's own being in him or her: the innkeeper, who is beside himself over the wineskins Quixote has just cut to ribbons while lost in the fantasy that he is slaying a giant; Sancho, who yearns to become governor of an island that doesn't exist, and then applies himself with abandon to solving that island's impossible and invented problems; or the bachelor Sansón Carrasco, who delights in egging Quixote on, and then cries real tears when the madman returns to sanity. To become the writer he was in his later years, Cervantes had to create a style of writing that went further than satire, one capable of internalizing his lifetime of mounting hopes and crushing disappointments, his countless encounters with people of different stations and cultures, and converting them into an unparalleled capacity to make characters come alive on the page.

BY 1567, WHEN HE TURNED TWENTY, Cervantes was living with his family in Madrid, which was not only the capital of Spain, but was also starting to feel like the center of the world. When Philip moved his court from Toledo to Madrid in 1561, he felt he was doing more than just fulfilling his father's wish to establish the capital in the land's geographic center. The city of some thirty thousand inhabitants, which would swell almost threefold by the end of the century, was to become the center of an empire that stretched around the globe. It was also, in Philip's mind, the center of God's kingdom on earth, a counterweight to a papacy that, for many of the Spanish faithful, had been weakened by both corruption and the Protestant revolt. It was thus, in this pure intermingling of earthly might and divine providence, that Philip located the essence of the empire he would now anchor in the physical center of the Iberian peninsula. Indeed, this combination was embodied in the royal residence and monastery he built to house the remains of his father, himself, and their descendants, the deservedly famous Escorial.

While still a backwater in comparison to the grandeur of Seville, Madrid had seen its population quintuple in the dozen or so years since Philip II had established it as his new capital. Its dusty medieval streets were growing pell-mell into the labyrinths of stone and tile one can still wander through today. And with one economic shock after another hitting the countryside, those streets were filled with legions of needy souls who would line up for the free soup ladled out by the churches.

Miguel's father, Rodrigo, had just led the family through a tumultuous, itinerant decade, driven by debt and the need to find steady work. Moving back to the central plains of Castile after several rocky years in the south, Rodrigo sensed that Madrid was an up-and-coming city, and a place where he could finally lay down roots and make a

The Escorial, from Joan Blaeu, *Der Aerdrycks-Beschryuing, welck vervat Spaenjen, Africa, en America*. Amsterdam: Blaeu, 1665. Vol. 8. George Peabody Library, the Sheridan Libraries, Johns Hopkins University

good life for his family. Added to this was the fact that his wife's mother had just passed away and, as her only child, Leonor stood to inherit a considerable fortune, if Rodrigo could for once manage to win one of his many lawsuits. As it turns out, he had some success in that endeavor, and the first years in Madrid were among the few times that Rodrigo had any money to show for himself—money he quickly squandered by lending an enormous sum to a friend, one Pedro Sánchez de Córdoba. Typical of Rodrigo's luck, he would still be trying to get that money back years later as attempts to earn a living as a barber proved less than lucrative.[14]

Even with scrambling for work and moving from town to town, Rodrigo had managed to take advantage of family connections and locations and provide Miguel with an education. Now a young man, Miguel was being accepted into the educated elite of his country's capital at a time when its imperial ambitions were growing in equal measure with its apparent wealth, power, and influence on the world stage. An aspiring poet and intellectual, Miguel was in his element at last. He had even risen to be a favorite student of the greatly admired teacher and scholar Juan López de Hoyos, who would soon be named rector of one of the city's publically financed academies, the Estudio de la Villa, and was thus in charge of preparing the city's youth for the university. It was also at this time that he started lifelong friendships with some of the established and up-and-coming poets of Spain. In the well-known poet Pedro Laínez he would find a mentor whom he would later acknowledge as one of his teachers in the art of poetry, and whose life and death would intertwine closely with his own. Poets who were more his contemporaries, such as Gabriel López Maldonado and Luis Gálvez de Montalvo, would later earn hefty words of praise from Cervantes in *Don Quixote*, as his characters debate the relative merits of works such as the former's *Cancionero* and the latter's *El pastor de Fílida*.

López de Hoyos would earn his place in history by being the first person to publish something by Miguel de Cervantes. Referring to him as "my well-beloved student," he included four of Cervantes's poems in a book intended to record for posterity the funereal ceremonies that followed the untimely death of Philip II's young wife Elizabeth of Valois in 1568. Her sudden death during childbirth, resulting in a still-born child, plunged the king into the depths of grief; he imposed the strictest mourning on the nation and, especially, its capital. For the city's artists and writers, though, official mourning was an opportunity to put their skills on display in the most public fashion, as the ceremonies celebrating the queen's life and marking her death were full of fanfare and attended by virtually all the city's residents.

In one of those poems, Cervantes wrote:

> *I will say that, against the hard evil, the dark mourning*
> *That Spain, in the arms of death, now faces,*
> *God did not mean to leave her without solace.*
> *He left her the great Philip, who sustains*
> *Like a firm foundation for the high firmament*
> *The good or misfortune that befalls her.*[15]

Composed with great feeling in an utterly conventional style, in imitation of the most respected poet of the age, Garcilaso de la Vega, these early verses radiate an earnest appeal to the idea of Spain as a unified body, and to her king Philip as protector and guide of her people. The young poet who penned those verses believed what he wrote, and wanted nothing more ardently than to belong to this great nation and sing its virtues.

That nation, though, was built on shaky ground. Philip's father, Charles, and his advisers had spent his reign consolidating not only an empire cobbled together from disparate peoples and interests, but even a country, Spain, that itself had very little internal coherence.[16] While Castilians were an essential part of Charles's armies as he established dominance in the Netherlands, Italy, and the New World, and clashed with England, France, and the Turkish Empire, they were never a majority of those fighting. And yet the often German- or Flemish-speaking troops would yell, "Santiago, España!" at the top of their lungs while racing into battle.[17] Another variant on that battle cry was "Santiago, and close Spain!," a practice that a much older Cervantes would have Sancho Panza wryly comment on when he asks Don Quixote why it is that Spaniards yell this when going into battle: "by some chance is Spain open so that it's necessary to close her, or what ceremony is that?"[18]

Charles financed the expansion of his empire—itself knit together from an incongruous tapestry of hereditary territories that retained their legal autonomy and customs under his rule—through a combination of taxes, loans from Flemish and Genovese bankers, and silver unloaded in Seville from the galleons returning from the New World. The last, which grew in impact after the development in the 1570s of the use of mercury in extracting silver from ore, accounted for an increasing proportion of the crown's resources throughout the rest of the sixteenth century, even as the influx of coin contributed to the explosion in prices and the general collapse of the economy.

While Spain's reputation for military and political might was cemented under Charles's son Philip, already in the second year of the latter's reign, in 1557, his government defaulted on its debts in the first of several general bankruptcies. While the famous destruction of Philip's armada against England in 1588 marks in the popular imagination the beginning of Spain's decline, in truth its ambitions had been unsustainable from much earlier.

The year that Miguel de Cervantes was born, 1547, was also the year of two events that are symbolic of the pivotal juncture that Charles's great empire had come to. In the Museo del Prado in Madrid there hangs a majestic painting of Charles on horseback painted by Titian in 1548 to commemorate his greatest military victory, in April of the previous year, over a league of Lutheran princes at the town of Mühlberg on the river Elbe.

The emperor's victory was achieved in typical style for Charles, by an army only about a fifth of whom were Castilian soldiers. While 1547 could thus be read as the ultimate affirmation of the "open Spain" of the first part of the sixteenth century—a society working in cooperation with other nations in a joint imperial endeavor under an international, enlightened monarch—another event took place on the peninsula then that would signal a decisive movement in a very different direction indeed.

In that year, the newly appointed archbishop of Toledo, Juan Martínez Siliceo, forced the town to adopt a statute of blood purity to be taken into consideration in the appointment of all high-ranking ecclesiastic and secular posts. Martínez Siliceo, who was of humble but "old Christian" origins (meaning, in the parlance of the time, that he could trace his family back numerous generations with no evidence of Jewish or Muslim ancestors), used this statute to ensure that a rival, a nobleman named Fernando Jiménez (whose father was a converted

Titian, *Ritratto di Carlo V a Cavallo*, 1548. Photo by the Print Collector/Print Collector/Getty Images

Jew, or *converso*, who had recently been investigated by the Inquisition), be barred from the post of canon in the diocese.[19]

This first official blood purity statute was built on a tension that had been simmering in the Spain of Charles V since before he assumed the throne. Charles, who was a thin and awkward teenager when he arrived for the first time in Spain for his coronation in 1517, was initially resented for his foreign advisers and his accented Castilian— French was his native language—as he would be later for his long absences from Castilian soil. The year after accepting the allegiance of the Courts of Castile, he was elected Holy Roman emperor to replace his grandfather Maximilian, who had died five months earlier. While Spaniards eventually came to accept and be distinctly proud of their emperor, the traditionalist, antiforeign sentiments that greeted his reign would present the first great challenge to his authority in the form of a popular revolt, and would eventually come to dominate Spanish social and political life as he compromised his own positions and practices to accommodate that faction.

The Revolt of the Comuneros, or "municipal governments," which has often been misunderstood as a progressive popular revolution, was in reality deeply conservative in nature, and targeted the perceived foreignness of Charles's government and sphere of influence. As a Dominican monk in 1520 proclaimed, exhorting his flock with a sermon in which he spoke directly to Charles, "It is of these realms that Your Majesty is true sovereign and proprietor, and you have bought with money the Empire, which ought not to pass nor be transmitted to your heirs; and Your Majesty has reduced the realm to the poverty in which it stands, and your followers have enriched themselves excessively."[20]

The same period that saw this violent reaction against foreign influence, however, also witnessed the arrival of new currents and ideas from Italy and Charles's native Netherlands, among which the ideas of Erasmus held a special prominence. In addition to being embraced by the community of intellectuals and proponents of a more open, internationally oriented Spain, the ideas of Erasmus may have held special appeal for the *conversos*, who had outwardly converted to Christianity in order to stay in Spain after their expulsion by the Catholic monarchs Isabella and Ferdinand in 1492, and who appreciated the idea of a religious practice that emphasized interior devotion over the public signs that, in practice, led to discrimination and distrust of their communities.[21]

When the Inquisition began investigating *converso* families for possible backsliding, the inquisitors would focus their interviews on precisely such publicly visible signs, asking neighbors whether they noticed families extinguishing their fires on Saturdays or avoiding pork. Charles, who was at first a supporter of the spread of Erasmus's ideas in Spain, found himself in a difficult position as he faced the new challenges posed by the rise of Lutheranism in the east, and felt for political as well as religious reasons that he needed to back the Inquisition and its proponents in Spain. In that regard, 1547 was a watershed year. Toledo's blood purity laws were followed in short order by similar statutes throughout the kingdom, and nine years later the freshly crowned king Philip II would approve the statutes with the words "all the heresies in Germany, France, and Spain have been sewn by descendants of Jews."[22]

This newly articulated calculus of self-worth was rapidly absorbed and superimposed on older, traditional indicators of social value, most specifically, the concept of honor. Honor had been associated with the nobility in feudal Castilian society, and its tight connection with noble virtues such as courage and truthfulness was reflected in late medieval literature. From the late sixteenth century, in contrast, and in particular with the rise of the fantastically popular public theaters, honor became seen as, in the famous words of the playwright Pedro Calderón de la Barca, the universal "patrimony of the soul"[23]—but only if the soul in question was of pure, old Christian blood. Commoners on the Spanish stage repeatedly touted their claim to honorable status on the basis of their blood purity,[24] but the stage would just as quickly discover the dramatic possibilities involved in the potential loss of honor should the purity of one's family be stained by illicit behavior on the part of one's wife or daughters.

The ideology of purity brought together into one crucible all the paranoid fantasies sustaining Spain's religious and patriarchal social structure. Honor was available to all men as long as they were free of even the slightest stain of suspicion concerning the religious purity of their ancestry or the sexual purity of their women. And this insidious ideology metastasized throughout Spanish society in inverse proportion to the control the Spanish crown actually had over its diverse constituents, its economy, and the state of its foreign policy conflicts. The arc that began with the blood purity statutes of 1547 reached its logical conclusion in 1609, when Philip III ordered, with wide popular support, the forced exodus of the entire Morisco population of Spain, resulting in the dispossession, extreme suffering, and death of hundreds of thousands of innocent people, solely because of their ethnic identity.[25]

AT THE MOMENT OF HIS FIRST literary triumphs in 1568, Cervantes would have been keenly aware of the fragility of his acceptance into this purified people, his zeal for his nation inflated by a desperate desire to belong. His grandfather Juan de Cervantes had been a successful man who kept his family, including four children, in relative luxury even as he moved from city to city to take up new government appointments. But his wealth and proximity to power meant that his children would grow up on the fringes of Spain's nobility while not truly belonging to it, a situation that engendered as many problems as it did privileges.

Juan de Cervantes's father was Rodrigo Díaz de Cervantes, a draper likely born in the 1430s in Córdoba. Córdoba was a town with a significant *converso* population that lived in a state of uneasy détente with its "old Christian" neighbors. In 1473, a few years before Juan's birth, a statue of the Virgin that was being carried through a *converso* area of town during a Lenten procession was doused by a pitcher of water thrown, inadvertently, one assumes, out the window of a prominent *converso* family's house. The rumor spread quickly that the liquid had in fact been urine, and in the mob scene that followed, a *converso* by the name of Pedro de Torreblanca was stabbed to death, which led to three days of riots and ethnic tensions throughout the city. The incident is of particular interest because about thirty years later, Juan, by then a freshly minted graduate in law from the University of Salamanca, married a physician's daughter who was possibly his cousin as well; her name was Leonor Fernández de Torreblanca.[26] Her last name, her father's profession, Juan's own chosen path as well as the evident means his father had with which to educate him—all the evidence, while decidedly circumstantial, points to Cervantes's family being new Christians.

While Juan's struggle for acceptability was certainly successful, his efforts brought him into conflict with the very echelons of power whose ramparts he was striving to breach. During his service to the Duke of the Infantado while living in Guadalajara, a regional capital of La Mancha some forty miles northeast of Madrid, Juan's daughter María become entangled in an illicit affair with the duke's bastard son Martín de Mendoza, who wooed her with promises of marriage. Such a liaison would have greatly benefitted Juan's aspirations, but his fortunes changed for the worse when the duke suddenly died and his sons discovered that Juan de Cervantes, his trusted adviser, had been complicit in the duke's own secret marriage to a commoner, to whom he had given an outlandish dowry and who now stood to inherit a large chunk of his estate. Partly as a result of this feud, Martín de Mendoza severed his engagement with María, thus reneging on his promise of marriage.

Juan fought back, using his legal acumen to exact a significant payment from the Mendozas, but not before being forced to spend a week in Valladolid's royal prison.

Juan used the Mendoza payoff to move his family to Alcalá de Henares, where he took the position of assistant magistrate. Alcalá would become one of Spain's great centers of learning during the sixteenth century, second only in renown to Salamanca, and home of the first complete and multilingual printed Bible, containing the Greek Old Testament, the Septuagint, and the Targum Onkelos, or Aramaic translation of the Torah. That Bible would be henceforth known as the Complutensian Polyglot Bible in honor of the Latin name for Alcalá: Complutum. The university at Alcalá would later be moved to Madrid, where it is now the largest university in Spain and one of the largest in the world, the Universidad Complutense.

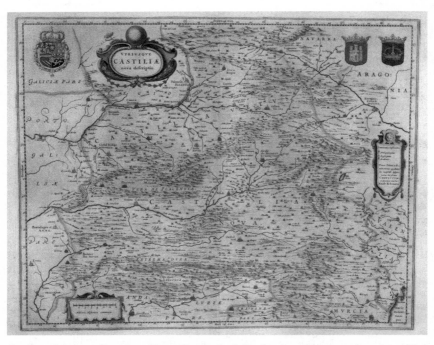

Castile and Aragon, from Joan Blaeu, *Der Aerdrycks-Beschryuing, welck vervat Spaenjen, Africa, en America*. Amsterdam: Blaeu, 1665. Vol. 8. George Peabody Library, the Sheridan Libraries, Johns Hopkins University

In Alcalá, Juan set his family up in a fine house, replete with servants, horses, and all the trapping of wealth and power; and his sons, especially Rodrigo, became accustomed to a leisurely lifestyle. His daughter María, who gave birth to a daughter whom she named Martina de Mendoza, bought another large house on the Calle de la Imagen, where the town's synagogue had been located.[27] This all began to change in 1538 when Juan de Cervantes left Alcalá, taking with him only his older son, Andrés, and leaving behind the rest of his family, including Rodrigo. Juan returned to his native city of Córdoba, where he struck up a new life of opulence with another woman while his former family was left to struggle in poverty. Estranged from his father, the source of his livelihood until then, Rodrigo stayed in Alcalá and in 1542 married Leonor de Cortina. The fact that none of her relatives appears to have attended the baptisms of any of the couple's children suggests that they may have been of higher social standing and thought this alliance beneath them.[28] Alcalá would become the birthplace of Miguel along with his younger brother, Rodrigo, and two older sisters, Luisa and Andrea. A first son, Andrés, died in infancy, and a final daughter, Magdalena, would be born in 1552, when the family had moved to Valladolid. Rodrigo, who was a surgeon by profession, which at the time meant little more than a bloodletter, tried to support his growing family by stitching the wounds and setting the fractured bones of Alcalá's students, but a surgeon's lowly wages were far from enough, and he quickly fell into debt.[29]

Rodrigo's attempts to support his growing family as a surgeon in a university town where, as Cervantes would later write, "of the five thousand students who studied that year at the university, two thousand were studying medicine,"[30] were likely doomed from the outset. His leisurely youth seems to have left him with little aptitude for hard work, although he may already have suffered from hearing problems, as he would be quite deaf in his later years. In any event, Rodrigo's money problems followed him to Valladolid, where he tried to insinuate himself into a wealthier clientele by padding the family's lifestyle on borrowed funds. In the summer of 1552, a few weeks before his daughter Magdalena was born, he was jailed for failing to pay his debts, and his property was impounded. During this time of extreme hardship for the Cervantes family, it was only the fortitude and wit of Leonor that allowed them to survive. A woman of seemingly boundless internal resources who had learned to read and write in an age when few women could, she bartered and sold what she could to keep her children fed, even during the final weeks of her pregnancy. The wealth of strong and independent women in Cervantes's fiction may have something to do with the fact that Miguel's first memories were of a time when his father languished behind bars while his mother kept the family afloat.

During this stint in debtor's prison, Rodrigo tried to take advantage of the inequities governing Spanish society at the time by getting a court to rule that he was of hidalgo lineage and not subject to debtor laws. As he claimed in a deposition at the time, his status was in question in Valladolid solely because his hometown was Alcalá. It was there that he had an estate and could easily access the funds to pay off his creditors, who were simply not willing to wait for him to do so; also, he was known to be a hidalgo, "and I have the information to show it."[31] At first he was unable to establish a legal basis for this, and the court dismissed his claims and left him in jail. This initial failure to establish his exempt status reinforces the claim that Cervantes's family, by and large educated and literate and descending as they did from Cordovan merchants, had Jewish forebears—an indelible stain in a culture where Judaism was outlawed and any traces of it were hunted out with paranoid ardor.

Finally he was able to obtain multiple affidavits stating that the Cervantes family had at least always been considered by others to be of old Christian blood, which the courts finally accepted as enough to establish his status as a gentleman, and he was released from prison. A free man, but with no more means of making a living than he had had before, and presumably somewhat less likelihood of borrowing more, Rodrigo decided to move his family to Córdoba, perhaps in the hope of parlaying his relation to his father into some gainful employment.

It was in Córdoba that a then-six-year-old Miguel de Cervantes would have had his first opportunity at a formal education, most likely at the hands of the Society of Jesus. The Jesuits opened a school in that city in 1553, and their schooling left a lasting impression on the young Miguel, who would later write with some affection of the Jesuits and their pedagogical methods. As one of the eponymous dogs of his novella *The Dogs' Colloquy* recounts to the other, a merchant he knew in Seville sent his two sons to study with the Society of Jesus, thus expressing in his offspring an ambition to get ahead in the world. The dog, watching at the door as the teachers dispatched their lessons, marveled at the "love, conduct, solicitude, and effort with which those blessed fathers and teachers instructed those children."[32]

Miguel, already stuttering, perhaps shocked into shyness by his family's forced exile at a time when it was unusual not to be rooted for generations in a single place, clearly bloomed in the world opened up to him by the Jesuits' love of learning. He had seen his father in prison, his belongings taken away by creditors. He had come to taste poverty, and was certainly already feeling the sting of his family's dishonor. As his father's failures and exclusions became increasingly clear to him, the world of letters and specifically literature that his teachers showed him would have beckoned with a comforting promise of escape from such mundane cares. Poets who later would be recognized and praised by Miguel, such as Pedro Sanz de Soria and Jerónimo de Lomas Cantoral, may have been in class with him in Córdoba, and it was there that he struck up a lifelong friendship with Tomás Gutiérrez de Castro, who would become a successful and wealthy actor, and would give safe harbor to Miguel in Seville during some of his darkest days.[33]

Juan de Cervantes died in 1556, after which Rodrigo may have moved his family to Cabra, a town some fifty miles distant from Córdoba where his younger brother Andrés was mayor and could easily have procured him a job in the local hospital. It is likely the family remained there until 1564, when Rodrigo's name appears on a lease in Seville. Andrés had taken up a position as a magistrate in Seville by that time, and his own son, also called Rodrigo, was close to Miguel in age, so it is quite plausible that they would have continued their education together at the Jesuit school of Seville, where the playwright Pedro Pablo de Acevedo had joined the faculty in 1561.[34]

Acevedo is considered the founder of the scholastic drama (plays written in Latin in imitation of classical models) in Spain. Jesuit schools were one of the few arenas in Europe where classical theater was being performed, as the Jesuits would have their students act out plays as well as discuss them in order to reveal their underlying moral messages.[35] Under Acevedo and other teachers, Cervantes would have been exposed to scholastic drama, and perhaps even performed some pieces, although his tendency to stammer kept him from pursuing a life on the boards.

In Seville he witnessed performances by the itinerant playwright and actor Lope de Rueda, an experience that seared in his mind a love of the stage that he would attest to many years later. As he wrote in the preface he penned for his *Eight Comedies and Eight Interludes Never Performed Onstage*, Lope de Rueda "was admirable in pastoral poetry, and in this way no one here has surpassed him, then or now; and although, because I was just a boy then, I was not able to judge properly the quality of his verses, from those that I remember now, seen from the maturity of my age, I find that what I write is the truth."[36]

An image begins to emerge of the young Cervantes, child of the itinerant and perpetually underachieving Rodrigo, attending school next to the son of his far more successful uncle, suffering from a mild speech impediment while looking on with longing at the rhetorical flourishes of actors on the stage. This young Miguel clearly sought solace in the written word, and it was in Seville that he would have first encountered the ideas of Renaissance humanism that had flooded Spain during the first half of the century, but that were already meeting with resistance from an increasingly conservative Church orthodoxy. Only a few years later, the Inquisition's first *Index Librorum Prohibitorum* would be published, and most of the books of Erasmus of Rotterdam would make the list. But Erasmus's teaching, along with the ideas of many Italian Renaissance thinkers, had great influence on Spanish intellectual circles in the first part of the sixteenth century,[37] and there can be little doubt that Cervantes was exposed to such ideas early and often.[38]

In short, the Cervantes, who by his late teens became López de Hoyos's beloved student, was the intellectual beneficiary of the open, tolerant current that flowed from the flourishing contact with Dutch humanism and that characterized Spanish culture of the 1520s. Beset by insecurities, he devoted his energies to developing extraordinary erudition and verbal brilliance. At the same time, there is no reason to doubt that Cervantes was both a dedicated and passionate defender of his crown and its religion. But his society's gradual adoption of an ideology of racial, religious, and even sexual purity, combined with his later disappointments over his government's foreign policy failures against the Turkish Empire and lack of recognition for his own military service, would eventually cultivate in him a deep-seated suspicion toward the official version of events. The Cervantes who years later would turn his hopes away from a government sinecure and start cobbling together an existence as a writer supported by intermittent government commissions would not only see clearly the discrepancy between his government's portrayal of Spain and its sad reality, but would also have to come to grips with the loss of his own faith in the system and its values. Just as Spain would close the door on different beliefs and different peoples, Cervantes would see his own options close. It would take literature to open them again.

The lofty sentiments of his teenage poems wilt before his take on Philip II's legacy in a poem he would compose many decades later on the occasion of the king's death in 1598, and that he would later declare among the very best of his writings. In that poem, one man stands before a funeral monument built in honor of the king and speaks, and then is approached by another, described as a bully, rogue, or rapscallion:

> *"I'd wager that the soul of the departed*
> *Has left high heaven, where he enjoys eternal*
> *Bliss, to enjoy this place." A bully, hearing this,*
> *Replied, "What Your Honor says is true, sir soldier,*
> *And whoever says it's not, lies like a dog."*
> *Whereupon he clasped his hat upon his head,*
> *Checked his sword, looked furtively, and left.*
> *And that was that.*[39]

Where his earlier poem gushed with praise for Philip, the later poem, unable to criticize the king openly, instead portrays someone praising Philip and then subtly undermines that speaker's credibility. Thus at the close of the seventeenth century, thirty years after those heady days in Madrid and now on the verge of his greatest breakthrough, the poet reveals in this withering portrayal of public attitudes toward authority the double-edged irony that would characterize his later and greater works.

It is not too difficult to see in this bully, who touts the king's virtues at the top of his voice and then reassures himself of his own status before slinking off the scene, a chastened version of the poet who three decades earlier had sung those words of praise. Checking his privilege while casting furtive glances to see if he has been observed, the bully, infected by a touch of Cervantes's own disappointments, rises from being the mere imprint of a doctrine to become a full-fledged character. Yes, he is the object of the poet's ridicule, but he is also imbued with his empathy. Cervantes has drafted him from within and without, and by doing so he has divided his readers as well, into spectators who both look on from the outside and project themselves, their feelings, and their desires onto the figures populating the space of the page.

The young aspiring poet who wrote those earlier lines in praise of Philip in 1568 had not yet become the older, wiser, disillusioned author of this plaint. His spirit, like his words, was naïve and full of fire and patriotic fervor. It is even likely that his sense of honor—the proverbial chip on the sloped shoulder of his stunted self-esteem—was attuned to the superficial expectations of the day. For generations, the next scent that biographers had of Cervantes's life after these first poems in 1568 was his surprise appearance two years later in Rome, as an employee in the house of a young nobleman by the name of Giulio Acquaviva, who that year would be named a cardinal by Pope Pius V. But in the nineteenth century a researcher working in the archives of the town of Simancas, near Valladolid, discovered a warrant issued on September 15, 1569, for the arrest of a student named Miguel de Cervantes for the crime of having wounded one Antonio de Sigura in a duel.

Dueling, which normally was provoked by a *pundonor*, or perceived besmirching of a man's honor, was severely prohibited by the government, and the punishment handed down in Cervantes's absence was a case in point: banishment for ten years and loss of his right hand. Whatever it was that Antonio de Sigura had said to Cervantes, or vice versa, the result was that a young man two weeks shy of his twenty-second birthday, with his first literary successes behind him and on the threshold of a promising future, risked his life and his freedom over a tossed-off insult or snide insinuation about his family's heritage or his sisters' moral character.

That bravado had an incalculable toll. Evading capture in Madrid, Cervantes made it first to Seville before leaving Spanish soil entirely and would not return for more than a decade. And though he would eventually count Spain his home again, the next thirty years of his life would be characterized by suffering and misfortune, by extraordinary acts of courage in the face of death, and by professional disappointments and the banal recompense of an ungrateful homeland. Imperial,

Counter-Reformation Spain, in all its fateful, tragic arrogance, had begun to close around young Miguel.

Cervantes would learn from these experiences, though. In every case—the exploits of war, the travails of captivity, the humiliation of prison—each of these hard knocks would bring their own texture and specific dimensions to what would be his life's work. It would take many years to realize, but the love of literature planted in that shy, stuttering newcomer in Córdoba would pay off in spades. As his own fate constrained and disappointed him; as he encountered and came to love real people whose lives were ruined by the fantasies of blood and honor; as he grew to see his sisters disgraced and himself imprisoned like his father and grandfather before him; Miguel de Cervantes would seek his freedom in an explosion of emotionally rich characters whose palpable reality would stem from their feeling excluded from and baffled by the righteous certainties of the society that framed them.

3.

Soldier of Misfortune

"And if this seems an insignificant danger, let us see if it is equaled or surpassed when the prows of two galleys collide in the middle of the wide sea, for when they lock and grapple, the soldier is left with no more than two feet of plank on the ram of the ship; despite this, seeing that he has in front of him as many ministers of death threatening him as there are artillery cannons aimed at him from the other side, only a lance's throw away, and seeing that at the first misstep he will visit the deep bosom of Neptune, despite this, with an intrepid heart, carried by the honor that urges him on, he makes himself the target of all their volleys and attempts to cross that narrow passage to the enemy vessel. And the most astounding thing is that no sooner does one man fall, not to rise again until the world comes to an end, than another takes his place, and if he too falls into the sea that waits like an enemy, there is another, and another who follows him, and their deaths come one after the other, without pause: no greater valor and daring can be found in all the perils of war."

Since the verses sung to posterity by the blind poet Homer and even before him, the two most constant themes of literature have been love and war. The epic poems that proliferated in the eleventh through fifteenth centuries were often about great knights doing battle against the infidel, and at first were mastered by minstrels who would travel from town to town earning their living by singing these tales. As the Crusades got under way, many of the themes, characters, and specific stories of famous Christian knights who had gone to the Holy Land were adopted into "songs of deeds" or *chansons de geste*, as they were called in French. Sometime in the eleventh century these songs began to be copied down by scribes who transliterated them into Latin script, creating the first written literature in vernacular Romance languages.

Many of the books that circulated during the literacy explosion of the sixteenth century were such epic tales of war. From the publication of Ludovico Ariosto's *Orlando furioso* in 1516, one of the first true international bestsellers,[1] to Torquato Tasso's *La Gerusalemme liberata*, or *Jerusalem Delivered*, from 1581, the epic poems recounting the great deeds of Christian knights set the standard for popular literature. Two of Tasso's great heroes, the knights Tancredi and Rinaldo, appear in the forty-fifth stanza of the first canto of *Jerusalem Delivered*, a canto devoted, in the style of classical epic poetry, to describing the gathering of heroes:

> Next comes Tancredi; and there is none among so many (except Rinaldo) who is a greater swordsman, or handsomer in manners and in appearance, or of more exalted and unwavering courage. If any shadow of guilt makes less resplendent his great repute, it is only the folly of love: a love born amid arms, from a fleeting glimpse that nurtures itself on sorrows and gathers strength.[2]

A mere twenty-four years after the enormously successful publication of this great poem, Cervantes has his own fearless and lovelorn knight step forth onto the glorious fields of Mars. Having spied "a large, thick cloud of dust coming toward them along the road they were traveling," Quixote says to Sancho,

> "This is the day, O Sancho, when the good fortune that destiny has reserved for me will be revealed! This is the day, I say, when, as much as on any other, the valor of my arms will be proved, and I shall perform deeds that will be inscribed in the book of Fame for all time to come. Do you see that cloud of dust rising there, Sancho? Well, it conceals a vast army, composed of innumerable and diverse peoples, which is marching toward us."
>
> "If that's the case there must be two," said Sancho, "because over in the opposite direction there's another cloud of dust just like it."[3]

Overjoyed at the prospect of at last showing his prowess by intervening in a battle between two great armies, Quixote urges Sancho up the nearest hill to get a better look at the armies. From their new vantage, the Don begins to narrate in terrific detail, as Ariosto or Tasso would have done, all the famous knights and giants he spots among the two armies, ludicrous inventions of his imagination replete with their signature arms, shields, and powers—all to the great bewilderment of Sancho, who cannot see anything because of the great quantities of dust in the air:

> Sancho Panza hung on his words but said none of his own, and from time to time he turned his head to see if he could see the knights and giants his master was naming; since he could not make out any of them, he said,
>
> "Señor, may the devil take me, but no man, giant, or knight of all those your grace has mentioned can be seen anywhere around here; at least, I don't see them; maybe it's all enchantment, like last night's phantoms."
>
> "How can you say that?" responded Don Quixote. "Do you not hear the neighing of horses, the call of the clarions, the sounds of the drums?"
>
> "I don't hear anything," responded Sancho, "except the bleating of lots of sheep."+

Cervantes's version of the gathering of heroes is blatant satire, of course. But his view of the battlefield doesn't differ from that of Tasso merely because of its comic bent, or because of the depths of its description, the beauty of its verses, or another purely aesthetic measure. It differs because Tasso's prose describes for Tasso and his readers the essence of war, while Cervantes's describes how people perceive and misperceive war. While both descriptions rise to Aristotle's definition of poetry as relaying not what did but what could happen, Cervantes, by moving his reader's experience into the space between his characters and how they see the world, has taken a decisive step toward what the modern world understands as fiction.

Having been there himself, Cervantes knew that really fighting in a war had none of the beauty, excitement, and pageantry that the tales of chivalry claimed for it. The stories we tell from afar about war, the view from above, are always belied by the experience of those whose lives are on the lines. For the men who die in such wars—the foot soldiers and musketeers firing into opposing lines, galley soldiers leaping from plank to plank under harquebus fire—their experience is more akin to that of bleating sheep lost in enormous clouds of dust, albeit far more deadly.

But Cervantes also had the greatest respect for the calling of arms, for the courage that led a man to risk his life for a higher cause, and for the enormous hardships suffered by those who had, like him, taken those risks and either fallen or survived. While relentlessly ironic in his treatment of war and those who profited from it, he also yearned for a time when those who distinguished themselves on the battlefield with honor and courage would be awarded the admiration and dignity they deserved. This conflict, like so many in Cervantes's personality, found its way into the odd friendship growing between his two most iconic characters. For every time that Quixote waxes poetic about war, Sancho's own unabashed preference for peace comes in to balance what he has said; and every unceremonious bashing one or the other receives provokes as many practical admonitions from the squire as it does pious justifications from his master. As Quixote proudly tells Sancho after his tilting at windmills has left him listing in his saddle,

> "If I do not complain about the pain, it is because it is not the custom of knights errant to complain about any wound, even if their innards are spilling out because of it."
>
> "If that's true I have nothing to say," Sancho replied, "but God knows I'd be happy if your grace complained when something hurt you. As for me, I can say that I'll complain about the smallest pain I have, unless what you have said about not complaining also applies to the squires of knights errant."[5]

With war as with all other things, Quixote and Sancho manage to reach a fragile détente across the battlefield of Cervantes's own conflicted feelings.

LIKE DEATH CHEATED, fate had found a way to take Cervantes's hand, even if not the right one claimed by the law. Two years after his hurried departure from Spain he would be hit three times by harquebus fire while boarding a Turkish galley off the coast of Greece, and would forever lose the use of his left hand. As he later wrote in his autobiographical *Journey to Parnassus*, with a customary wink at fortune's cunning, "I lost the movement of my left hand for the greater glory of my right."[6] Upon the wounding of Sigura in a duel, the terrified twenty-one-year-old had quickly fled Madrid and the literary life he aspired to there, first returning to Seville, but soon coming to the realization that nowhere on Spanish soil could he find safety from a sentence that commanded that he be sought out and captured wherever Spanish rule held sway.

So it was that in December of 1569 Cervantes found himself in Rome, where he applied to serve as a chamberlain in the household of the son of the Duke of Altri, a priest named Giulio Acquaviva only a year his senior. Back in Madrid his father, Rodrigo, requested documentation of his son's blood purity and status as a hidalgo— a member of the lower gentry, literally, the son of someone—a necessity for holding such a position in a prelate's household. He was successful, and in February of the following year Cervantes began his service. It was not to last long, however, as the powerful young Acquaviva was appointed cardinal in May of 1570, and Cervantes left his service.

Living in Rome, a city under the jurisdiction of the papacy rather than the Spanish king, gave Cervantes some measure of safety from his sentence, even as he walked through the streets of what his friend Luis Gálvez de Montalvo called a den of iniquity, with "its prisons full of Spaniards, the streets full of prostitutes, and the city full of priests."[7] Still, he knew that extraordinary service would be needed in order to cleanse his name and permit his eventual return home; so when the opportunity for such service was created the following year by the Turkish Empire, the reluctant exile jumped at the chance to go to war for his faith.

Growing in power and influence in the Mediterranean and eastern Europe since the beginning of the sixteenth century, in the summer of 1570 the Turkish admiral Uluç-Ali, backed by an armada led by Piali Pasha, attacked the island of Cyprus, putting to the sword thousands of its Christian inhabitants.[8] Venice, the European power with the greatest presence on the island, at once began diplomatic efforts to form a coalition to come to Cyprus's defense. Specifically, Venice turned for help to the papacy and to Philip II, who was preoccupied with Muslim pirates attacking Spain's southern coasts and simultaneously engaged in the suppression of a rebellion of Moriscos on Spanish soil. In May of 1571 the three powers put their mutual distrust aside enough to declare the formation of the Holy League and begin preparations for a major counteroffensive against the Turkish fleet.

With the massive mobilization under way, Cervantes made his way to Naples. It must have seemed to him that half of Spain was already there. Most important, his brother Rodrigo had arrived with the company of Diego de Urbina. Urbina's outfit had been one of those fighting against the rebellion in the Alpujarras Mountains near Granada, and was now recruiting new soldiers to replace those it had lost in the violence there. Cervantes must have been overjoyed as he and his brother embraced after an absence of several years, and looked ahead to serving side by side in a great and noble adventure.

In Urbina's company Cervantes was assigned the role of harquebusier. This meant that, in addition to acquiring the heavy, clumsy weapon he would wield in battle, he was given a splendid uniform of red-and-yellow striped pants, ruff collar, leather doublet, red shirt, stockings, and buckled shoes. So outlandish was the outfit that the harquebusiers were called *papagayos*, or "parrots."⁹

On August 8, Miguel and Rodrigo made their way down the steep streets to the port in the Bay of Naples, looking out in wonder across the shimmering water toward the islands of Ischia and Capri as the bay filled with the incoming ships of Don Juan of Austria. Don Juan would stay for that week to receive the jewel-encrusted baton symbolizing his command of the Holy League's fleet and to gather the troops who had assembled in Naples. At the end of that week the fleet headed south toward Messina, Sicily, the last port of call before sailing around the boot of Italy to engage the Turks. This time the Cervantes brothers were with him.

In Messina the festivities and preparations for war were reaching a fever pitch. There, Miguel and Rodrigo were joined by friends from home and relatives from far away. Miguel was reunited with some of his literary circle, poets such as Juan Rufo, Gabriel López Maldonado, and even the older man he would later call his mentor in poetry, Pedro Laínez.¹⁰ After more than two weeks of last-minute planning, loading ships, oiling guns and cannons, and waiting out storms in the harbor, on September 16 all of Messina came out to witness the spectacle of more than three hundred ships weighing anchor under the flying colors of Spain, the papacy, and Venice, as well as those of many other nations and city-states that had lent their people to this crusade.

After such a send-off, life on board the *Marquesa* was a great disappointment. No doubt the experience colored Cervantes's later description of ships as "maritime dwellings where one is most often abused by the bedbugs, robbed by the criminals, angered by the sailors, ravaged by rats and wearied by insects."[11] One of those insects was to do more than weary him. Within two weeks, as the armada made its way cautiously across the Adriatic in search of Uluç-Ali's fleet, Cervantes was belowdecks convulsed with fever. Life in the belly of a galley like the *Marquesa* would have been almost unbearable under the best of circumstances; one can only hope that, in the throes of malaria, Cervantes was delirious for most of that time. The stench of human waste and poor-to-nonexistent ventilation would have been overwhelming; the food, revolting; and the nausea from motion sickness would have been exacerbated only by the great number of seasick men, themselves recently graduated landlubbers.

To top it all, infighting among the Christian leadership was on the verge of scuttling the entire mission. In fact, it might well have, had not news arrived on October 4 that Cyprus, in whose defense the League had been launched, had already fallen two months earlier. More tragically, the League learned that the Turkish leader Mustafa Pasha, enraged by how many men he had lost in his long siege of the island, had violated the surrender terms, sending his captives into slavery and killing the Venetian leadership. Marcantonio Bragadino, the Venetian commander who defended the island and negotiated the surrender, had suffered a particularly horrifying end: he was flayed alive, and his skin was stuffed with straw and the effigy hung from the mast of Mustafa's ship.[12] Their differences erased by their communal outrage, the feuding members renewed their commitment, this time in the name of vengeance.

On the morning of October 7, the Holy League's armada engaged the Turkish fleet off the shore of Greece in the Gulf of Lepanto. At that time, just prior to the development of the broadside warship that would revolutionize naval warfare by the end of the sixteenth century, sea battles tended to be fought near to shore between long, low-slung galleys powered by the rowing strength of hundreds of shackled slaves. Battles could be won only by ships being boarded and their crews subdued, so the key to any offensive was for the soldiers to come sufficiently close to shoot and kill enough of the enemy for them to board and take over the ship.

Cervantes's actions at this point show something of his mettle, a courage that many others would later testify to. When Diego de Urbina ordered him to remain belowdecks on account of his illness, he refused, shouting, "Captain, put me in the most dangerous post there is. I will stick to it and die fighting!" Seeing his evident resolve, Urbina assigned him to a position on the side of the ship known as the skiff, "the highest and the most exposed part of the whole galley and the most dangerous."[13] So intense was the fighting that day, and so many were the dead and wounded, that the gulf's waters turned

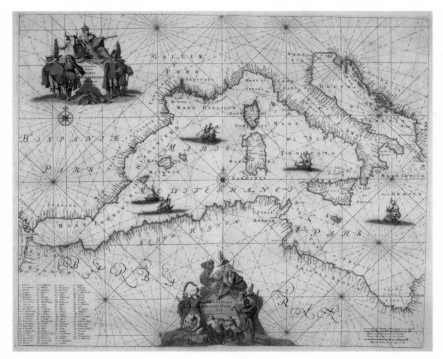

Map of the Mediterranean, from *Atlas* by Frederik de Wit, Amsterdam, 1695. The John Work Garrett Library, the Sheridan Libraries, Johns Hopkins University

crimson. By the end of the battle, the League's forces emerged victorious, and some fifteen thousand Christian slaves were freed from below the decks of the enemy vessels. Cervantes, who endured an arduous sea journey back from Lepanto to Sicily and spent the next six months recuperating from his wounds in a hospital in Messina, became a hero of that momentous battle, which would go down in history as one of Spain's greatest victories, and would remain for Cervantes a glorious reminder of what true valor, sacrifice, and honor meant.

HOW CAN WE BEGIN to imagine the ambivalence that Cervantes must have felt for war? On the one hand, his experiences at Lepanto made manifest the depth of his convictions and the strength of his courage; they revealed to him the unparalleled bravery of the comrades who fell around him, and those who survived to fight on. His most intimate sense of self-worth was tied to his exploits as a soldier. On the other hand, by the time he returned to Spain a broken man, wounded and unrewarded, he had also seen the fruits of his and others' sacrifices churned up and unceremoniously spat out by the relentless machine of the early modern state's military industrial complex.

My allusion to Eisenhower's valedictory warning to the United States is not gratuitous. As the eminent historian Geoffrey Parker put it, by the early seventeenth century, "the expansion of military administration formed a powerful stimulus to bureaucratic growth in Europe."[14] At the same time, the growing apparatus of war was entirely funded by an international banking industry addicted to the interest payments on its massive loans to governments that were repeatedly on the verge of going bankrupt. Indeed, Philip's first bankruptcy was followed by six more from the end of the sixteenth to the middle of the seventeenth centuries. The result was a continent where most nations were at war most of the time, and in which the Spanish Empire, for the first half of the seventeenth century, never knew a year of peace.[15]

That ambivalence, however, as difficult as it may have been for him, lay at the heart of Cervantes's literary innovation. While he deals with war in many of his writings, in *Don Quixote* it appears mostly in a kind of negative form, as the Don fantasizes about battles and great armies where none are, in fact, present, and as he mistakes goatherds or merchants for soldiers and knights, to their great bemusement and, more often than not, to the exacerbation of his own sorry state.

In a justifiably famous passage from *Don Quixote*, the mournful knight broaches a beloved subject of Renaissance rhetoric. Sitting at the head of a long table over dinner at an inn, Don Quixote, having finished his meal, launches into an impromptu harangue on the superiority of arms over letters, of the soldiering life over that of the scholar. He begins by establishing the purpose of each way of life. The life of letters, he declaims, serves "to maintain distributive justice, and give each man what is his, and make certain that good laws are obeyed." Granting that this is "generous and high and worthy of great praise," he nonetheless insists that it is "not so meritorious as arms," and concludes with spectacular righteousness that peace is the true purpose of war.[16]

When Don Quixote speaks, he is almost always funny. This is even the case when he speaks with eloquence, as he is often capable of doing. In this case the comedy comes from the earnestness with which the knight pronounces, as if they were totally convincing points, arguments that his readers would recognize as a *reductio ad absurdum*, given how war in Cervantes's time had taken on a kind of industrial permanence. For the knight's earnest defense of war *is* an expression of Cervantes's own conviction that the greatest valor is to risk or lose one's own life for a greater cause. At the same time, in a suspension of opposing sentiments permitted by the very form his writing created, we readers are faced with the utter absurdity of the early modern state's creation of a never-ending culture of war, and the circular justification of its permanent investment in the machinery of war.

Fiction allows Cervantes to express his agonizing ambivalence about war because it is a form of language that permits him to produce sentences that are simultaneously true and false, with the conflict within them provoking us to think about why and how they can be both at the same time. The knight's discourse is full of admiration for the life of the soldier and the toughness with which he survives it, all the while and in the same breath ridiculing the practice of war that forms the very basis of the soldier's life, and slyly skewering the state that puts the soldier in harm's way while depriving him of his due rewards.

Of the soldier, Don Quixote says,

No one in his poverty is as poor as he, for he depends on his miserable pay, which comes late or never . . . If merciful heaven protects him and keeps him whole and alive, it may be that he will remain in the same poverty as before, and he will have to go through one engagement after another, one battle after another, and emerge victorious from all of them in order to prosper only a little; but these miracles are not seen very often.

Indeed, Don Quixote concludes, the only just reward for them is impossible, for it would entail taking "the very wealth that belongs to the lord they serve."[17]

A public speech or pamphlet advocating that soldiers be paid from the pockets of the nobility, much less the king, would be subject to severe censorship; but a mad knight discoursing on the relative worth of arms and letters has far more leeway.[18] Continuing his speech, Don Quixote shows remarkable knowledge of exactly that theater of war in which Cervantes lost limb and almost life, as he waxes poetic on the unparalleled bravery of a soldier in a pitched battle at sea in the passage with which I began this chapter. Here Cervantes and Don Quixote speak together, expressing reverent astonishment before a scene in which, as he writes, "no sooner does one man fall, not to rise again until the world comes to an end, than another takes his place."[19]

The scene Don Quixote describes so vividly is certainly accurate. So many of the broad, flat galleys of the Spanish fleet filled the Gulf of Lepanto on that October morning in 1571 that many more were forced to wait at the entrance, unable to fit among the already abutting planks that covered the water's surface. At least eight thousand of Cervantes's companions died that day, and another eight thousand were counted among the injured. And the loss of Turkish life was well above those numbers, estimated by some historians to be as high as thirty thousand.

As hellish as the Battle of Lepanto was, the machinery of war evolved into an ever more efficient purveyor of death in the thirty years separating that event from the appearance of Cervantes's great novel. On land, battles gave way to extended sieges, encouraged by architectural innovations that allowed cities and towns with the proper armaments to withstand direct assaults. Such cities could be taken only by siege, for which enormous resources were required. On the sea, the galleys like those Cervantes sailed on, which turned a body of water into a kind of extension of a land battle where soldiers would spring from plank to plank to engage one another in combat, were eventually replaced by broadside ships carrying massive artillery, such that opposing ships would be sunk before the troops on either side could engage one another.

It is this mechanization of war that the Knight of the Mournful Countenance most regrets:

"Happy were those blessed times that lacked the horrifying fury of the diabolical instruments of artillery, whose inventor, in my opinion, is in hell, receiving the reward for his accursed invention, which allows an ignoble and cowardly hand to take the life of a valiant knight, so that not knowing how it comes or from where, a stray shot is fired into the courage and spirit that inflame and animate a brave heart, sent by one who perhaps fled in fear at the bright flare when the damned machine discharged it, and it cuts off and ends in an instance the thoughts and life of one who deserved to enjoy many more long years. When I consider this, I am prepared to say that it grieves my very soul that I have taken up the profession of knight errant in an age as despicable as the one we live in now."[20]

Here as in many places Cervantes puts words both praising individual deeds of bravery and condemning the modern practice of warfare into the mouth of an errantly foolish knight capable of moments of great wisdom and lucidity. Clearly Cervantes was justly proud of the valor that led him to face death and survive; but just as clearly these words spring forth from a figure who is comical in his devotion to ideals that the world around him fails to value or even to recognize.

This ambivalent attitude toward the evils and, at times, glories of war is pervasive throughout Cervantes's work. While he was proud of his own service, by the time he published *Don Quixote*, Cervantes had long been disabused of any expectation that honorable feats in war bring just deserts in life. In his writing, though, he translated this disappointment into a theme that animates his entire literary production: the inevitable and irresolvable clash between ideals and reality, a clash now sewn into the fabric of everything we recognize as fiction.

There can be no doubt that ideals suffer mightily in this conflict, but despite the author's justified cynicism, they are never entirely demolished; in truth, what often strikes us as most worthy of our respect is when our fellows hold to their ideals despite the ravages dealt by an unyielding reality. What fiction permitted Cervantes to do in a way that no author before him managed was to juxtapose ideals and their inevitable disappointment in such a way as to force the reader simultaneously to acknowledge their value and to recognize the comic tragedy of their defeat. And because portraying the disappointment of expectations required him to draw on his own experience to imagine how those expectations would feel to those who held them, the shuttling back and forth between expectation and disappointment, between belief and its betrayal, or simply between different points of view in turn animated the characters he created, pulling them into relief by virtue of the difference between their views and those of their counterparts.

Don Quixote's comment that the importance of letters as opposed to arms is that they are used "to maintain distributive justice, and give each man what is his, and make certain that good laws are obeyed," takes on a new importance when seen in the light of how the Spanish state was using the law to maintain the power and privileges of society's most elite echelons. In a scene from the first chapter of the second book of *Don Quixote*, the knight's friends the barber and the priest visit him in his house following his return from the adventures recounted in the first book. After some conversation on politics and the law in which the Don makes fun of the concept of reason of state,[21] acquitting himself so cogently that all present are almost convinced he is cured, he finally turns to the topic of knight errantry and reveals that his delusion continues unabated.

As the narrator tells us, "in the course of their conversation they began to discuss what is called reason of state and ways of governing, correcting this abuse and condemning that one, reforming one custom and eliminating another."[22] Quixote confirms the political connotations of the concept when, reflecting on rampant speculation concerning the possibility of renewed attack by the Turkish Empire, he offers advice to King Philip concerning a much-needed "precautionary measure that His Majesty is very far from considering at present."[23] The immediate and negative responses of his interlocutors show how, by offering unsolicited advice to the crown, Don Quixote is venturing into a hotly debated arena. While the priest thinks to himself that Quixote has, with the mere mention of offering advice that the king may not have thought of, "leaped from the high peak of your madness to the profound abyss of your foolishness," the barber tells him outright that his is one of "the many impertinent proposals that are commonly offered to princes."

Quixote's proposal—that the king call up all the knights errant in the land, as "there might be one among them who could, by himself, destroy all the power of the Turk"—is the one readers had been awaiting for a decade, for it reignites the madness that so delighted them in the first book. But while rendering Quixote's advice anodyne by virtue of its fantastic nature, Cervantes is simultaneously drawing attention to the fact that "what is called reason of state" is far from divinely inspired, and that the king's subjects were in fact constantly identifying abuses and hence disputing the notion that policies and laws were justified by virtue of their provenance from the king's decree.[24]

For Spain's newly crafted state and its attendant bureaucracy had devised and implemented a massive network of ideas and laws supporting the existence and expansion of its engine of war in the face of all economic and moral reasons. These ideas and laws were in turn nourished by the production of an official version of Spanish history that had been continually commissioned by the crown since the early years of Charles's reign and well on into Cervantes's time.[25] In fact, one of the most influential official historians under Philip III was Antonio de Herrera y Tordesillas, the very same censor charged with approving Cervantes's manuscript in the summer of 1604. Thus the man who would write that it is the prerogative of "princes to give the laws and order to the kingdom, and not the kingdom to the prince" was also the one who gave *Don Quixote* the right to see the light of day, with the passing comment that "the public will find it both pleasing and entertaining."[26]

The purpose of these official histories was to retrofit against the reality of Spain's conflicted and multicultural present the idea of a unified religious and cultural origin that had been disrupted by

HISTORIA

DE LOS REYES
GODOS QVE VINIERON
DE LA SCYTHIA DE EVROPA
CONTRA EL IMPERIO ROMANO; Y A
ESPAÑA: CON SVCESSION DELLOS, HASTA
LOS CATOLICOS REYES DON FERNANDO
Y DOÑA ISABEL.

POR IVLIAN DEL CASTILLO.

PROSEGVIDA DESDE SV
principio có adiciones copiofas de todos tiem-
pos, hafta el del Catolico dó Filipe IIII. nuef-
tro feñor, Rey de las Efpañas, y de ambos or-
bes: y añadidas muchas familias iluftres
tocantes a la Hiftoria.

POR EL MAESTRO FRAY
Geronimo de Caftro y Caftillo, hijo del Autor, mo-
rador y Predicador del Conuento infigne de la
Santifsima Trinidad de Madrid.

AL EXCELENTISSIMO SEÑOR DON
Manuel de Fonfeca y Çuniga, Cauallero del habito de Santiago, Conde
de Monterrey, y de Fuentes, Gentilhombre de la Camara de fu Ma-
geftad, Prefidente de Italia, de los Confejos de
Eftado y Guerra.

CON PRIVILEGIO.

En Madrid, Por Luis Sanchez, impreffor del Rey N.S.

Año M.DC.XXIIII.

Julián del Castillo, *Historia de los Reyes Godos*. Madrid: Luis Sanchez, 1624. George Peabody Library, the Sheridan Libraries, Johns Hopkins University

Muslim invaders in the early eighth century, and was beset even today by enemies foreign and domestic. One 1624 book's very title page established a direct lineage between the pre-Romanic inhabitants of the Iberian Peninsula and Philip IV, thus implicitly casting the seven hundred years of Arabic habitation as exceptional.

This ideology was so successful that it continues to be an implicit and at times even explicit justification for Spanish and European policies in post-9/11 geopolitics, as when former president José María

Aznar of Spain, in a speech given at Georgetown University in 2004, positioned Spain at the crossroads of a transhistorical war on terror dating back to its Reconquest of medieval Iberia from the Muslim invaders, saying, "The problem Spain has with Al Qaeda and Islamic terrorism . . . has nothing to do with government decisions. You must go back no less than 1,300 years, to the early 8th century, when a Spain recently invaded by the Moors refused to become just another piece in the Islamic world and began a long battle to recover its identity."[27]

One of the decisive tools in disseminating this powerful system of justification of the monarchy's consolidation of power was the concept of reason of state, Niccolò Machiavelli's term for the right of princes to subordinate the means of their use of power to the ultimate end of what they determined to be in the interest of the state. While Machiavelli's naked advice to princes on how best to assert themselves in the realm of realpolitik had earned his work censure on moral grounds and a place on the *Index of Prohibited Books*, Giovanni Botero's concept of reason of state, which he expounded in a book by the same title first published in 1589, began to make the case for a state's legitimacy based on a concept of justice that was rooted in popular sovereignty.[28] Although Botero was reacting both to Machiavelli and to Jean Bodin, in his view, once the state's sovereignty was seen as just, what the sovereign then determined to be in its vital interest was enough to trump any and all external moral standards. In this sense his theories were a continuation, in softer garb, of Machiavelli's justifications of a sovereign's machinations.[29]

Botero's thesis was translated into Spanish in 1598, and the author of that translation was none other than, again, Antonio de Herrera y Tordesillas, the official historian and censor who would, a few years later, approve Cervantes's manuscript for publication. When his translation was reprinted in 1603, Herrera y Tordesillas replaced the original dedication letter in which he had excoriated Machiavelli with a new one that didn't mention him at all, and thus severed any connection between the theory of reason of state and Machiavelli's tainted thought.[30] This repackaging of a concept that had once been anathema was commensurate with an increased circulation of the concept within intellectual circles, as political theorists and lawyers as well as judges sought to deploy it as justification for their own potentially idiosyncratic interpretations of the law.[31]

Having listened in astonishment to Quixote's harangue, the barber tells a story intended to ridicule Quixote's ability to appear sane when on any other topic than chivalrous adventures. In his anecdote, a madman is on the verge of being released from an asylum when he reveals his madness by claiming to be Neptune. Grasping the barber's meaning immediately, Quixote fires back with this flash of passion wrapped in eloquence:

"I, Señor Barber, am not Neptune, the god of the waters, nor do I attempt to persuade anyone that I am clever when I am not; I only devote myself to making the world understand its error in not restoring that happiest of times when the order of knight errantry was in flower. But our decadent age does not deserve to enjoy the good that was enjoyed in those days when knights errant took it as their responsibility to bear on their own shoulders the defense of kingdoms, the protections of damsels, the safeguarding of orphans and wards, the punishment of the proud, and the rewarding of the humble. Most knights today would rather rustle in damasks, brocades, and the other rich fabrics of their clothes than creak in chain mail."[32]

Cervantes, who risked his life on many occasions for his country and religion, is able here to ridicule his own naïveté while simultaneously eviscerating a society so enslaved to appearances and reputation that it betrays any ideals worth fighting for. But he also lowers the reader into the sea of his characters' consciousness, precisely by allowing their differing takes on the world to clash. The barber intends his tale to enlighten the confused old man as to his failure to perceive his own lunacy; Don Quixote, however, shows him that he knows exactly what he is saying, and counters that it is rather the world that is in error for having sacrificed true valor for the false idols of vanity and appearances. The barber, a bit crestfallen at the reception of his story, responds apologetically that "this is not why I told my story, and as God is my witness my intentions were good, and your Grace should not be offended."[33]

One of Cervantes's most curious tales, *The Glass Licentiate*, tells the story of Tomás Rodaja, a blank slate of a young man who is picked up by two students in Salamanca to be their servant, and thus gains a level of learning that would have been unavailable to him. Having acquired an education in books, Tomás joins the company of a soldier named Diego de Valdivia, who persuades him to accompany his troupe to Italy by regaling him with tales of the bright side of soldiering while editing out its evils:

> He praised to heaven the free life of the soldier and the freedom of Italy; but he told him nothing of the cold of watches, of the danger of the assaults, of the horror of battle, of the hunger of sieges, the destruction caused by mines, with others of those sorts of things that many take as add-ons to the soldiering life, but that in fact are its main feature.[34]

Rodaja decides to go with him, but exacts a promise that he won't be required to enlist and thus will not incur any of the obligations of the soldiering life.

Upon returning to Salamanca, Tomás rejects the advances of a worldly woman, who responds by feeding him a love potion that poisons him and leaves him with a curious delusion: he becomes convinced that he is made of glass and will break at the slightest touch. In this persona Tomás becomes a kind of idiot savant, bestowing advice in the form of refrains and one-liners, the gist of which is conveyed by his response to the invitation of a nobleman to join him at court: "I am not a good one for the palace, because I have shame and don't know how to flatter."[35] In a sense, Tomás becomes something like Erasmus's Folly, uttering the truths that polite society refuses to air.

When Tomás is finally cured of his insanity, he is unable to bear the crowds that continue to beset him for advice, and he declares his decision to leave with a word of warning about courtly life, that it "fulfills the hopes of bold claimants and dashes those of the virtuous but modest, abundantly supporting shameless clowns and starving the discretely shameful." Thus does he decide to join his friend Valdivia in Flanders, this time truly engaging in war, and dying "a prudent and most valiant soldier."[36]

As strange as this story first appears, when seen in the context of Cervantes's attitudes toward war, service, and honor, its logic becomes clear. Valdivia's speech to Tomás severs the reality of war from the illusory trappings of a life of adventure. Tomás, unlike a real figure, unlike

Cervantes himself, opts for only one side of this split, eschewing the reality of war for the illusion of the soldiering life that faultily represents it. While he thus collects the experiences he desires, his return to Spain is marred by the intrusion of his illness. Yet again Tomás lives a split reality: this time he deals in truth but can do so only through a falsity, an illusion.

Tomás, we could say, has become an embodiment of fiction, one taken largely from the blueprint of Cervantes's life experiences, and one nourished by the disappointment of the ideals that drove him to risk life and sacrifice limb in the service of his king. In the end, Tomás opts for the reality of war, and receives the prize most often earned there, the prize Cervantes's own brother Rodrigo had earned years earlier on the fields of Flanders, and that cannot have been far from his mind as he penned those last words: "earning fame with his death as a prudent and most valiant soldier."[37]

FROM THE STONE RAMPARTS enclosing the cathedral high on the hills of Messina on the northeast corner of Sicily, you can gaze across the straits to the jagged shores of mainland Italy, which at times look so close as to be within your grasp. The beauty of those aqua waters bely the treacherous currents beneath, which have struck fear in the hearts of generations of sailors, giving birth to the legend of the cliff-dwelling monster Scylla and the permanent whirlpool Charybdis that conspired with so many other travails to keep the valiant Odysseus from returning home for ten long years after the epic and tragic losses Homer sang of in *The Iliad*.

As he convalesced from the injuries that would remain for the rest of his life a sign of his courage and a reminder of the injustice of his fate, Cervantes would have had many occasions to gaze across those same straits and wonder if his own odyssey would soon end like that of the mythic hero, with that long-awaited return to what the Greeks called *nostos*, the home that animates the nostalgic recollections of a past we can never quite regain. But destiny had other, darker plans for him.

As bad as the journey out to Lepanto had been, the return trip was worse. Miraculously recuperated from malaria, Cervantes was severely wounded, and languished for weeks under the decks with so many other casualties of war, his still-bleeding wounds at constant risk of infection. When he finally arrived in Messina and was given a bed in the hospital, his lot was not much improved. It was well known that more people died in hospitals than survived. And yet, still, somehow, he pulled through. Finally able to sit up and take nourishment, he and other veterans were visited by Juan of Austria, who bestowed on him a pitiful pay raise authorized by one of his fellow military leaders, the Duke of Sessa, in honor of his service and bravery. Cervantes took the occasion to request letters of recommendation from both leaders, which he hoped would pave the way for a successful return home to Spain and the erasure of the disgrace that had forced him to leave.

The victory at Lepanto was received as an almost prophetic event in Christendom. The aging Pope Pius V's entourage feared he would die from happiness when he heard the news (with good reason, it seems, as he died in May of the following year), and the Pope sent word to Philip that he would personally crown him emperor of the East should Philip press on and take Constantinople as well.[38] Juan of Austria, encouraged by his success at Lepanto, urged his older brother to convert their victory there into a total Turkish capitulation, and he personally led the force that took the city of Tunis and established a Spanish garrison of eight thousand men there in 1573.[39] But Philip did not press on, as his attention was drawn northward to the continuing revolts in the Netherlands, and westward toward further expansion in the New World; the victory at Lepanto would be short-lived.

The Turks, for their part, shocked by the immensity of their defeat at Lepanto and by the loss of Tunis, immediately set to rebuilding their navy, and by the summer of 1574 had amassed an even larger armada than the one that had been decimated before. With this armada they sailed on Tunis. Cervantes had long since recovered from his injuries and realized he would never regain the use of his left hand. Despite this, he decided to stay with Juan of Austria's troops, eagerly awaiting a chance to sail from Sicily, where the fleet had wintered, to defend the newly established garrison across the narrow stretch of the Mediterranean Sea.

He was to be deeply disappointed. Storms impeded Juan's armada from leaving until it was too late, and the Turkish fleet retook the fortress of Goleta and the city of Tunis in what was to be a devastating defeat and a stinging rebuke to Spain's pretensions to dominance in the Mediterranean. The piracy that Philip had hoped to put an end to by authorizing the campaign returned in full force, and the jubilation and optimism that Lepanto had sparked among Christians gave way to fear and confusion. Very soon it became clear not only that Spain was unable to ward off the threat of Islam from the south and east, but that it was all it could do to maintain order in the Netherlands, Philip's birthright, where religious dissent was combining with unrest due to burdensome taxation to provoke some of the most serious uprisings Philip would have to contend with.

The unavoidable truth was that Spain's military commitments and imperial ambitions were economically unsustainable. By the second half of the sixteenth century, an estimated one hundred fifty thousand Spanish troops were permanently deployed in various locations around the world. And the per capita cost of supporting these troops tripled between the middle of that century and the end.[40] Moreover, the seemingly endless revolts against Spain's authority, which in turn provoked increasingly brutal repressions, especially in the Netherlands, were sapping Spanish morale on the front and at home. Under the command of Philip's lieutenant, the fearsome Duke of Alba, Spanish troops were permitted to exorcise their deep frustrations on the population of Dutch towns that tried to resist them, and in 1572 they systematically executed an entire garrison of two thousand men in the city of Haarlem, leading even Spanish officers to protest to the crown over the excesses of the war and its exorbitant human and economic costs.[41]

While Cervantes could not know it at the time, the endless war in Flanders would eventually come home to affect him personally in the most devastating way. After successfully serving together with him in Italy and surviving years of captivity with him in Africa, his closest family member, his brother Rodrigo, would die in battle in the Flemish wars. Cervantes would not be alone in losing a brother to the conflict; Philip's brother Juan of Austria would also lose his life on the fields of Flanders, albeit in somewhat less heroic circumstances, succumbing to septicemia after an operation on his inflamed hemorrhoids. For Cervantes, who would continue his military service in the Mediterranean for four more years, the battle against Islam was the one true Holy War. It was a matter of religious conviction, of beliefs that defined who he was and what his country and his king stood for.

In those years, Cervantes saw firsthand the reality of war. He witnessed the death and mutilation of thousands, barely surviving himself, and far from intact. But he also witnessed how easily the sacrifices that real men make for God and country could be forgotten, how expediency trumps valor, and how the real gains purchased with the lives of those he loved would be left behind, abandoned for other causes, because the coffers were empty even as the poor were taxed to starvation and the nobles' wealth was left untouched. To a valiant veteran like him, the art of war had degenerated from one depending on the exploits of valorous men to a mechanized drudgery of states and their bankrollers. As the political theorist Giovanni Botero would write in the same year Cervantes published *Don Quixote*, these days "war is dragged out for as long as possible, and the object is not to smash but to tire, not to defeat but to wear down the enemy. This form of warfare is entirely dependent on money."[42]

In the fall of 1574, Cervantes returned to Naples where he seems to have for once attained a happiness he would never experience again. We know little of this time aside from the possibly autobiographical snippets from the poem ostensibly dedicated to his own life, the *Journey to Parnassus*. Naples here is tinged with the nostalgic beauty of a life left behind and sorely missed. It is possible that Cervantes fell in love in Naples with a woman he would call Silena. In his *La Galatea*, the novel he would publish ten years later, she appears as the love object of the poet who is his namesake in that roman à clef, Lauso. Laínez is there, too, as he was during that year in Naples, along with many of the other poets who would drift in and out of Cervantes's life.

While we cannot know if there was a real Silena in Naples, Cervantes hints that he may have fathered his only son with her, a boy he would refer to in the poem as Promontorio:

> *I cleared my vision and it seemed to me*
> *I was in the midst of a famous city.*
> *Such amazement and disquiet this provoked in me;*
> *I looked again, to make sure that fear or illusion*
> *Was not taking advantage of my good reason,*
> *And I said to myself: "I am not mistaken:*
> *This city is the illustrious Naples,*
> *For I walked its streets for more than a year;*

Glory of Italy, and even light of the world . . ."
As I was thus engaged, there came furtively to me
A friend named Promontorio,
Youthful in his age, but a great soldier . . .
My friend embraced me tenderly,
And, holding me in his arms, said,
That much he doubted that I was really there.
He called me father, and I called him son . . .
Promontorio said to me: "I sense,
Father, that some great cause
Brings your gray hairs, now almost in the grave, so far away."
"In my fresher and earlier hours, my son,
I lived in this land," I told him,
"With livelier and more robust strength.
But the will that moves us all,
I mean, the desire of heaven, brought me
To a place that pleases me more than afflicts me." [43]

If it is true that he found love and happiness in Naples, we can only wonder why, a year later, he decided to leave for Spain in the company of his brother, Rodrigo. Perhaps the relationship went sour; perhaps he intended to establish himself in his homeland and call for lover and child there. In *La Galatea*, Lauso's tributes to Silena are wracked with the pain of jealousy, the plague of a young man in the throes of passion. These words of yearning, in contrast, come to us from a wiser man, a man at the end of a very full life, chastened by experience, suffering, and loss. If the younger man fathered a child, the older man looks back in sorrow, and appears to wish that he had raised a son, even as he comes to terms with where his fate has led him.

Whatever his intentions may have been, when he embarked from Naples in September of 1575, not only would he never return, never see Silena or Promontorio again, but it would be another five long years before he would arrive in Spain. The weather was favorable for sailing as Miguel and Rodrigo embarked that September day, doubtless looking forward to a speedy arrival in Barcelona. But storms arose as they neared Corsica, and the passenger ship they were sailing on, the *Sol*, was separated from the three other ships in the convoy that might have offered some modicum of protection against pirates. Sure enough, before they were reunited with the others, and before they could pull into the safety of a Spanish harbor, they were set upon by Barbary corsairs, whose speedy ships could outrun all others and were the scourge of the Mediterranean.

The brothers and their fellow passengers and crew fought bravely. Many were injured and killed, including the captain of the *Sol*, before the battle was over and the remaining survivors were taken in chains aboard the ship of the famous and feared pirate, the Greek renegade Dalí Mamí. It was then that the remaining ships of the convoy came into sight, too late to stop the faster vessels as they sped toward Algiers and slavery. As a character in a play inspired by his time in captivity (one that Cervantes would write some years later) says upon drawing into view of the port of Algiers, "When I arrived a captive and saw this land, so renowned in the world, which in its breast covers, welcomes, and encloses so many pirates, I could not hold in my sobs and, without knowing what it was, I saw my withered face covered in water."[44] It is hard to believe that this is not exactly how Cervantes felt himself as he contemplated his fate.

4.

A Captive Imagination

"Although hunger and scant clothing troubled us at times, even most of the time, nothing troubled us as much as constantly hearing and seeing my master's remarkable and exceptionally cruel treatment of Christians. Each day he hanged someone, impaled someone, cut off someone's ears, and with so little provocation, or without provocation at all, that the Turks knew he did it merely for the sake of doing it and because it was in his nature to murder the entire human race. The only one who held his own with him was a Spanish soldier named something de Saavedra, who did things that will be remembered by those people for many years, and all to gain his liberty, yet his master never beat him, or ordered anyone else to beat him, or said an unkind word to him; for the most minor of all the things he did we were afraid he would be impaled, and more than once he feared the same thing; if I had the time, I would tell you something of what that soldier did, which would entertain and amaze you much more than this recounting of my history."

As the Christian captives were brought before the ruler of Algiers, the man who would one day invent fiction must have believed that he was about to die. The one who would decide his fate, Hasan Pasha—pasha was the title in the Ottoman Empire granted to regional governors—was a renegade from Italy also known as Hasan the Venetian, renowned for his brutality, his thirst for Christian blood whetted by a convert's zeal. Facing the pasha, Cervantes had every reason to suspect that his death would be slow and painful. Hasan regularly impaled slaves on sharpened wooden poles and left them to die slowly in public view, as a punishment for attempting escape. Lesser offenses could easily lead to a slave's ears being sliced off.

For his part, Cervantes had not only just attempted escape for the second time; he had also hidden a group of Christian captives for seven months in a cave on the extensive grounds of a *ka'id*, or governing official of one of the districts of Algiers, caring for them there while they waited for the arrival of a rescue ship he had arranged to pick them up. While the companions were hidden away, Hasan Pasha had assumed his new position and taken ownership of those slaves who were considered worthy of ransom.

The daring plan for escape was hatched a half year earlier, in April of 1577, when negotiations were undertaken by monks of the Mercedarian Order for the ransom of a large number of Christian captives, including Cervantes's younger brother, Rodrigo. Believing Rodrigo would soon be in Spain, the brothers agreed that, upon his arrival there he would hire an armed frigate and return immediately to spirit away Miguel and his companions. The appointed meeting place was where the *ka'id*'s garden met the shore some three miles up the coast from town.[1] The gardener, a Christian slave named Juan, agreed to keep their presence there a secret while Cervantes went back and forth between the city's bagnios (the prisons where the slaves were normally housed) and the cave, supplying them with provisions. Little did the group expect that the negotiations would take so long; it was not until August 24 that Rodrigo and 105 other freed captives set sail for Spain.

While it seems strange to our eyes that a Christian slave would have the freedom to move about as he did, this was in fact common in Algiers. Slaves not owned by private citizens were kept in one of several public bagnios. The bagnio was a network of interconnected rooms several stories high surrounding a common courtyard. In the largest, the royal bagnio, there could be found as many as two thousand prisoners living at any time. The conditions were atrocious; but unless they were being punished or consigned to specific work, as they often were, the slaves were free to roam the city's streets during the day, identifiable as slaves by the irons that remained on their legs.[2]

It was not until the end of September that Cervantes joined the captives for good and prepared to meet the expected frigate. But the rescue attempt was foiled by a combination of bad luck and treachery.

For on their first attempt to land, a number of the Spanish sailors were sighted and captured, and the frigate was forced to retreat. In the meantime, one of the conspirators, a man known as the Gilder, who had been helping convey food from the city, lost his nerve and betrayed the escape plans to Hasan Pasha in the hope of saving his own skin. The pasha immediately had the garden surrounded, and the men were taken into custody.

Cervantes had ensured that his valor and exceptional service in His Majesty's army were duly recognized in letters bearing the seal of such dignitaries as Don Juan of Austria, King Philip's brother and the admiral of his Mediterranean armada, and the Duke of Sessa, both of whom were largely responsible for ongoing diplomatic efforts to achieve a lasting peace between Spain and the Ottomans. As Don Juan had honored him for his service as he convalesced from his wounds in Sicily, the praise the letters showered on Cervantes conveyed to his Moorish captors the sense that this must be a man of no small importance.

Holding such stature in his captors' eyes was a mixed blessing for Cervantes. While there is no doubt that he benefitted enormously from not being sent to work in the fields, he was deeply discouraged by the five hundred gold escudos his captors set as his ransom, an astronomical sum that would take a normal family such as Cervantes's many years of ceaseless labor to accumulate. In fact, he tried to persuade his captors on several occasions that he was not of a wealthy family and that there was little chance they would ever cash in on such a hefty ransom—to no avail. They refused to believe that a man carrying such impressive credentials wasn't worth every penny they'd asked for.

As he stood before the terrible governor of Algiers, Cervantes must have thought that his luck had finally run out. When he had attempted escape once before—that time venturing through the desert toward the city of Orán, some two hundred miles away, until his guide abandoned him, and thirst and hunger forced him to return—the previous governor, Ramadan Pasha, had spared him his life and, indeed, any serious punishment (although the chains and beatings he was subjected to were certainly brutal treatment by most modern standards). His owner at the time, the pirate Dalí Mamí, who had captured him when taking his ship, the *Sol*, was away on the seas, and Ramadan, cut of a different cloth from Hasan Pasha, was known as a wise and beneficent ruler—although he, too, could be brutal and vindictive, responding to news of the death of a Morisco in Spain with the order to execute a captive priest in Algiers by burning him alive.[3]

Given how different Hasan's reputation was, Cervantes had every reason to try to hide or minimize the role he'd played in the most recent escape. Instead, according to affidavits later signed by a dozen witnesses, he stepped forward, looked the pasha in the eye, and claimed all responsibility for the escape attempt. He even insisted that the other men were entirely blameless, and that he had cajoled and tricked them into joining him on this foolish venture.

Hasan Pasha could not but have been struck by the audacity and valor of this crippled but handsome man with the piercing eyes, hooked nose, and light brown beard. Hasan Pasha was bisexual, having a wife and children while maintaining relations with younger men, just as he had grown up in the sexual service of older, powerful men. But there is no evidence that he had any such feelings for the bedraggled, undernourished prisoner who, at almost thirty years old, was far from the clean-faced youth who would normally have entered into such a relation with a man like Hasan. Cervantes, for his part, had nothing but scorn for prisoners who gave in to the temptations of either sex or apostasy to get for themselves a better life. In a play he would write years later exploring the trials of captivity in Algiers, he gave the name Sayavedra (so close to the second surname he would later adopt himself) to a character who declares he would "die before deviating a stitch from the honest way to live."[4]

Whatever the reason, Hasan defied expectations and neither killed nor tortured any of the captives. Only the unfortunate Christian gardener, Juan, who had helped hide them and brought food to the cave, paid for his generosity with his life. He was executed using the barbarous "death of the hook," in which the victim's foot is pierced by a metal hook and he is suspended upside down and tortured until he dies choking on his own blood.[5] It was not a quick death, and Cervantes and his companions were forced to stand and watch until the end. While he was surely relieved to have escaped such an end himself, a man of Cervantes's deep moral convictions must have suffered enormous guilt at the punishment meted out in his place.

Born in Venice in 1544, Hasan Pasha was captured as an adolescent by corsairs and raised as a Muslim in Tripoli before passing into the

Giannizzero Soldato, from Cesare Vecellio, *Degli Habiti Antichi e Moderni di Tutto il Mondo*. Venice: Giovanni Bernardo Sessa, 1598. George Peabody Library, the Sheridan Libraries, Johns Hopkins University

ownership of Uluç-Ali, admiral of the Ottoman fleet. He was likely subjected to pederasty, as was common in relationships between older janissaries (see Figure 5, page 34) and Barbary pirates and their younger "bearded wives." From his favored position in Uluç-Ali's household, he rose to become himself leader of the Turkish fleet before being appointed governor of Algiers.

THE ISLAMIC WORLD under the Ottomans was far more tolerant of religious and ethnic differences than the Christian world was. Social mobility was available to Muslim men of all provenance, and the Mediterranean was full of so-called Turks by profession, a play on words referring to renegades or converts to Islam who integrated themselves into the empire's military and commercial life and flourished at least in part by "professing" their new faith. By some estimates, more than half the population of Algiers in the mid-sixteenth century was renegade. Even by those standards Hasan's rise was meteoric. After converting to Islam he rose quickly in the Turkish bureaucracy, starting as a tax collector and eventually serving as bey, or governor, of Algiers two times.

Algiers in the sixteenth century had developed a terrible and awe-inspiring reputation among Europeans and, especially, Spaniards. By 1570, it was a prosperous and bustling Mediterranean capital, but its wealth was due almost entirely to the highly profitable trade in slaves and booty from piracy. About one square mile within its ramparts and with a population of around a hundred thousand, Algiers was a lattice-work of narrow bending streets separating houses made of beige stone and decorated with multicolored tiles. Larger estates, farms, and orchards dotted the countryside immediately surrounding the city's walls. The city's Muslim elite built lives of luxury around their bagnios, which were brimming with populations of slaves that at times numbered up to twenty-five thousand, who lived in abject and squalid conditions and were regularly subjected to beatings, torture, and execution.[6]

Piracy, or privateering, as its state-sponsored version is called, had become a staple of Mediterranean life.[7] Corsairs prowled the sea but also made regular raids onto the shores off Christendom, and the villages and towns along Spain's southern coast were very much in the danger zone. As captives were brought back to Algiers, they underwent a kind of triage: children and women could be sold to households, sometimes into sexual slavery, and at times young boys would be adopted by janissaries and raised in that culture where, like Hasan Pasha, they could achieve great heights. In that sense, Muslim culture of the sixteenth century allowed for greater social mobility than did its Christian counterpart with its intense fear of crypto-Muslims and Jews and its rigid class hierarchies.[8]

Slaves with special skills, from goldsmiths to bricklayers, were put to work in the city, and those deemed least valuable were either sent to do manual day work in the fields or, for the least fortunate, assigned to row on the Barbary galleys. For these slaves, their short lives almost certainly stretched on much longer than they would have wished. They were chained to benches in ghastly conditions and forced to row incessantly, with little food or water. Those who were exhausted or sick would be beaten mercilessly, and when they finally expired, their bodies would be tossed over the side of the ship like so much unwanted debris.

Noblemen and prisoners deemed to be of high social value were destined for a very different treatment. They were kept apart from the others and forced to write to their families and supporters at home. A ransom was set on their heads, and broad-reaching charitable networks arose in Spain among the Trinitarian and Mercedarian orders for the purpose of funding the ransom and return of captives. While they would at times be sent to work with the city slaves, this was mainly to give them added incentive to write home for money. Their purpose was to be ransomed and to generate the coveted incomes that kept the elites of Algiers in their accustomed splendor. Because of the letters of commendation he carried on his person and had strived so hard to obtain, Miguel de Cervantes was among this last group.

THE FIVE YEARS Cervantes spent in Algiers left an indelible mark on his creative genius. Many of the poems published in his first novel, the pastoral romance *La Galatea*, may have been written during his time in the bagnios. Another captive and close companion of Cervantes in Algiers, the Portuguese priest and scholar Antonio de Sosa, had much occasion to read and write during his captivity, and reported that Cervantes often worked on his poems as well. In 1581 de Sosa returned to Spain from Algiers, where he had been in captivity for about four years. During that time, he observed the city that was his prison and its inhabitants with an ethnologist's eye, recording in great detail the beliefs and appearances, the customs and even the ways of speaking, of its inhabitants. Those observations would be published under another man's name in Spain in 1612 as the five-volume compendium entitled *A Topography and General History of Algiers*, which serves to this day as one of the most valuable sources of knowledge about life in one of the early modern Mediterranean's most prominent sites of intercultural exchange, and the European perspectives on Muslim society at the time.[9]

Their passion for books and reading helped keep men such as de Sosa and Cervantes alive during their captivity, but there were also real dangers to being a bibliophile in a society ruled by one of the religions of the Book. Early in his captivity, when de Sosa caught sight of a man carrying a beautifully embossed book in the marketplace, he ran over to him and asked to see it. When the man saw a Christian slave attempting to touch what turned out to be a copy of the Koran, he beat him severely for his curiosity, as it was considered sacrilege for an infidel to handle the sacred text.[10]

It was shortly after Cervantes's release and return to Spain that his first novel, *La Galatea*, was published and several of his plays were staged. In one of those theatrical works a character named Sayavedra appears for the first time in Cervantes's writing. Characters with that name or its quasihomonym Saavedra will make two more appearances in later works, all in conjunction with the time in Algiers. This was not simply a case of Cervantes inserting himself in a cameo appearance from time to time, like Alfred Hitchcock's stepping onto a bus or appearing in profile at the back of a scene in one of his films. For, at the time of the writing of that play (between 1581 and 1583), Saavedra was not yet one of Cervantes's names. Rather, he adopted it shortly *after* it first began to appear in his work. Once adopted, it appeared from then on as his second last name on his published works and was the name he gave his illegitimate daughter, Isabel, when he officially recognized her in 1584.[11]

While neither his mother nor father was named Saavedra, a distant relative who was also a poet and a soldier carried the name, although there is little evidence that Cervantes and that relation spent much time together. The greater motivation for his choosing the name was its almost mythical association with a soldier from the fifteenth century named Juan de Sayavedra, who had been captured by the moors during the final years of the Reconquest of Granada and whose deeds were immortalized in a popular ballad of the time, "El Romance de Sayavedra." In that ballad the historical Sayavedra fights heroically against the Moors; but perhaps more vital to his fame, and a reason for Cervantes's choice of his name, was his capture by the enemy and his perseverance in retaining his Christian values in the face of threats and enticements to apostatize.

After appearing in the play *Los tratos de Argel*, or *The Business of Algiers*, a character called Saavedra appears in a story called "The Captive's Tale," which, while an essential part of the novel *Don Quixote*, was most likely composed much earlier, around 1589, and only later included in the novel. The third appearance of the name was in one of Cervantes's later plays, published as part of a collection of plays and interludes. In that play, called *The Valiant Spaniard*, the character Don Fernando Sayavedra has the starring role and is most similar to the historical Sayavedra, in that he is a soldier stationed in North Africa who learns the Moorish culture while defending Orán against a Turkish siege.

In *The Business of Algiers*, Sayavedra is the exemplary Christian captive, representing a virtue untainted by the temptations of the flesh or apostasy. Confronted by news of the brutal execution of a Christian slave in retaliation for the reported killing of a Morisco in Spain, Sayavedra counsels stoic restraint: "Stop your moaning, my friend; we should not mourn those who go to heaven, but those who remain: for though what he suffered may seem an offense for human eyes, having ended with such a death he may begin a better life."[12]

While Sayavedra names actual characters in both *The Business of Algiers* and *The Valiant Spaniard*, in "The Captive's Tale" in *Don Quixote* the name Saavedra is mentioned briefly in passing, albeit tellingly in the context of Cervantes's strange relationship with Hasan Pasha. In the epigraph with which I begin this chapter, the captive, recently returned to Spain, tells the gathered travelers at the inn about his time in Algiers, and draws their attention to "a Spanish soldier named something de Saavedra" as being the only one who stood up to Hasan Pasha, and did so without ever being mistreated by him.[13] In a story he invents about the love between a Christian captive and the beautiful daughter of a wealthy government official, Cervantes memorializes his own legend in Algiers by inserting a name that, at the time of his captivity, was not yet his.

But he also does something more, something that allows us to see into the inner workings of fiction almost at the moment of its invention. As the narrator deviates from the tale he is telling in order to sing the praise of a stand-in for the author, the perspective of the prose subtly shifts from without to within, from an external description of the man to one offering a privileged view into his consciousness and his emotions, reporting that Saavedra "more than once he feared the same thing." This injection of the author's subjective recollection into the objective recounting of an invented tale reveals the architecture of Cervantes's new style. His method generates an experience of solidarity between the reader and the world opened up by the pages of a book, by almost surreptitiously coaxing the reader into the frame of the story, and doing so by way of an illusion of depth: the reader steps into the pages of the book in order to discuss with other characters a book, tale, or character located even deeper in the story.

This creation of depth by delving into the space between tale tellers and the tales they are telling is the technique that animates all of *Don Quixote*. The result of making his work focus so closely on questions of how people portray the world and how they react emotionally to theirs and others' perceptions, was to produce a kind of writing that more closely mirrors our own world, because it includes both our representations of the world and how we experience those representations. His novel became much like what you see if you look into a mirror while holding another mirror up in front of you. Like that mirror, his book portrays characters discussing books and characters, including the book *Don Quixote* and its characters and even its author. The central source of the book's charm becomes the blindness of those characters to the perspectives and motivations of other characters around them and the empathy that blindness evokes. In other words, they have become a lot more like us readers; people struggling to understand the world around them, limited by how much they can see and know, and responding to those limits with their emotions.

This connection between emotions and the limits of human knowledge is borne out by modern science.[14] Brain researchers believe that human beings share a series of basic emotions with "lower animals, but [that] the derived or nonbasic emotions tend to be more uniquely human."[15] In fact, these later, more distinctly human emotions are tightly related to the limits and barriers that separate us from the feelings and desires of others. We feel rage in response to the impingements on our limits, such as slights to the ego; we feel sadness that arises from loss of a beloved object, or from the sense that the ones we love do not love or desire us; we feel shame when something is exposed that we wished to keep hidden. An essential dimension of our affective experience is, it seems, the horizon of opacity that characterizes our experience of other people. Cervantes plugged into that dimension with his narrative techniques.

In developing those techniques, Cervantes was also translating into prose a profound shift in the way Europeans thought about and portrayed their place in the world. In the Middle Ages, writers, thinkers, and artists tended to portray human agents as fully integrated aspects of the cosmos rather than as observers or even inhabitants of an independent reality. By the seventeenth century the various fields of human creativity had begun to assume a very different role for the individual, with the individual's perspective and experience becoming a central concern in works of literature as well as in painting and architecture.[16] At the same time, natural philosophers were starting to conceive of the cosmos not as an extension of human existence, closed in around the earth at its center, but as a vast and even infinite expanse of space, in which the earth held no position of privilege.

In the plastic arts, the emergence of individual perspectives is even more clearly observable. Toward the beginning of the fifteenth century the architect Filippo Brunelleschi, designer of the famed Duomo atop Florence's Cathedral of Santa Maria del Fiore, built on earlier studies in optics in order to produce a painting that could fool its viewer into thinking it was real. In a famous experiment, Brunelleschi placed a painting of the baptistery that he had made following the rules of linear perspective in the doorway of the unfinished cathedral, facing outward. He then drilled a hole at the painting's vanishing point and invited viewers to look through the hole toward the baptistery. Unbeknownst to them, what they were viewing was not the baptistery but a mirror positioned a few feet away that reflected back to them the image Brunelleschi had painted.

While previous painters had produced works using linear perspective, after Brunelleschi's experiment, the practice caught fire, spreading through Italy and the rest of Europe. Unlike the paintings of the Middle Ages, in which figures differed in size according to their importance or sanctity, now pictures would use relative size to convey a sense of depth and space to the viewer. At the same time, linear perspective depended for its effect on the viewer occupying a very specific point with regard to the painting. As stage designers would later notice when they applied the techniques of perspective to the burgeoning theater industry, scenery constructed according to the rules of perspective accords only one ideal vantage point, the one directly in front of the scenery's vanishing point. Stage productions created for royalty would quickly take advantage of this discrepancy in vantage points, ensuring that just the king had the ultimate realistic view on the stage, and that all others would be removed from that perspective in proportion to their actual rank in society.[17]

The increasing focus on the distinctness of individual perspectives on the world can be readily seen in the development of portraiture. Portraitists such as the German Albrecht Dürer began to focus their attention on what was specific to the subjects as individuals, rather than on expressing the grandeur of their position, rank, or importance through the use of conventional imagery. Dürer's experiments included a great number of self-portraits that betray what was for the time an unprecedented focus on the person of the artist. This focus resulted in a tendency both to self-aggrandizement, as when the artist appears to be taking on the iconography of Christ, and to an undermining of any sense of the work as an unmediated expression of the world.[18]

Albrecht Dürer, *Self-Portrait*, 1500. Photo by Archiv Gerstenberg/Ullstein Bild via Getty Images

His cameo appearance in paintings of other themes, such as a sketch of him at work that he made on the reverse side of a canvas carrying a more finished self-portrait, appear to be reminders that these representations are the creations of a single man; the man is thus elevated, but his creations are simultaneously humanized, put into perspective as the products of a single, and hence limited, perspective.[19]

By the turn of the seventeenth century painters such as the Spanish court portraitist of the Hapsburg family, Diego Velázquez, were using the techniques of perspective to express a new way of understanding the world and the place of humans in it.[20]

Gazing into the courtly world of Philip IV that Velázquez's astounding *Las Meninas* opens up for us, we see how the plane of the painter's canvas within the painting forms the border between two views that cannot be simultaneously occupied; one cannot turn away from the scene without confronting the realization that no single

Diego Velázquez, *Las Meninas*, 1656. Photo by Universal History Archive/Getty Images

viewer can see it all.[21] Velázquez's painting occupies such an essential place in the history of European art because it revealed a new way of organizing and understanding knowledge that was taking hold at the time.[22] But the other great example of this change is Cervantes's *Don Quixote*.[23]

Both Cervantes in his writings and Velázquez on his canvases play out the drama of a world that was discovering the distinction between how *I* see the world and how that world *really* is, how it is for God or for some other human being. The world had been uprooted, put into a box for each individual, but this uprooting entailed a far more complex and consequential experience as well. Once the world has been made portable, once media such as print, theater, or painting are conceived of as offering a distinct perspective on the entirety of the world, they also inevitably turn back on themselves. By incorporating the world into their frame they necessarily incorporate that frame, too, as well as the person performing the framing.[24]

A similar progression in Cervantes's writing style emerged in tandem with his successive versions of his time in Algiers. Gradually we can see him bringing his individual perspective on the world into relief and incorporating it back into the world he portrayed. It seems that Cervantes was using the traumatic memory of his captivity to create fiction, and he in turn used fiction to help him heal from the wounds of his long captivity.[25] In writing invented stories (as opposed to confessions) to deal with intensely personal pain, Cervantes was inaugurating a particularly modern use of literature. In the words of Karl Ove Knausgaard, the Norwegian author of the six-volume auto-biographical novel *My Struggle*, "What I discovered when I began to write my first novel was that I could disappear in my writing. The self, and all the difficulties and pain associated with it, vanished." He attributes this dissolution of self in writing to a quality particular to literature, for "like no other medium, literature is able to break the boundaries erected by society."[26] And "literature" in this instance may best be read as "fiction," that mode of writing that specializes in breaking boundaries and perhaps even palliating the pain that those boundaries can engender.

Victims of severe trauma often begin to deal with the pain of their experience by means of a defense mechanism called externalization, in which the victim tells a story or draws a picture that evokes the event without including him in it directly. Another character may be designated as a stand-in for the victim, thus enabling the story to be told while limiting the extent to which the victim has to relive the emotional pain it produces. In some cases this process can be understood as a kind of splitting of the self, in which one portion is assigned the burden of the trauma while the other can experience it from a distance. In assuming the name Saavedra and proceeding to incorporate it into his writings at key moments, Cervantes may have been initiating a process of working through his traumatic captivity in Algiers.[27]

But even as Cervantes was dealing with the trauma of his own memories, the way he did so reverberated throughout the course of his writing and had an immense impact on the development of fiction. He would tell and retell episodes of his captivity, each time with variants, as if splitting his person enabled him to divide reality itself into multiple versions. Each version could be true, in that it portrayed some essential aspect of his experience, and at the same time be false, in that the different versions would contradict one another in important ways. Taken as a whole, they would explore not only what happened, but also what could have happened differently, and why. They would explore not only reality, but also the desire that always seeks to change it, and that sometimes succeeds and sometimes fails.

Furthermore, by moving the same story across genres, Cervantes managed to innovate in one genre by incorporating aspects of another. Specifically, he took a partially remembered, partially invented episode from his time in captivity and turned it into a piece of theater, creating multiple characters to explore different aspects of the experience. When he then went to write the same story in prose, essential qualities of the theatrical version moved with the story into the prose version, qualities that today we consider standard aspects of fictional characters.

The most telling example of this transposition is the story of a Moorish woman's love for a Christian captive, which lies at the heart of two plays and "The Captive's Tale." In *The Business of Algiers*, Sayavedra's resolve serves as a contrast to the temptation of the protagonist, Aurelio, who has become the love interest of the beautiful and wealthy Zahara. Aurelio's own beloved, Silvia, is also a slave, and has in turn caught the eye of Zahara's husband, Yzuf. Against the backdrop of the suffering of the Christian slaves, *The Business of Algiers*

focuses on this love quadrangle, exploring the nature of the temptation faced by every slave to abandon his or her religious, cultural, and
personal commitments. By using the techniques of the stage, Cervantes
allowed his characters alternately to conceal and expose their motivations, both to one another and to the audience.

Cervantes returned to this North African love intrigue in one of
the plays he published in written form many years later, around the
time of the publication of the second part of *Don Quixote*. In that play,
The Bagnios of Algiers, Zahara has become Zara, and her story becomes
one of secret conversion to Christianity and love of a Christian slave.
Their story comes to a happy conclusion, with the Christian Lope
engineering their escape and Zara renaming herself Maria. The final
words of the play are Lope's, which he addresses to the audience:
"This business was not taken from the imagination, for truth forged it
far from *fiction*. This love story of happy memory, survives in Algiers—
thus should truth and history delight the understanding. And even
today one may find the window and the garden there. And here this
business comes to an end, though that in Algiers has none."[28]

Here Cervantes uses the term fiction, *ficción*, in its traditional sense,
merely opposing it to truth. At the same time, though, he perverts the
Horatian mandate (that poetry should delight while instructing) by
insisting that it is truth and history that are doing the delighting,
precisely *not* poetry or some work of the mere imagination. But a
history delights us (that is, engages our emotions in a positive way)
when the truth it conveys is of a different order than the mere accurate
rendering of what happened—that is, when it conveys a personally
meaningful truth, a truth about ourselves. We delight in fiction not, as
we might think, because we are trying to escape reality, but because we
are drawn to a different order of reality: emotional, subjective truth, the
truth about ourselves.

The word rendered as "business" twice in this passage is *trato*, which
is the same word in the title of the play *The Business of Algiers*: *Los tratos
de Argel*. *Trato* means "dealings," "business," or just "goings-on in
general," but here it allows Cervantes to refer to the story he has just
recounted, to the title of his previous play, and to the real *business*
of Algiers itself, namely, the slavery that is so seared in his memory.
Here, in the final lines of the play, an imagined character announces
that what has just been presented was not imagined but true history;

that this history so rendered can take over the function once relegated to poetry of delighting while instructing; and that with this creation, he is putting to rest his own business with Algiers, even if the business of Algiers itself continues unabated. In this one statement, then, Cervantes is describing his invention of fiction out of the denial of that word's traditional meaning: in the form of a lie I reveal the truth, and thereby exorcize my personal demons by creating a work that will delight others while bringing them to greater understanding.[29]

By splitting himself in order to write about his trauma, and then borrowing techniques from the theater to help enable that splitting, Cervantes succeeded in fusing two of the most essential elements for the invention of fiction: the suspension of frames of reference dividing what is true from what is imagined, which would eventually become known as the suspension of disbelief; and the ability of the narrative to move the reader's point of view and emotional identification among an almost unlimited array of characters. It is this ability that bestows on fiction that quality that we recognize as a kind of literary empathy, the sense of stepping into someone else's shoes. By using this technique to express to others the pain of captivity, Cervantes could start to work through his own trauma, but more important, he also cultivated the ability to imagine the circumstances and suffering of others. Fiction, by presenting imagined realities as if they were true, became the perfect vehicle for Cervantes to transform the past, all the while creating the means for reimagining the present.

In this sense, the techniques of fiction have become in the modern world essential tools for even such nonfictional work as journalism. As the reporter Matthieu Aikins put it in an interview with NPR's Terry Gross after he won the Medill School of Journalism's James Foley Medill Medal for Courage in Journalism, "What motivates me is to try to render non-Western lives into, you know, a narrative, so that they come alive as human characters that we care about." To be able to render the lives of those who are different from us in a way that makes us care for them, a journalist such as Aikins first has to be in those places, side by side with the people about whom he is reporting. But to make his readers feel for them, to make their lives and their suffering—using a term he borrows from the philosopher Judith Butler—"grievable," Aikins needs to make them "come alive as characters we care about." In fact, recent studies have confirmed that reading literary fiction primes readers to feel empathy for other people.[30] This is what Cervantes was doing when he turned his experience in Algiers into the world's first full-blown work of fiction.

For the telling of "The Captive's Tale" in *Don Quixote*, the knight and his companions have settled in for the evening at an inn. After entertaining the gathered company with that eloquent speech on the differences between the life of learning and the life of soldiering that we have already had occasion to discuss, Don Quixote asks the newest arrival, a man accompanied by a mysterious veiled woman, to tell his story. The man turns out to be one Captain Viedma, recently returned from a long captivity in Algiers, who tells the travelers of his daring escape with the help of the fantastically beautiful Zoraida, daughter of one of the wealthiest men of Algiers, Agi Morato.

Agi Morato is Cervantes's transliteration of Hajji Murad, who was a wealthy and powerful citizen of Algiers. When the widely admired Abd al-Malik, who would later become the Sultan of Morocco, came to dine with Hajji Murad, Cervantes may have dined with them. Abd al-Malik was extremely learned both in Arabic and Turkish culture and in European letters, speaking Italian and French fluently. Cervantes clearly admired him, and referred to him on occasion as a man of great wit and generosity who liked to eat at a table in the European fashion. As it happens, Hajji Murad really did live with a daughter renowned for her beauty, who would later marry Abd al-Malik and become sultaness herself. The daughter's name was Zahara, a fact that leaves us with the tantalizing suggestion of a love affair, real or imagined, between the captive Christian and a beautiful, wealthy Moor. In the real world, when Abd al-Malik died in 1578, Zahara remarried Cervantes's nemesis and last owner, Hasan Pasha, moving with him to Constantinople.

During the time she was still in her father's house, Cervantes would have had plenty of occasions to see Zahara and even interact with her, because Christian slaves were given access to households where women went unveiled, and were allowed far more freedom to communicate with Muslim women than Muslim men were. The penalties for a Muslim woman caught in sexual relations with a Christian could be disastrous, though, and the man would be faced with the immediate choice of conversion to Islam and marriage, or death. Nevertheless, the real Zahara never fled to Spain, and thus whatever Cervantes's characters may claim to the contrary, that key aspect of the story is the fruit of his imagination. So when we hear the ex-captive Viedma tell those seated around him that they are about to "hear a true account that could not be equaled by fictions written with so much care and artfulness,"[31] we know we are again entering Cervantes's special world.

In "The Captive's Tale," Zoraida has eyes only for the captive Viedma; unlike in *The Business of Algiers*, where her love is a temptation that must be resisted, in this version she herself is a captive of sorts: a Moorish woman who has converted to Christianity in secret. She sees Viedma and decides he is the one to save her and bring her to Spain. The two must overcome the challenges of language, possible betrayal, and the vigilance of her father before finally escaping by ship to Spain, where they arrive at the inn while on their way to Viedma's hometown to marry.

As in *The Bagnios of Algiers*, the story of the love between Viedma and Zoraida finds its fruition in a happy, requited form, and their escape is successful. Thus while we have no way of knowing if the real Zahara was ever tempted by Christianity or the love of a Christian man, the success of Viedma's escape is very clearly the work of Cervantes's captive imagination, reality and memory becoming the raw material for new and improved versions. In fiction, failure can be transformed into success, just as tragedy can be experienced vicariously.

At the same time, fiction allows for the reader's identifications and sympathies to shift between opposing viewpoints, and even to be shared among them. Like any Christian Spaniard of his time, Cervantes was indoctrinated to consider Islam a heretical religion and the Moors of North Africa his natural enemies. Despite this fact, his writing is full of sympathetic portrayals of individual Moors. Few passages of literature can match in poignancy the despair expressed by Agi Morato as the Christians leave him safely onshore after their escape, and he watches as his only daughter leaves her family and homeland of her own free will: "Come back, my beloved daughter, come ashore, I forgive everything! Give those men the money, it is already theirs, and come and console your grieving father, who will die on this desolate strand if you leave him!"[32] Equally moving is Zoraida's powerful conflict, torn as she is between her Christian conscience and desire for Viedma, and her tender love for her father, who is portrayed in every scene as a sweet and gentle man. Having been subjected to five years of captivity and suffering in Algiers could easily have led Cervantes to develop a corrosive hatred of its people and culture. That he instead would produce such loving portraits lends further credence to the picture of Cervantes as an unusually compassionate man.

The transposition across time and genres of this story of love and captivity provides an intimate snapshot of Cervantes's creation of fiction. In his theater, Cervantes transformed the trauma of the violence and constraints of his imprisonment and his desperate yearning for freedom into the verses sung by an array of characters in whom he distilled different aspects of his experiences. These characters strive to know the desires and intentions of those around them, alternately hiding their motivations from one another and revealing them to the audience with asides. This technique allowed Cervantes to move in and out of their perspectives, creating depth of emotion and experience. By translating these characters into prose, he retained that sense of depth and complexity while adding to it the narrator's ability to shift a reader's sympathies and insights between different characters at different times. Throughout it all, the desire to transcend constraints and restrictions one has not chosen for oneself remained one of his central themes.[33]

IN SEPTEMBER OF 1579, Cervantes convinced a Valencian businessman named Onofre Exarque to purchase a large ship and have it ready for a quick departure, while he in turn organized some sixty captives in the bagnios to board the ship under the cover of night. Unbeknownst to him, a renegade former monk named Juan Blanco de Paz found out about the plan and, resentful of having been excluded, sought an audience with the pasha, at which he told him about Cervantes's plans. Enraged by yet another insurrection attempt, the pasha ordered Cervantes to be kept in tight confinement for a half a year. Algiers, he said, could be safe only with Cervantes under lock and key.

During his five years in captivity in Algiers, Cervantes made a total of four escape attempts, every one of them a failure. On September 19, 1580, he was loaded onto a ship with other captives belonging to Hasan Pasha, who had received orders to return to Constantinople. Had Cervantes left with that ship, he almost certainly would never have attained his freedom. That very day, a friar of the Trinitarian

Order named Juan Gil presented himself to the pasha with the purpose of obtaining the release of a number of captives, including a nobleman by the name of Jerónimo Palafox. Frantic negotiations ensued, with the pasha's men insisting on the unheard of price of one thousand escudos. Lacking such funds, the priest added two hundred escudos to the three hundred he had brought from Cervantes's family to pay his ransom. At the last possible minute, Cervantes found himself freed from his shackles. Hasan Pasha, we may surmise, was not sad to see him go.

As he watched the departure of the ship that would have carried him to his doom, and was certainly carrying others in his place, Cervantes must have endured the internal conflict of one who obtains his freedom after a long imprisonment. He yearned to return to Spain, but suffered mightily for those he was leaving behind. On so many occasions Cervantes had put the lot of others before his own, counting on his own strength of character to survive. Now he himself was free, while others would remain in bondage.

Also, there was business to attend to before he left. Blanco de Paz, who had betrayed him on the last escape attempt, now feared for his reputation and his life, and was hoping to clear his name by maligning Cervantes, claiming that he had misled the others and was responsible for their eventual capture. Cervantes needed to make sure that his reputation was entirely clean on his return to Spain, especially given that captives were often suspected of having apostatized or agreed to be spies in order to obtain their freedom. The report he generated before departing, consisting of his own relation of events along with affidavits from a dozen of his fellow captives, remains the most in-depth pictures we have of his time in Algiers.

On October 24, 1580, Miguel de Cervantes embarked for Spain, the first time he would step on his native soil in more than ten years. On that day, looking back at the fearsome walls of the Port of Algiers as the billowing sails slowly pulled him to freedom, he surely thought that his homecoming would be like the one he would give to Captain Viedma years later, when he wrote that, upon seeing Spain, "all our sorrows and hardships were forgotten, as if they had never existed, so great is the joy one feels at regaining lost freedom."[34] As another of his great literary descendants, Ernest Hemingway, would write in the final words to *The Sun Also Rises*, his own achingly beautiful tribute to

Spain, "Isn't it pretty to think so?"[35] For far from being forgotten, the sorrows and hardships of his years of captivity would remain with him for the rest of his life, haunting his imagination and shaping every aspect of his literary creation.

5.

All the World's a Stage

Miguel: *I have six plays and another six interludes.*

Pancracio: *Well, why aren't they being performed?*

Miguel: *Because the directors are neither looking for me nor am I looking for them.*

Pancracio: *They must not know that you have them.*

Miguel: *Sure they know; but as they have their poets on bread and water and that suits them well, they don't go in search of something they don't need. But I intend to have them published, so that what is seen in a hurry and hidden or misunderstood when it is performed, can be read slowly.*

As he looked over the placard adorning the entrance to the *corral*, or "theater," that would be performing *The Business of Algiers*, with its text in large letters announcing A PLAY BY MIGUEL DE CERVANTES, HIMSELF HELD IN CAPTIVITY THERE FOR SEVEN YEARS,[1] Cervantes could have felt only the deepest sense of pride. Pride for his success in having made a name for himself as a playwright a few short years after returning from his long captivity—but more significantly, pride for his perseverance in having survived to return and tell his tale, which may account for the exaggerated time in captivity the announcement claimed for him.

Returning from captivity had not been easy, and Cervantes had even more trouble to contend with than what could be expected from the trials of reintegration into a quickly changing society. He disembarked in Valencia in the fall of 1580, and while he must have felt an intense longing to see his family in Madrid, he remained there until December, ensuring that the decade-old charges against him had faded from official memory. Even as he reunited with his family at the end of the year, their financial woes, exacerbated by his father's age and deafness and yet another failed relationship for his sister Magdalena, evidently weighed on him, for his first action was to apply to the Council of Castile for a program intended to help ransomed captives pay back their debts.

From this point on, debt would be the overriding concern in Cervantes's life, much as it was for his father. His mother, Leonor, also put her considerable wiles to work on the problem, applying for and receiving a license to export some two thousand ducats' worth of commercial goods from Valencia to Algiers, intending to use the profits to pay back the costs of Miguel's ransom, but that scheme failed as well. So with little time to rest, and not even having seen his brother, Rodrigo, who had since reenlisted and was deployed in the Duke of Alba's forces amassing on the Portuguese border, Cervantes set off for Portugal as well—but in his case, to join another army: that of the petitioners in search of an appointment from King Philip.

Philip at that time had temporarily moved his court to Badajoz, near the Portuguese border, preparing for the annexation of that kingdom to his realm following the death of its king, Sebastian, at the battle of Alcazar-el-Kebir. Sebastian had embarked on a quixotic venture of his own in Morocco, essentially a disorganized crusade resulting in the destruction of his army and his own death. His body, however, was never recovered, which led to Elvis-like speculation about his eventual return and the rise of Sebastianismo, a quasi-messianic cult that was fostered by anti-Hapsburg sentiments in Portugal.[2] When the throne passed to Sebastian's great-uncle Henry, who as a man of the cloth had never married and was already quite old, Philip II suddenly found himself with a realistic chance of staking his own legitimate claim. Sure enough, Henry died two years later, having failed to convince Pope Gregory XIII (who was, not surprisingly, a close family ally of the Hapsburgs) to grant him a dispensation from his vows so he could marry. The Portuguese nobility, suspicious of their powerful Castilian neighbors and traditional rivals for Atlantic power, in turn backed the claim of Don Antonio, Philip's cousin on his mother's side. For this reason Philip bolstered his own claim with a show of real power; by the end of the summer of 1580 some twenty thousand troops under the Duke of Alba's command had wrested control of the kingdom and driven Don Antonio from its borders.

In an appeal to restore the confidence of the nobility and bring Portugal more securely under his control, Philip eschewed the traditional practice of replacing local appointees with Castilians seeking favors, and instead allowed the best local positions to go to those preferred by the Portuguese nobles themselves. At a time when, by Philip's own accounting, he received more than a thousand petitions a month and signed hundreds of documents a day,[3] it was most unlikely that a Castilian veteran with very few connections at court would have much success. In fact, Cervantes had only one viable connection: a man named Mateo Vázquez de Leca, the king's personal secretary and one of a few advisors who was privy to the king's most important matters of state. Such secretaries wielded enormous influence, not least of all by acting as gatekeepers determining who could have access to the king. One of the very first works Cervantes composed during the period immediately following his return was a letter to Mateo Vázquez, entirely in verse, that is both a testimony of his own captivity and an attempt to gain entry into his government's circles of power. Many of the verses set out in the letter made their way into his play *The Business of Algiers*.[4]

While Cervantes was unable to secure a permanent position, he did receive an assignment for which his experiences in North Africa and the special cultural competency they gave him made him eminently qualified. So it was that June of that year found Cervantes again on the road, this time traveling from Lisbon down the coast to Cádiz, a stone jewel of a city jutting out into the Atlantic from Spain's southwestern shore, from where he would cross the Strait of Gibraltar into Africa, this time on a mission for his government.

At the very least, his five years of captivity in Algiers prepared him well for the brutal heat of high summer in the Maghreb. During the month he spent there, he first met with Don Martín de Córdoba, commander of the garrison at Orán, the city Cervantes had twice tried to reach in his unsuccessful attempts at escaping from Algiers. Recounting to Don Martín his failed attempt to contact him from across the desert, Cervantes must surely have been thinking of those many Christian souls still languishing there. From the comfort of

Spanish dominion he then set out into enemy territory, to the city of Mostaganem, which the Turks had wrested from Spanish control in 1558 and was now itself home to thousands of Christian slaves. Cervantes hoped that his mission there—to retrieve information regarding Turkish plans for the eastern Mediterranean from the *ka'id*, himself a secret convert to Christianity and a spy for Philip—would eventually result in a military strike on Mostaganem and even Algiers, and thus the eventual liberation of those captives. But by the time he finished his mission, news of the Turkish admiral Uluç-Ali's return to Constantinople had allowed Philip, momentarily relieved of the pressure of Turkish buildup in Spain's Mediterranean backyard, to turn his attention yet again away from the captives, the war with Islam, and Cervantes.

Upon his return Cervantes made another plea for a government position, this time appealing to the Council of the Indies for an open appointment in one of the regions of the New World that are now Guatemala, Colombia, Nicaragua, and Bolivia; but his petition was returned with the words *Let him look for something over here* scrawled across it.[5] The frustration of his repeated failures was now clearly starting to weigh on him. As he wrote in a letter to Antonio de Eraso, a member of the Council of the Indies who had sent him to speak with one of the king's secretaries,

> Illustrious sir: Secretary Valmaseda received me as I expected, in view of the favor that Your Grace was going to do for me. But neither his consideration nor my diligence can overcome my bad luck. The bad luck that I have had with my affairs is that the post I applied for is not being filled by His Majesty, so that I am forced to wait for the dispatch vessel [from the Indies] to see whether it brings news of some vacancy . . . In the meantime, I am entertaining myself by bringing up Galatea (which is the book I told Your Grace I was writing). When she has grown a little, she will come kiss Your Grace's hands and receive the polish and improvement that I have not been able to give her.[6]

Frustration was already feeding his creativity, and in fact, Cervantes would publish his first novel, a pastoral romance called *La Galatea*, some four years later. But as he returned to Madrid in late 1581 after almost a year of petitioning in court with nothing to show other than one hundred escudos paid to him for his freelancing spy work, what Cervantes needed was work that would pay, and fast. For a man whose greatest passion had always been writing, and above all poetry, there was one industry that promised that kind of income: the theater.

LATE-SIXTEENTH- AND SEVENTEENTH-CENTURY Spain was, along with England, the birthplace of the modern theater industry, which was built on the importation of theatrical texts and architectural models from Italy. First, itinerant theater troupes and eventually more permanent establishments catered to the ever-growing desire of the urban masses for new entertainment. Theater tickets were cheap, and the crowds flocked in, sometimes several times a week, to see the latest play by a slew of new writing talents, the most successful of whom would become known as "the Phoenix," Félix Lope de Vega y Carpio.[7] Theater had existed as a popular pastime in Spain since the middle of the sixteenth century, but it had begun to take root as an institution with the development of permanent theater spaces only from 1579 on. In Madrid the first theater, or *corral*, was opened in 1579, although it was forced to shut down for a year following the death of Philip's wife, Queen Anna of Austria, in the fall of 1580. But by the time Cervantes returned to Madrid in 1581 it was again operational, and a second one had opened, too—playwrights were needed.

The job of a playwright was different from what it is today. The plays they produced were not thought of as the protected intellectual property of the author, but were purchased and used by the theater company's director, himself known as the *autor de comedias* (literally, "author of the plays"), as a working copy from which to stage his productions. While it may seem strange from our perspective for a poet with literary ambitions to make such a choice, it's important to remember that the theater in the late sixteenth century was undergoing an explosion in popularity. The closest example for us today might be the golden age of Hollywood, when writers, composers, and actors all flocked to California for a chance to ply their trade in a new and booming industry. We tend to forget nowadays, but writers as canonical as F. Scott Fitzgerald and William Faulkner, and more recently Michael Chabon and Dave Eggers, all spent some time writing for the silver screen.

The Spanish theater of the 1580s was as new and exciting as the American cinema of the 1930s was, and the greatest literary talents in a culture packed with literary talents were all vying to put their work on the stage. Reestablishing himself in Madrid after his long absence, Cervantes regained contact with his previous circle, including his former teacher Juan López de Hoyos as well as a group of established poets such as the author of the bestselling pastoral novel *El pastor de Fílida*, Luis Gálvez de Montalvo.

These were writers in the classical humanist vein, who valued poetry above all and specifically the kind of poetry mastered by the great Spanish poet Garcilaso de la Vega, who himself wrote eclogues, or bucolic lyrics, in the spirit of Virgil. As such, they were little prepared to serve up short-order plays for fast public consumption, and preferred to rely on traditional systems of noble patronage. Even successful playwrights would continue to rely on noble patrons, who in turn supported their protégés for the pleasure and personal promotion of seeing popular works publicly dedicated to them. Cervantes himself sought the patronage of an Italian nobleman named Ascanio Colonna, a friend of his former employer the Cardinal Acquaviva; Colonna would eventually himself be appointed Cardinal of Aragon, and Cervantes would dedicate his first novel, *La Galatea*, to him.

If his closest literary companions didn't deign to write for the stage, Cervantes harbored no such hesitations. While only two of his plays from that period survive, he claimed to have written twenty or thirty, and names about ten of them in the postscript to his autobiographical *Journey to Parnassus*. In a reminiscence shortly before his death in 1615 he writes,

In the theaters in Madrid were seen performances of *The Business of Algiers*, which I composed, and the *Destruction of Numancia* and *The Naval Battle*, where I dared to reduce plays to three acts from the five they previously had. I showed or, to say it better, was the first to portray the imaginings and hidden thoughts of the soul, bringing moral figures out onstage, with general and pleasurable applause from the audience. I wrote in those times up to twenty or thirty plays, which were recited without there being offered gifts of cucumbers or other thrown things: they ended their runs without whistles, shouts, or uproar.[8]

Cervantes's recollections are tinged with regret, and perhaps a little resentment. While successful in the short run, his foray into the theater largely failed to ignite the enthusiastic following of the masses of theatergoers who years later would flock to see the work of his junior competitor, the man Cervantes would refer to as a "monster of nature," Lope de Vega.

While Cervantes sought to cast himself as the theatrical innovator, it was really Lope who changed the Spanish stage, for better or worse, and who wrote the kinds of plays people wanted to hear. (Until the middle of the seventeenth century, audiences still went to *hear* rather than to *see* a play, and indeed our word *audience* still carries that connotation.) Lope's plays were fast, strong on action, and not so concerned with characterization. They dealt mainly with the topics that fascinated and titillated the audiences of the day: the destruction of honor and reputation by sexual intrigue and innuendo, and its reparation through violence or marriage. Lope himself would brag about his disregard for the classical rules of composition and his popularity among the masses in a poem dedicated to the subject of how to write plays, which he called *The New Art of Writing Plays in Our Time*.[9]

From the vantage of his later years, Cervantes would find this blatant pandering to the public's base tastes to be a betrayal of artistic integrity, although his scorn for it was seasoned with some envy of Lope's success. As a character says in one of the many literary debates that fill the pages of *Don Quixote*,

> "This can be seen in the infinite number of plays composed by one of the most felicitous minds in these kingdoms, which displays so much grace and so much charm, such eloquent verses and such fine language, such grave thoughts and so eloquent and lofty a style, that his fame is known throughout the world; because these works attempt to accommodate the taste of the theater companies, not all of them have reached, though some have, the necessary degree of perfection."[10]

This sentence was clearly intended as a backhand compliment to Lope, who took it as such, and was duly offended.

Cervantes probably would have given his one good hand to see his popularity equal that of Lope's, but after his initial success his plays were often not even performed, and instead, he found himself the target of Lope's, at times, quite public ridicule. Their disputes reached such levels of rancor that years later Lope would write that, of his contemporary poets, "there is none so bad as Cervantes or so stupid as to praise *Don Quixote*."[11] But what failed for the stage ironically paved the way for the massive success of Cervantes's prose; for the techniques he learned as a lover of theater and his ability to import every imaginable influence into his prose generated some of the most vital aspects of Cervantes's new genre.

What is most interesting about Cervantes's claim to originality on the stage is the specific mention of "moral figures" and how he uses them. In fact, there was nothing new about allegorical figures representing virtues or vices. They were a holdover from medieval dramas, where they were often the dominant figures, and had already been mixed in with straightforward human characters by earlier playwrights such as the court dramatist Juan del Encina.[12] Where Cervantes's claim holds more water, however, is in how he justifies their use.[13] Using such figures to reveal or present "the imaginings and hidden thoughts of the soul" shows that Cervantes was ultimately concerned with his characters' status as persons, in the etymological sense of the word.

Person stems from the Latin word *persona*, which in turn comes from the Greek *prosopon*, which originally referred to the masks worn by actors on the Greek stage to signify their role in the drama being performed. The Spanish word for character, *personaje*, comes directly from this root as well. By creating allegorical, moral figures who would reveal the true thoughts and emotions that the human characters were hiding from one another as well as from the audience, Cervantes was experimenting with ways of exploring interior depth on the stage, even if the methods he tried out would ultimately be rejected in favor of other conventions, in particular the aside and the soliloquy.

In the final lines of one of his earliest plays, *The Destruction of Numancia*, Cervantes has the great Roman general Scipio look on as the last Numantian child chooses death over submission to the Roman invaders and throws himself from the highest tower of the city. In the monologue that follows, Scipio speaks to the boy directly, and tells him, "You, with this fall, raised your fame and laid low my victories." But his speech is greeted by the entrance of the figure of Fame, which then speaks to the gathered Romans, instructing them to "raise your inclined heads" and "carry from here this body, which was able at such a young age to strip from you the triumph that would have brought you such honor."[14]

Here Cervantes uses the figure of Fame as a kind of window onto Scipio's soul, translating his private feelings of respect for a fallen enemy into the greater meaning that this sacrifice will hold for future generations. As it turns out, the particular innovation of Cervantes's use of allegorical figures did not catch on, but the idea of using the form and architecture of the theater and its characters as a way of exploring how each person houses an interior world that he or she can alternately close up or reveal to others—this idea had an abiding impact on his writing.

LIKE MANY ASPECTS of public life, the theaters in Spain were highly regulated, with censors scouring the contents of the plays performed there before they could see the light of day. The crown and its allies among the nobility and the Church quickly saw in the nascent theater industry a potential tool to help keep in check a populace that was constantly, to their mind, being tempted away from orthodoxy while bristling at the ever-growing impositions on its economic well-being. Spain's economy in the second half of the seventeenth century was squeezing all but the wealthiest nobles, as the ceaseless war financed by silver from the New World drove prices higher and higher and made taxes more and more punitive, while the nobility and the Church were spared from fully sharing the burden. The monarchy quickly saw in the theater its version of a Roman circus, and ticket prices were kept low for the commoners even as the seating arrangements reinforced class and gender divides.[15]

There were two theaters, or *corrales*, in Madrid, El Corral de la Cruz and El Corral del Príncipe. These were constructed in plazas between inhabited buildings, where the apartment owners in those buildings would often rent their rooms with windows as some of the best seats in the house.

Other expensive seating was built to the sides of the stage, which was a rectangular elevated platform extending from the back of the plaza out toward the center. A curtain separated the stage from a space

The reconstructed Corral de Comedias de Almagro. Photo by Antonio Leyva via Creative Commons

backstage, where there were dressing rooms and various entrances and exits, and the windows above the curtain would serve as balconies or any space that a playwright designated as "on high."[16] There was an elevated area to the back of the viewing area that was cordoned off for women who could afford to spend at least a little more on tickets. This was wryly referred to as the *cazuela*, or stew pot. Finally, there was the general admission area for those who couldn't afford comfortable seats; these were known as *mosqueteros*, and were the ones who would most likely launch those rotten cucumbers and other missiles that Cervantes and his colleagues so feared.

After censors under the jurisdiction of a court appointee known as the *protector* had cleared a play for performance, officials known as *alguaciles* would police the performances to ensure that standards of public morality were maintained, that nothing was performed that had not been cleared in advance, and that people remained in the sections that were designated for them.[17] Thus the theater both offered a spectacle for the general public to enjoy and situated that same public in a way that enforced the state's powers of surveillance and control.

This assertion of control by the state via one of the most popular media of the time was itself reinforced by the sorts of stories that were popular on the stage, the kinds that Lope bragged about mastering in his *New Art of Writing Plays in These Times*. The obsession of the new theater was the theme of honor. Until the middle of the sixteenth century, honor had been widely considered an attribute of the nobility. It referred to the strength and valor of men who made a profession out of war, men who served kings and were permitted to wear swords in public.

To be sure, by the end of the sixteenth century the nobility still wore swords—although limitations on these and other sartorial displays were often set by the monarchy—and they also considered honor to be an exclusive attribute of the aristocracy. Yet the popular culture promulgated by the theater, very much with the blessing of the state, begged to differ.[18]

"Spagnuolo nobile," from Cesare Vecellio, *Degli Habiti Antichi e Moderni di Tutto il Mondo*. Venice: Giovanni Bernardo Sessa, 1598. George Peabody Library, the Sheridan Libraries, Johns Hopkins University

For the new theater and its mass audiences, honor had very little to do with valor or force of arms. Instead, a man's honor, that attribute he prided himself on more than any other, was entirely dependent on the purity of his Christian bloodline and the sexual morals of his wife, sisters, and daughters. Evidently neither of these factors is really in a man's control, but more important, both of them depend utterly on the perception of other people. As the theater would demonstrate in hit play after hit play, "honor is pure crystal, which the merest breath will shatter."[19]

The flip side of honor's fragility and dependency on outward appearances was its newfound universality. No longer an exclusive pertinence of the nobility, honor was something that all men were expected to aspire to. A man could be poor, but as long as he could boast that his blood was Christian as far back as anyone could delve, then he could hold his head up proud and consider himself as good as any other man, and better than many.

It is not hard to see how the spread of this belief would benefit a state that depended for its livelihood and the continued prosecution of its multiple foreign wars on the smothering taxation of the common classes. On the one hand, the monarchy needed the combined allegiance of the Church and the aristocracy in order to maintain its central control, and it could not risk upsetting these allies by trying to tax them at the rates it would need to in order to finance its endeavors. On the other hand, the highly visible privileges of this gentry exacerbated unrest on the part of a population that was barely scraping by even without shouldering the burdens of higher taxes. Billeting the king's troops as they moved through towns and villages was another obligation that commoners had to accept even as the nobility was spared it. The doctrine of honor spread by the Spanish stage essentially told those commoners that these daily humiliations were palatable because they had honor. Honor was the invisible, intangible coin with which the new state bought the loyalty of its abused populace.[20]

This loyalty or obedience in the face of widespread suffering was encouraged as well by the very metaphors the theater helped make commonplace, especially the idea that the world was itself a kind of stage. The theme of the world as stage was not at all new in the late sixteenth and early seventeenth centuries. In fact, it was already a common metaphor in medieval theology for depicting the relation between humans and their maker, and was derived from the classical Latin dictum *quod fere totus mundus exerceat histrionem* ("for almost the whole world performs as actors"), attributed to the Roman author Gaius Petronius Arbiter. In this medieval model, later used by the great Spanish playwright Pedro Calderón de la Barca as the organizing theme to his most famous sacramental play, *The Great Stage of the World*, God is figured as the eternal playwright or director, assessing our mundane actions from behind the scenes. Our job is to play our roles to the best of our ability. If we perform well in our appointed role, be that of king or pauper, we will be rewarded in the afterlife. If we perform poorly, we will be punished.[21]

The metaphor of the world as stage and the idea of honor as a universal patrimony of the soul were in fact fused to great effect by the theatrical industry. In play after play, failures of the honor system, even those involving noblemen and kings, would be set right by the end of the play, thus showing that while humans can make mistakes, and even sovereigns may lose their way, ultimately all honor flows from the king, and to the king from God. In this way the theater industry provided a powerful support at the popular level for what political theorists were at work defining as the divine right of kings.[22] Faced with a dishonor committed by the king, a character in one play asks, "And if the King should twist the law with violence?"—to which his companion replies, "The King is the King; be quiet and have patience."[23] All in all, the message was this: the world appears topsy-turvy; time, to put it in Hamlet's words, is out of joint; but these are ultimately only appearances, much like those we see every day on the stage. In the end, God, who is guiding our sovereign and who has assigned us our roles in life, will make everything work out.

Cervantes knew this metaphor well, and even has some fun with it in his great novel. Following an episode in which Quixote and Sancho confront a cartful of actors in disguise, including one dressed as the personification of Death, Quixote has this to say about the theater:

"I want you, Sancho, to think well and to have a good opinion of plays, and to be equally well-disposed toward those who perform them and those who write them, because they are all the instruments whereby a great service is performed for the nation, holding up a mirror to every step we take and allowing us to see a vivid image of the actions of human life; there is no comparison that indicates what we are and what we should be more clearly than plays and players. If you do not agree then tell me: have you ever seen a play that presents kings, emperors, and pontiffs, knights, ladies, and many other characters? One plays the scoundrel, another the liar, this one the merchant, that one the soldier, another the wise fool, yet another the foolish lover, but when the play is over and they have taken off their costumes, all the actors are equal."

"Yes, I have seen that," responded Sancho.

"Well, the same thing happens in the drama and business of this world, where some play emperors, others pontiffs, in short, all the figures that can be presented in a play, but at the end, which is when life is over, death removes all the clothing that differentiates them, and all are equal in the grave."

"That's a fine comparison," said Sancho, "though not so new that I haven't heard it many times before."[24]

Sancho's wry comment deftly puts the idea of the world as stage in its place: in the dustbin of overused metaphors and unquestioned conventions. Indeed, as Quixote has just revealed despite himself, it is the comparison itself that performs such a great service for the nation. For Cervantes, in contrast, when he compares human beings to actors and characters, it is for a very different reason.

When modern theater developed in the sixteenth century, one of its main innovations was the technique known as the stage within the stage. Once dramas began incorporating plays, actors, and playgoers into their story lines, a complex and fascinating new dynamic developed. Spectators had to learn something that is second nature to us now but was entirely new to audiences at the time: they had to learn how simultaneously to believe a statement and know it was false; they also had to learn to suspend what we can call a sentence's *performative* function, all the while understanding what the sentence meant.

As the British philosopher John Austin argued, sentences that from their structure seem to describe a reality can also have the ability to affect that reality. He called these performative sentences, and he gave as an example the sentence pronounced by a priest at the wedding between a man and woman, "I now pronounce you man and wife." While it sounds like a description of what the priest is doing, namely, pronouncing something, in fact the sentence creates the very situation it is describing. By hearing it pronounced, a roomful of attendees participates in the change of status of two people from single individuals to a married couple. As Austin also pointed out, when speech acts take place in literature or on the stage, we are able to suspend their function, making such uses less interesting for his purposes. For us, however, they are key. For what is it exactly that enables us to know when to suspend the performative power of a sentence?

In a play by Lope that was first staged in 1608, *Lo fingido verdadero*, or *True Pretense*, this very scenario is enacted by the main character, a Roman actor named Genesius, who performs a series of plays for the amusement of the emperor Diocletian. Before moving on to the main drama of the play—in which Genesius portrays a Christian martyr with such intensity that he starts to believe himself, and is converted—Lope first plays with the problem of characters acting on the stage before an audience played by other actors, and does so by having the actors play characters who are in love and who make declarations of love to one another, while the actors playing them are also in love.[25] In this way Lope is able to explore how the interior characters suspend or fail to suspend the performativity of their declarations of love, all to the enjoyment of those in the real audience, who must simultaneously understand their pronouncements and suspend their performativity as well.

When it comes to Genesius's performance as a Christian, after he has in fact converted and is therefore no longer acting but in fact believes everything he is saying, a spectator of the interior play and member of the emperor's entourage exclaims about the play he is watching that "there's no difference between this and the real thing."[26] Of course, in order for this sentence to make sense to us, the real spectators, we *must* be able to see the difference between the play we are watching and the interior one, and thus we must simultaneously believe and disbelieve the character's claim.

Cervantes was also fascinated by this essential paradox of acting—namely, that a perfect performance eradicates the very idea of a performance; that theater strives for an illusion that it can't sustain without ceasing to be theater. In fact, the paradox and how he handles it goes to the heart of his invention of fiction and its impact on the modern world. The setting is once again an inn. Having just heard an amusing tale about two local villagers who can imitate a donkey's braying so well that they can't tell the difference between a real donkey's bray and their imitation of it, the inn's guests learn with excitement that a well-known puppet master, Master Pedro, has arrived with his puppet cart and his soothsaying monkey. After using his trick with the monkey to fleece Quixote and Sancho for a few reales, the puppet master (in fact a disguised rogue whom Quixote had freed from a chain gang in the previous book) and his assistant set to enacting a story of chivalry—at which point the puppet show, for the delusional knight, begins to bleed into reality:

> Don Quixote, seeing and hearing so many Moors and so much clamor, thought it would be a good idea to assist those who were fleeing; and rising to his feet, in a loud voice he said:
> "I shall not consent, in my lifetime and in my presence, to any such offense against an enamored knight so famous and bold as Don Gaiferos. Halt, you lowborn rabble; do not follow and do not pursue him unless you wish to do battle with me!"
> And speaking and taking action, he unsheathed his sword, leaped next to the stage, and with swift and never before seen fury began to rain down blows on the crowd of Moorish puppets, knocking down some, beheading others, ruining this one, destroying that one, and among many other blows, he delivered so powerful a downstroke that if Master Pedro had not stooped, crouched down, and hunched over, he would have cut off his head more easily than if it had been so much marzipan.[27]

Cervantes knew how characters work in the theater. They are masks whose illusion the audience accepts even as we project emotions onto the stage with them. While we don't leave the theater believing the two leading actors are really in love, for the time they are on the stage we act as though we do, and we believe our own acting enough to feel joy for them, or to cry tears when their love is unrequited. The entire emotional impact of a character thus stems from that partial belief, that splitting that allows some part of us to step out on the stage with them.

Quixote's defining trait as a character is that he cannot split himself in that way, at least when it comes to chivalry. He cannot suspend disbelief; he cannot suspend the performativity of a play or a story. When he sees Master Pedro's puppets, or encounters any event that he can interpret through the lens of his stories, the barrier between reality and fantasy fades away; his emotions take over completely without the guiding hand of reason—that awareness that we have, even when awash in vicarious feelings, that what we are reading is solely a story, that the figures on the screen are only actors playing a part. By making his greatest character one whose defining trait is precisely his inability to split himself in that way, Cervantes was drawing a blueprint for fiction even as he was taking advantage of it to make his characters come alive.

The Master Pedro episode has such charm in part because it shows us Quixote on both sides of this split, even though he cannot occupy both simultaneously. Seeing how distraught Master Pedro is over the destruction of his puppet show, the softhearted Sancho rushes to comfort him, even as he comes to his master's defense:

> "Don't cry, Master Pedro, and don't wail, or you'll break my heart, and let me tell you that my master, Don Quixote, is so Catholic and scrupulous a Christian that if he realizes he's done you any harm, he'll tell you so and want to pay and satisfy you, and with interest."
>
> "If Señor Don Quixote would pay me even in part for the figures he has destroyed, I would be happy, and his grace would satisfy his conscience, because there is no salvation for the man who holds another's property against the will of the owner and does not return it."
>
> "That is true, said Don Quixote, "but until now I did not know that I had anything of yours, Master Pedro."
>
> "What do you mean?" responded Master Pedro. These relics lying on the hard and sterile ground, what scattered and annihilated them but the invincible strength of that mighty arm? And whose bodies were they but mine? And how did I earn my living except with them?"
>
> "Now I believe," said Don Quixote at this point, "what I have believed on many other occasions: the enchanters who pursue me simply place figures as they really are before my eyes, and then change and alter them into whatever they wish. I tell you really and truly, you gentlemen who can hear me: it seemed to me that

everything that happened here was actually happening, that Melisendra was Melisendra, Don Gaiferos Don Gaiferos, Marsilio Marsilio, and Charlemagne Charlemagne; for this reason I was overcome with rage."[28]

Here we are witness in the clearest way to how Cervantes has mastered the paradox of the theater in the service of his new art: for just as he pulls the knight back from behind the curtain of his illusion, he has subtly pulled us behind his own—because nowhere is Quixote more human, nowhere is his befuddlement and regret more palpable, than when he is forced to confront his failures. In those moments of rueful clarity, Cervantes exercises the magic of fiction even as he's just shown us the card up his sleeve.

IN THE POSTSCRIPT TO HIS *Journey to Parnassus*, Cervantes stages a conversation between a would-be dramatist named Miguel and one Pancracio, who asks the dramatist about his plays and why they are not performed. After some back-and-forth on the reasons, Miguel declares his intent to "have them published, so that what is seen in a hurry and hidden or misunderstood when it is performed, can be read slowly."[29] Early on, Cervantes tried hard to get his plays performed, but they were rejected by all the *autores* he approached, and he felt a deep frustration with the theater industry at the time. Following these early failures, though, it may be the case that Cervantes intended his later theater to be read as opposed to seen,[30] for he was convinced that a reader, as opposed to a theatergoer, would have the time to digest his work slowly, and to think carefully about what was being represented.[31] This intent also fit with his criticisms of the sorts of plays being put on at the time, their speed and tendency to go for cheap thrills and to be written for the taste of the lowest common denominator.

Returning to Madrid after his failed attempts to secure a government position in Portugal, Cervantes nevertheless seemed to have gained something, even if he was unaware of it himself. His experience among the retinue of flatterers striving to make themselves heard at court had clearly left a lasting impression, one we hear echoing in that line from his tale *The Glass Licentiate*: "I am not a good one for the palace, because I have shame and don't know how to flatter." The insight he brought with him to the stage was that the world was indeed like a theater, but not because we are all playing roles for the benefit of God, who will reward or punish us for how well we play them. Rather, the world is a stage because humans are constantly playing roles for one another.

The brilliance of Cervantes's theater is that it is a theater about how we are always playacting, how we do so mostly in others' interests, and how to do so in our own.[32] There are clearly two ways to explore this theme, and Cervantes does both: either he shows characters who act out roles written in others' interests, and how they fail, or he shows characters who learn to become *autores* of their own destinies. In the case of his play *The Diversion*,[33] one of the principals is Cristina, a kitchen wench who tries to better her social position by marriage, and now sports delusions of being a lady as she follows the rules of courtly love and the honor code. As she says to the lackey Ocaña (who along with the page Quiñones vies for her hand while she rejects them both in the hope of reeling in a higher-ranking mate),

> *Am I a woman to serve a page?*
> *Do I come from such lowly lineage?*
> *By keeping intact the flower of my virginity*
> *do I not have more claim to be a maiden*
> *than El Cid has to be a warrior?*[34]

Not only does Cristina presume to follow a code that would, in the real world, pertain only to ladies far above her station, but her suitor Quiñones makes a great deal of the fact that, as a page, he is of a higher rank than Ocaña. Ocaña, for his part, recognizes his station, but also sees the folly of playacting according to rules set for others' benefit. As he puts it in a dialogue with the nobleman Don Antonio, "The wise man is a concord engendered by skill / the fool a dissonant disparity."[35] Concordance between one's interests and the roles one plays begets wisdom; dissonance between those roles and interests, foolishness.

Cervantes then sets Cristina's machinations against those of the student Cardenio, who, in order to win the love of Cristina's mistress, the noble Marcela, pretends to be the wealthy *indiano*—*indianos* were Spaniards living in the New World—cousin to whom she is betrothed, and whose arrival from Peru they are awaiting. Again the words of caution are offered by a servant, in this case Cardenio's man Torrentes, who assures Cardenio that his deceit is

> *a tower built on toothpicks,*
> *or a little house of cards.*
> *Tell me, where are the pearls?*
> *Where are the bezoars,*
> *the parakeets or parrots?*
> *Where is the practical knowledge*
> *of the Indies, of the ports and seas*
> *to choose and navigate?*
> *Where is the flannel and the tailor?*
> *If you desire a happy ending to your affairs*
> *I advise you always to bear the truth before you.*[36]

In the play, almost all the characters are pretending to be something they are not in order to obtain something or someone that is not theirs to have. The comedy results from how miserably they all fail and, more important, from the fact that they *all* fail—unlike in the vast majority of the more lighthearted plays of the period, where at least some of the characters win out and obtain their desires. In *The Diversion*, in each and every case the reason for the characters' failure is that they buy into social illusions *as if* they were real.[37] "It's the illusion, stupid," Cervantes seems to be telling us. And theater is the perfect medium to show us that.[38]

In the theater, we can see a character unmasked in one moment and quickly donning his or her role in another. The ploy of the aside allows the audience to hear the character's "real" thoughts and contrast them with what the character then says to his counterpart. But while all the theater being produced in Europe at the time takes advantage of these inherent characteristics, Cervantes pushed the technique to another level, using the very idea of theater to explore the complexity of social role playing and its effects on the perception of reality.

In that light, a quirky comedy such as *The Diversion* turns out to be built on a mind-bogglingly intricate web of various nesting levels of playacting. The centerpiece of the web is a theatrical interlude put on by Cristina and authored by Ocaña for the entertainment of the entire household. There are many play-within-a-play structures in the early modern period, but none quite as complex as this one. Here we have Cervantes writing a play in which actors play characters who, in turn, put on another play—this much is common enough—to which two of the ostensible audience members react in jealousy by fighting and wounding each other. Even this last would be far from unprecedented, a scenario similar to the short circuit between a play and "reality" in Hamlet's famous *Mousetrap*; except that here the audience members, Ocaña and Torrentes, are only *pretending* to fight as payback to Cristina for setting them against each other. Thus a scene with wounding and blood that, against the backdrop of an interlude within a play, would seem to be asking to be interpreted by all spectators as *real* turns out to be fake. As Don Antonio blurts out in anger upon learning that the mayhem was a joke, "By God, I'm of a mind to turn illusion into reality!" Well, Cervantes seems to be saying, that's what we've all been doing all along.

Appropriately, Cervantes ends his play with two asides, coming from those characters who were the least bamboozled by attaching their desires to illusory dreams. After a comical stream of declarations of despair from the long string of characters who, in stark contrast to the customary ending, will *not* be getting married, Marcela simply states that "I will maintain my integrity, not seeking the impossible but things appropriate to our nature." Ocaña, for his part, delivers the moral:

> *What happens in this story*
> *is no one marries in the end—*
> *some because they're not in love*
> *and some because they can't.*
> *I ask you to bear witness*
> *to this well-known truth:*
> *our diversion does not end in marriage!*[39]

In real life, in other words, our diversions, what we do to pass the time, to have pleasure, do not conform to the dictates of social mores; in plainer language: sex does not always lead to marriage. But by buying into that code and its impossible standards of purity, we run the risk of ruining our chances for love, satisfaction, and self-determination in the real world.

While the characters of *The Diversion* suffer devastating and comic failures because of their slavish adherence to the roles dictated by social custom, Cervantes also dreamed up characters who have markedly more success in manipulating the performances that make up everyday life. One such character is the rogue or trickster figure Pedro de Urdemalas from the play of the same name.[40] Pedro lives by his wits and aims to better his station in society, sometimes by solving peoples' problems and sometimes by conning them out of their gold. In one of the scenes from the first act that establishes Pedro's bona fides as a trickster, two lovers take part in a ritual wherein the woman, Benita, stands in a bucket of water and listens for a name to be whispered by the wind, with the understanding that she will marry a man with the name she hears. When a sexton called Roque tricks the couple by whispering his own name before her true love Pascual can, Pedro solves the problem by suggesting to Pascual that he take advantage of the sacrament of confirmation to change his name to Roque, thus literally writing his own destiny.

The play intertwines the story of Pedro with that of the gypsy girl Belica, who dreams of being a noblewoman. And it turns out that Belica is indeed the illegitimate child of a noble family, and related to the king. In the play's final act we see Belica move to the palace, as she has always dreamed, whereas Pedro finds his rightful place in the theater, as an actor in an itinerant troupe. The troupe then begins to perform before the court, and Pedro, having renamed himself as Nicolás de los Ríos, addresses Belica, now called Isabel, with these words:

> *I say that you have before you*
> *the one you knew as Pedro*
> *converted from gypsy to famous actor,*
> *to serve you in more plays than you can imagine . . .*
> *your hope and mine have reached their conclusion,*
> *mine only in* fiction, *yours as it should.*[41]

Here we see *ficción*—which, recall, in Cervantes's time connoted only pretend or playacting—becoming his name for all those ways in which people aspire to greater social recognition than they will ever have in the real world. In reality, solely those born noble attain the privileges accorded to the nobility and may dress the part, no matter what the theater tells us.[42]

Commoners in Cervantes's time would learn from the popular culture that they were titular members, by virtue of their old Christian heritage, of an elite whose doors were in fact forever closed to them. But in recognizing the power the theater and its fictions has over us, a character such as Pedro learns to succeed in his own way, to write his own ticket. The play ends with Pedro preparing his fellow actors for the play they will perform: not a typical cape-and-sword comedy that will "end in marriage, a common thing seen a hundred thousand times";[43] no, the play to be performed, free of all such worthless content, will be none other than the one Cervantes has written, *Pedro de Urdemalas*.

BY 1584, CERVANTES was already a celebrity of sorts, having brought many of his exploits onto the boards of Madrid's theaters. Records show that he was paid a small but respectable sum that year for two plays, both now lost, and he later claimed to have had his plays produced on numerous occasions, if not exactly to rave reviews. While he may not have been making a killing with his work on the stage, he was in his element, trading barbs with fellow writers in Madrid's literary salons and clinking glasses in cheap taverns with playwrights and actors—and even with actresses who, unlike their British counterparts,[44] were permitted to grace the Spanish stage despite the stains that thereby accrued to their honor, if that were ever a worry to begin with.

On one of those nights of revelry Cervantes clinked glasses with a woman some seventeen years his junior by the name of Ana Franca de Rojas, whom he met at the tavern she owned and operated with her husband. Ana Franca was by all reports a dark-haired, charismatic beauty who had at sixteen married an older shopkeeper from the northern region of Asturias. For his part, the Asturian, "one of the scramblers thrown up by the thousands by every large city,"[45] was interested mainly in the modest dowry a recently departed aunt had left Ana Franca; in fact, he used it to open the tavern where she and Miguel eventually met and started their affair. Soon she became pregnant and later that year gave birth to a daughter named Isabel.

At first Ana Franca's husband appears to have been none the wiser and accepted Isabel as his daughter, but Cervantes would eventually recognize her with that fabled name he adopted as his own and that adorns his later writing: Saavedra.

Shortly after the birth of Isabel, Cervantes took a trip to Esquivias, a small winemaking village close to his native city of Alcalá, where his friend the poet Pedro de Laínez had settled and had suddenly passed away. On that visit he met another young woman, Catalina de Salazar y Palacios Vozmediano, the daughter of a recently widowed landowner from the lesser nobility and in December of that year, they were married. Perhaps the seemingly hasty vows were inspired by his desire to keep his relationship with Ana Franca and their daughter a secret; perhaps a young wife and a property in the country appealed to Cervantes, now thirty-seven years old, well into upper middle age in those times.

Whatever the reasons for the decisions he made, Miguel de Cervantes—this son of a father who had struggled to stake a claim for an old Christian lineage but always remained under suspicion; this father of an illegitimate daughter and brother to women, in the case of his sisters, Andrea and Magdalena, who would have, in the eyes of their society, long since lost their honor due to multiple and failed love affairs—had clearly already lived a life in which the attribute of honor, so touted by the Spanish stage, would have been decidedly out of his grasp. Whatever his motivations, donning the guise of a comfortable country gentleman and moving out to Esquivias was also the move of a man who had learned that the world was indeed a stage, and that, for that very reason, the trick was not to play the roles you were given, but to write them for yourself.

6.

Of Shepherds, Knights, and Ladies

"Fortunate the age and fortunate the times called golden by the ancients, and not because gold, which in this our age of iron is so highly esteemed, could be found then with no effort, but because those who lived in that time did not know the two words thine and mine. In that blessed age all things were owned in common; no one, for his daily sustenance, needed to do more than lift his hand and pluck it from the sturdy oaks that so liberally invited him to share their sweet and flavorsome fruit. The clear fountains and rushing rivers offered delicious, transparent waters in magnificent abundance. In the fissures of rocks and hollows of trees diligent and clever bees established their colonies, freely offering to any hand the fertile harvest of their sweet labor."

For modern readers, pastoral has, to put it mildly, gone out of style. There are good reasons for this. Pastoral plots consist largely of handsome shepherds pining for virtuous shepherdesses in, well, pastoral idylls, grabbing any excuse to pull out a lute and belt out a bit of the poetry known as an eclogue. Here are some lines from an eclogue:

> *Hair, what changes*
> *I have seen since I saw you*
> *And how badly this green*
> *Color of hope suits you.*
>
> *I once thought, hair,*
> *Although with some fear,*

That no other shepherd
Was fit to be near you.[1]

In this case, the handsome shepherd doing the pining is called Sireno, and he is singing to a lock of hair he has lain out on the grass in front of him, and is now bathing with his tears. The hair belongs to the virtuous title character of Jorge de Montemayor's great pastoral novel *Diana*, which was the most popular book in Spain when Cervantes decided to make his first attempt at writing a novel.[2] Even if the translation fails to do justice to the original, the point remains: for modern tastes, the idea of getting rich by writing pastoral sounds a bit like trying to launch a pop career by singing Barry Manilow covers.

It was different in Cervantes's time. Literacy rates in Spain had been rising rapidly throughout the sixteenth century. In the early part of the century, very few Spanish men could read, and the majority of these were in the clergy, academia, or administration. By the end of the century, rates for men had risen considerably, and more significantly, evidence from Inquisition trials and wills indicates that literacy had spread widely among the common classes and even among women, both in cities and in the countryside.[3] The burgeoning literate populations demanded entertainment, and while the theater was the number-one draw, books were increasingly in demand.

Even so, reading was a very different activity from what it is today. Curling up alone with a good book was not common; books were heavy, rooms were dark, and the practice of reading silently to oneself was still a relatively recent innovation. While more and more books were being bought for private enjoyment, most copies sold were destined for more than one reader, and often were read out loud in a tavern or inn, as we see occurring in *Don Quixote*. As one innkeeper explains with regard to the few books he has and his perplexity at how anyone could find them objectionable,

"I don't know how that can be; the truth is, to my mind, there's no better reading in the world; I have two or three of them, along with some other papers, and they really have put life into me, and not only me but other people too. Because during the harvest, many of the harvesters gather here during their time off, and there's always a few who know how to read, and one of them takes down one of those books, and more than thirty of us sit around him and listen to him read with so much pleasure that it saves us a thousand gray hairs; at least, as far as I'm concerned, I can tell you that when I hear about those furious, terrible blows struck by the knights, it makes me want to do the same, and I'd be happy to keep hearing about them for days and nights on end."[4]

The innkeeper's preference is clearly for the tales of chivalry, but pastoral was selling well, too; more to the point, it was selling a lot better than poetry was. Cervantes had harbored the wish to be a poet since long before leaving Spain, and pastoral was a genre in which he could insert a good number of the eclogues he had been writing over the years, many of them during his time in captivity.

Poetry is very much at the heart of why Cervantes decided to write *La Galatea*. As he admits in his dedication to the novel, he always had a strong inclination to poetry, and he was pained at the apparent disfavor it had fallen into. Too much a lover of good poetry to suffer bad verse lightly, even his own, Cervantes in later years looked back on these earlier poems with some chagrin, dismissing his first novel as "better versed in misfortunes than in verses."[5] But in 1585, Cervantes was ready to take a full swing at the one genre that would allow him to showcase his poetic talents. While the results were not as revolutionary as his later work, we can already see in this early book a distinct tendency to buck convention.

While the setting in pastorals before *La Galatea* served mainly to frame the poetry, the story in Cervantes's treatment takes on a new importance. Poetry is still at the heart of the matter, but what the characters say about poetry and how they use poetry are far more central than the poems themselves. The poems are no longer simply interspersed in the text as in earlier pastoral; instead, the characters gather around the stage as an audience, commenting on and reacting to the verses being sung. Having failed to make a living in the theater, already in his first novel Cervantes has started to take the theater with him into prose.

The centerpiece of *La Galatea* is a poetic competition among four shepherds. As Cervantes writes of his protagonists, "many times they had come together to praise each one the cause of his torment, each trying to show as best he could that his pain was greater than that of any of the others, holding the greatest glory to be that of suffering the most. And *they were all so talented, that is to say, suffered such pain*, that however they represented it, they showed it to be the greatest imaginable."[6] Pastoral romances such as the *Diana* were about love. Their purpose was to provide a setting for a full spectrum of poetic expressions of that passion in all its glory and agony. In Montemayor's classic formulation, "those who suffer most are the best."[7] Cervantes's pastoral romance was certainly about love, but it was also about *how well or poorly poetry explores love*.[8] Hence his subtle joke in the lines just quoted, where the poets' talent and their pain are treated as one and the same thing.

True to form, and to the disappointments coloring his life experiences, *La Galatea* is in some ways the antipastoral romance, instilling from the very outset a sense that something in Arcadia is amiss. Rather than the weeping and pure-hearted shepherds who populated the *Diana* or *El pastor de Fílida* that Gálvez de Montalvo had just published two years earlier to great success, *La Galatea* treats its readers almost at once to the story of deception, betrayal, and death told by Lisandro, a nobleman who arrives among the shepherds intent on avenging the treacherous murder of his beloved Leonida. While Cervantes's rural characters do indeed pine, weep, and sing in true pastoral form, their awareness of the ever-present possibility of deception colors the novel from beginning to end. Much like audiences watching actors put on a play, the shepherds constantly wonder about the reality of the emotions and desires they hear expressed by others or see played out on their faces.

While the novel has countless characters and intricately interwoven subplots, its core story revolves around the love of Elicio for the beautiful shepherdess Galatea, much as Montemayor's novel dealt with the love of Sireno for the beautiful Diana. But the similarity ends there. Where Sireno's drama concerns his love for a married and hence inaccessible woman, the tension animating *La Galatea* turns on the impossibility of perfectly reading or ultimately understanding the beloved's true feelings, and thus its exploration of the poetry of love transforms the novel from the beginning into a kind of machine for the manufacture of psychological depth and hidden emotions. Here is how Cervantes describes his principals' feelings for each other:

It seemed to Galatea, since Elicio loved her with such regard for his own honor, that it would be too ungrateful not to repay his honest thoughts with some honest favor. Elicio imagined, since Galatea did not entirely disdain his services, that his desire might have some success; but when these fantasies awakened his hope, he found himself so happy and carefree that a thousand times he almost revealed to Galatea those feelings he had hidden with such care. But Galatea's own discretion recognized, in the movements on his face, what Elicio carried in his heart, and showed as much on her own face, such that the shepherd's words froze on his lips, and he was left only with the flavor of that first movement, it seeming to him that it would be an insult to Galatea's honesty to speak of things that might carry even the shadow of not being so honest that honesty itself would transform itself into them.[9]

What Cervantes manages in such sentences is to be at once slyly humorous and utterly insightful about the play of concealment and revelation at the heart of a new love relation. The intricate interplay of hopes elicited by expressions read on the face of the beloved is pushed to comic extremes; but as mannered as the scene may seem, it also presents its readers with a new kind of realism, one based on a detailed psychology of masking and revealing deeply felt emotions.

Where the shepherds of pastoral romance before Cervantes would use their poetry to express the pain of their unrequited love, Cervantes's shepherds go from singing poems that emphasize how their poetry cannot express the depths of their true pain to realizing that all they are ever talking about is the poetry itself.[10] But in that realization, the poets have suddenly become real themselves. No longer the standard cutouts of pastoral convention, the poets in La Galatea become characters precisely to the extent that they become aware of their conventional trappings.

In a similar way to his experiments with theater, Cervantes used his first foray into extended narrative to undermine not only the conventions of a literary genre, but also the social pretensions that genre supports; and the techniques he used to accomplish this task are the very ones that are central to what we now call fiction. By setting before his reader not just a problem or a passion or a crime, but the way in which that problem, passion, or crime is being presented, explored, and understood by the literature and theater of his day, Cervantes had subtly begun the process of teaching his readers to divide themselves in two, to become at once the readers *within* the texts, whose emotions treat what's happening as real, while remaining equally *without*, aware that it's all just a story.

AFTER THE DEATH OF LAÍNEZ, his much younger widow, Juana Gaitán, the inheritor of his estate and several of his unpublished manuscripts, remarried a man closer to her in age. Her new husband, a merchant's son named Diego de Hondaro, would spend much of Laínez's estate over the years, leaving Juana in poverty by the time she joined Cervantes's family in Juan de Navas's house in Valladolid some two decades later. But in 1584, Juana could still count on the wealth of Laínez's estate to host in style the friends from her late husband's literary circles. And so in September of that year, Miguel came to visit Juana's house in Esquivias, now formally a guest of Diego de Hondaro.

The town of Esquivias was not quite the middle of nowhere, but it was close enough to inspire those opening lines from so many years later that would carry their author into posterity: "Somewhere in La Mancha, in a place whose name I do not care to remember . . ."[11] Of its one hundred eighty families, five were Morisco; thirty-seven were gentry, albeit mostly those who had fallen on hard times: the impoverished hidalgos of literary lore, the most famous of which would be none other than Don Quixote himself. In fact it was at a wedding in Esquivias that Cervantes encountered an elderly man whose name was Quijana, and who would become the inspiration for his famous knight.

On September 22, Juana Gaitán gave power of attorney to Cervantes to seek privilege and license to publish Laínez's *Cancionero* (which, it turns out, he never managed to do). The business at hand done, the friends likely gathered at the little restaurant in the village square owned by Diego Ramírez. There, Cervantes may well have met a friend and neighbor of Juana's, the daughter of a local hidalgo named Fernando de Salazar Vozmediano, whose house was just down the street from Juana's, across from the village church. On December 12, a mere two and a half months later, Cervantes and Doña Catalina de

Salazar y Palacios Vozmediano would be married in that church by her uncle, Juan de Palacios.[12]

Cervantes's decision to wed Catalina after a courtship of a few short months may be at least in part explained by the situation back in Madrid. He had never abandoned his ambition to be recognized as a great and honorable man, and remaining in an illicit liaison with a married tavern keeper was sure to leave a stain on his reputation. Catalina de Salazar, while not wealthy, had inherited several acres of olive trees and grapevines in the countryside around Esquivias, and thus could count herself among the minor landed gentry. By marrying into this family and moving to Esquivias, Cervantes was distancing himself from the impurities of the big city in favor of the simplicity, honor, and charm of rural life.

So he moved into Catalina's house and became the titular head of the family. The country life, as hard as it was, would certainly have held some attraction for him. The house in the center of town, across from the church where Cervantes would hear mass, had an orchard behind it with a stream running by it. From the home's windows he could gaze out at hillsides covered with olive trees. The wine his grapes produced must not have been too bad; at least he implies as much when he compares it to that of the local gentry and finds it "more illustrious."[13] In Madrid, Cervantes had to deal with an illegitimate child by an Austrian innkeeper's wife, along with literary squabbles and the constant scraping to make ends meet. In Esquivias, he could settle down with a young and, by all accounts, beautiful bride and play the country squire to his heart's content. He might not even have to scramble for patronage anymore, if the landholdings coming to him in the dowry could be counted on.

Whatever he hoped to gain by this turn in his life, it did not work out as planned. Rather than a tranquil haven away from the burdens of his urban existence, Esquivias would offer Cervantes only more worries. While the eleven acres of land he now controlled was a considerable dowry, Catalina also brought her widowed mother and two underage brothers to the marriage, and her recently deceased father had left, as it turned out, a great deal of outstanding debt—all of which now were now added to Cervantes's cares. The olive plantation and vineyards that Catalina brought to the marriage also yielded far less than Cervantes had hoped for. His marriage would be equally barren, at least in terms of offspring. Catalina would have no children, and Ana Franca's daughter Isabel would remain Cervantes's only known descendant. All in all, Cervantes's move to his own private Arcadia failed to yield the good life he had hoped for; the payoff in literary terms would be, however, truly golden.

One reason that pastoral had gained new popularity was because of the growing vogue for stories and plays that held up the simple virtues of country life in contrast to the corruption of court and the filth of urban centers. As a widely read book circulating at the time put it, "the privilege of living in the countryside is that there no man lives or could live, or who is called or could be called, a king's or lord's land-lord."[14] The widespread praise of the simple life and the common classes in books and plays painted over a very different reality, though, in which commoners living in miserable conditions were exploited by the government to support an idle nobility that paid no taxes.

Some of the literary backlash against the court and in favor of rural life was a natural reaction to the court's obvious corruption, but it was also encouraged by the government as a way of counteracting the perverse incentives that were sapping the countryside of potentially productive occupants and crowding the court with indolent influence peddlers. In countless books and plays of the time the same theme is revisited ad nauseam: for every corrupt, effeminate, and immoral courtier the literature of the time created, there was a proud and honorable townsperson or country commoner, living productively on the land and unwilling to sully his principled beliefs in the dirty business of politics. The pastoral theme, it seems, was popular for a reason: it soothed a nation in decline with images of a golden past that had never really existed in the first place.

"All peoples that have a history have a paradise, a state of innocence, a golden age," wrote the great German poet Friedrich Schiller, and Renaissance Europe was no exception.[15] Renaissance poets turned to Ovid and Virgil for models of poetry that depicted a bucolic paradise of innocent shepherds singing against idyllic backdrops of pristine nature; Renaissance men of letters such as Lorenzo Valla theorized an unspoiled nature as being identical to God himself; and political thinkers posited a state of nature very much the opposite of Hobbes's nightmare of eternal internecine war. In their view, the golden age was a utopia of shared wealth, spoiled by the advent of property and the covetousness it instills in men. Like the Genesis story of the expulsion from Eden, the Arcadia dreamt by the Greeks and adopted by the Renaissance posited a time before time as both a lost ideal and a model for heaven on earth.

It is perhaps not as surprising as it might seem at first glance that Renaissance society itself was so different from the ideals of Arcadia it created and admired.[16] In Spain the interest in pastoral literature increased with the decline in enthusiasm for the romances of chivalry, but it coincided with the emergence and growth in popularity of the picaresque novel, a literary genre that exposed the seamy underside of humanity, everything that pastoral would seem to eschew.[17]

In some ways pastoral and the picaresque were responding to the same set of growing concerns in Spanish society. As living conditions became harsher for those in the small towns and countryside and those who were engaged in the farming and industry that Spanish society depended on for its wealth, more and more people were attracted to the centers of commerce and the court itself. The landed classes would also increasingly gather around the centers of political power, spending their time and political capital on the sort of politicking that could keep the taxes exacted from them by the Spanish government low, while in turn increasing the state's dependence on tax revenues from the non-noble landowners and commoners working the fields. Thus, as urban life grew more crowded and corrupt, Spanish writers responded by showing poverty, crime, and corruption in some works, while in others dreaming up an unsullied alternate reality of perfect equality and justice.

Cervantes's apparent ambivalence toward pastoral literature has long been a source of curiosity. On the one hand, he was clearly a great admirer of his good friend Gálvez de Montalvo's pastoral classic *El pastor de Fílida*, and despite later words of criticism about his own poetry, also clearly thought that his *Galatea* was a good book.[18] On the other hand, he could be pointed in his criticisms of pastoral literature, as when he has the dog Berganza in his *Dog's Colloquy* (a novella told in the form of a conversation between two dogs) wryly comment that what he has heard said about the lives of shepherds doesn't seem to fit well with his own experience.[19] But in truth there is nothing surprising about this ambivalence; it is to be explained by the way he approached the idea of the lost golden age in his own fiction.[20]

Just like the ideas of chivalry and honor that were so popular in the literature of the time, the idea of the golden age functioned as a kind of illusion or mask that hid the corruptions of his times. Life may be corrupt, dirty, and dangerous now, went the logic, but that is only because people have left the land; because local administrators are blinded by their own avarice; because foreign elements have interfered. Go back to your land, follow the king's law, and keep the one true faith and you will see that we are already living in the true golden age. Exactly like the ideal of honor or the mode of chivalry, the ideal of Arcadia was an illusion that served to distract people from the inequities of their lives, to convince them that country life was purer and better, despite the fact that the court was sucking their livelihood away.

But just as Cervantes balanced his cynicism over the degeneration of honor and the mechanism of war with a resilient idealism and adulation of courage, his ironic treatment of literature's bucolic idylls is tempered by an earnest exaltation of that literature's ostensible focus: love. For if his characters come alive in a way that few others before his did, it is precisely because his speakers' sense that the conventions that imprison them (the Fílidas and Filenas and Dianas bequeathed by the traditional forms of courtly love poetry) do not adequately express the depths of their feelings or the uniqueness of their ladies.

Cervantes's own alter ego in the novel, Lauso, hints at this when he allows that his Silena may be nothing more than a conventional mask for the real woman who has stolen his heart. As the narrator writes of Lauso in *La Galatea*, "although he believed no one understood [his song] because they did not know the disguised name of Silena, more than three of those who accompanied him there knew her and were even amazed that Lauso's modesty would allow him to offend someone, specifically the disguised shepherdess, in whom they had seen that he was so in love."[21] Her identity in fact becomes a kind of riddle, "since Lauso named Silena in his song . . . and no shepherdess by that name was known, and since Lauso had traveled through many parts of Spain and even all of Asia and Europe, the shepherdess who had conquered his will was probably a foreigner."[22] The poet's inability to capture his love in words is here grafted onto the identity of a real love, now lost, whose very absence lifts both the lover and the beloved out of stale convention and inspires them with the breath of mystery.

In this way, when Lauso plaintively sings to Silena,

In blind darkness I walked when
your light was missing, oh beautiful eyes,
here and there, without seeing the sky, I wandered
among sharp thorns and thistles;
but then, in the moment that my soul
touched the cluster of your bright rays,
I saw clearly the pathway of my delight open and clear...[23]

While the poetry is not the most polished, the sentiment of a bewildered lover who feels he sees clearly only when in the presence of his beloved rings profoundly true. The poetry reaps this vitality from the framework Cervantes installs around it, a story in which the characters are straining to burst free from their conventional skins.

For unlike their literary forebears, the shepherds of Cervantes's pastoral fiction are painfully—and at times hilariously—aware of their own conventional status, and in the very throes of passionate declamations about love, more often than not they make pointed references to the conventions they are using, even going so far as to make them the central theme of their poetic games. In one scene in *La Galatea*, the shepherds engage in a game of riddles. The final riddle, spoken by Elicio, runs something like this:

It is very obscure and very clear;
It has a thousand contradictions;
It hides the truths from us
And in the end uncovers them.
It is born at times of wit,
At other times of great imagination,
And it tends to engender obstinacy,
Although it deals with airy matters.

All know its name,
Even small children;
There are many and they have
Owners of a different sort.
There's no old lady who doesn't burn

With one of these;
They are the pleasure of a few hours;
Whether they weary or satisfy us.

There are sages who uncover them
To draw out their meanings,
And some are embarrassed
The more they brood on them.
Be it foolish, be it curious,
Be it easy, be it intricate,
Be it something or nothing at all,
Tell me what this thing could be?[24]

Timbrio, his poetic rival, answers right away that this thing the riddle is asking about is nothing but the riddle itself. By having their efforts constantly run up against the limits of their poetic genres, Cervantes turned the poets who populate *La Galatea* into characters who recognize they are generic and thereby exceed those genres, and whose feelings of love, pain, and loss thus spring to life.

JUST AS BOOKS ABOUNDED extolling the virtues of country life and excoriating the corruption of court life, there were plenty of critical voices pointing out that in reality there was little difference between the towns and the court, that Spanish society was putrid to the core.[25] What Cervantes was doing so differently with his fiction was representing the golden age as, simultaneously, a false model and hence one to be ridiculed, and a lofty ideal and hence a reminder of the imperfections of the here and now. Moreover, the way he did so was by allowing readers to inhabit characters as they went about believing in those ideals and being betrayed by them. It was with fiction that Cervantes could *both* proclaim the value of the model and ridicule the application of that model to the present, all the while inserting his readers into the perspective of someone who existed at the juncture of an ideal and its failed reality.[26]

While *La Galatea* was his first exploration of the theme, he touches on it in numerous other places in his work, including in both volumes of the *Quixote* and in the posthumously published *Trials of Persiles and Sigismunda*. Toward the very beginning of the first volume of *Don*

Quixote, the knight and his squire happen upon a hut outside of which a small group of goatherds is settling on the ground for a simple meal. The goatherds invite the travelers to join them, and Quixote sits down in their midst while Sancho stands at his side to serve him, as a squire normally would. At this Quixote corrects him, telling him, "I want you to sit here at my side and in the company of these good people, and be the same as I, who am your natural lord and master; eat from my plate and drink where I drink, for one may say of knight errantry what is said of love: it makes all things equal."[27]

If the sight of the goatherds and their simple meal invokes in Quixote the image of a golden age prior to any distinction of class or social status, his desire is immediately tested by Sancho's frank embrace of his own rusticity. As he responds, "As long as I have something good to eat, I'll eat it just as well or better standing and all alone as sitting at the height of an emperor." He then points out that he anyway prefers not to be limited by the sorts of manners that would require him to "chew slowly, not drink too much, wipe my mouth a lot, not sneeze or cough if I feel like it, or do other things that come with solicitude and freedom."[28] So while Quixote projects the fantasy of court society of a simple country life free of intrigue and class distinctions, where all are equal and, specifically, equally noble, Sancho's answer pulls the reader back to earth, to the reality of those people for whom Quixote's image of social equality would make no sense whatsoever.

As if to drive the point home, Quixote, after physically pulling Sancho down next to him, launches into a harangue inspired by the simple fare in front of him, in which he expresses every possible cliché about the golden age in ever more hyperbolic progression: from a society without the words "thine or mine," to bees "freely offering to any hand the fertile harvest of their sweet labor," to beautiful shepherdesses wandering around dressed only in "a few green burdock leaves and ivy leaves combined" and yet who, despite "wearing only the clothes needed to modestly cover that which modesty demands," could wander "wherever they wished, alone and mistresses of themselves, without fear that another's boldness or lascivious intent would dishonor them."[29] The speech is patently ridiculous, and the narrator immediately dismisses it, pointing to the acorns Quixote is eating as having "brought to mind the Golden Age, and with it the desire to make that foolish speech to the goatherds, who, stupefied and perplexed, listened without saying a word."[30]

If we imagine ourselves as readers in Cervantes's time, the absurdity of the speech, and hence of the idea of believing in the ideal of the golden age expressed in pastoral literature at the time, is never in question. The question becomes what is its relation to our own social reality and to that of the other characters sitting around him? If Quixote is making a speech that we readers are laughing at and that the "real" shepherds sitting around him are perplexed about, it is because we readers and those shepherds share a common ground, a reality or "realistic" portrayal of it from which we can scoff at Quixote's absurd belief in the myths bandied about by pastoral poetry. And here is where Cervantes shows us the full force of fiction, for that moment of shared perplexity with the shepherds has animated them as characters; they become modern, fictional characters the moment we imbue them with our own realization of how and why Quixote's speech is so ridiculous.

Moments after finishing the absurd speech, Quixote, along with Sancho, is urged by a companion of the goatherds to accompany them the next morning to the funeral of Grisóstomo, a nobleman who dressed up like a shepherd to woo the impossibly beautiful and unapproachable Marcela, a woman of independent wealth who has renounced society and gone to live the life of a shepherdess in the countryside. Right away, then, Cervantes's fiction also forces us to ask how we and the shepherds can laugh at the inanity of Don Quixote's fantasies about the golden age from the vantage of our cold, hard, reality if it turns out that, in that same reality, people are running around doing exactly what is done in Quixote's impossible pastoral fantasies. And, in fact, the effect of Marcela on the many noblemen who have descended on the area dressed in shepherd's garb is described by the shepherd Pedro in exactly the same hyperbolic and absurd language that Quixote had just used to obvious ridicule:

"Here a shepherd sighs, there another moans, over yonder amorous songs are heard, and farther on desperate lamentations. One spends all the hours of the night sitting at the foot of an oak tree or a rocky crag, not closing his weeping eyes, and the sun finds him in the morning absorbed and lost in his thoughts; another gives no respite or rest to his sighs, and in the middle of the burning heat of the fiercest summer afternoon, lying on the burning sand, he sends his complaints up to merciful heaven."[31]

That the "real world" is just as fanciful as Quixote's pastoral nonsense is underlined when, on the way to the funeral, Quixote and Sancho are joined by travelers who, hearing Quixote declare himself a knight errant, quickly grasp that he is insane, all the while taking entirely seriously that the region is flooded with noblemen dressed as shepherds pining for an impossibly beautiful, utterly unattainable shepherdess. What Cervantes puts into question is not the truth or falsity of scenarios presented within his story's frames, but the social reality that we readers believe we share and inhabit. With his fiction he is pointing out to us how that very reality has stitched into its fabric certain illusions that are in every way as laughable as Quixote's madness. At the same time, and again in a way that his fiction not only enables but thrives on, the patent nonsense of the pastoral convention gives way to characters who explode with real emotion and fiery conviction—to the very extent that they fail or refuse to fit the conventional roles expected of them.

As the goatherds, the fake shepherds, Gristóstomo's friends, and the travelers gather around his burial site and listen to his friend Ambrosio reading the last poem that Grisóstomo wrote to Marcela before his death, Marcela herself comes into view over the hilltop and approaches the gathering. To Ambrosio's accusations of homicide she then gives an extraordinarily eloquent defense of a woman's right to be free from the desires and expectations projected on her by men, declaring with fierce pride, "I have wealth of my own and do not desire anyone else's; I am free and do not care to submit to another."[32] The chapter then ends with Quixote vowing to defend her against all present and declaring that "she should be honored and esteemed by all good people in the world, for she shows herself to be the only woman in it who lives with so virtuous a desire."[33] Like the shepherds who come alive when we are forced to see the absurdity of an illusion through their eyes, Marcela is lifted off the page and into life by her fiery refusal to play the role assigned to her by the assembly of pining men. Suddenly we see the world through her eyes, another character ripped from the mold of convention, born of her own disillusion.

* * *

PASTORAL WAS ONLY A PRACTICE RUN, it would turn out. Cervantes would find his real home in a genre much closer in style and content to his own adventurous life: the immensely popular stories of knights in shining armor known as the romances of chivalry. The most popular by far of such romances was Rodríguez de Montalvo's *Amadís of Gaul*, published in 1508, which spawned multiple sequels throughout the sixteenth century. Amadís is a mythical knight errant, akin to those of Arthurian lore. Similar to Arthur, Gawain, and Lancelot, Amadís rescues princesses, battles giants and dark magical forces, and distinguishes himself for his bravery and purity. Montalvo's chapter titles spell out the itinerary of his heroic protagonists from one supernatural adventure to the next, and include such episodes as "How Galaor fought with the great giant the Lord of the Crags of Galtares and defeated and killed him," and "Of how Don Galaor, Florestan, and Agrajes went in search of Amadís, and of how Amadís, having abandoned his arms and changed his name, retired with a good old man in a hermitage to live a solitary life."[34]

In the chapter following this last one, the great Amadís has abandoned his arms and fellows, changed his name to Beltenebros, and gone to live a solitary life of penitence until his death, all in reaction to an infelicitous letter from his lady love, Oriana. Montalvo describes his travails in this way: "Beltenebros was, as you have heard, doing his penitence with much pain and great thoughts continually in his mind of how if God would not respond with the mercy of his lady, that death would be closer to him than life, and he spent most nights beneath some thick trees that were in an orchard near the hermitage, so as to go about his mourning and wailing without the hermit or the servants hearing him."[35]

This is also one of the passages that most caught the attention of that great reader of chivalric romance, Don Quixote. In a chapter Cervantes fittingly titles "Which tells of the strange events that befell the valiant knight of La Mancha in the Sierra Morena, and of his imitation of the penance of Beltenebros," the Don explains to Sancho his intention to achieve chivalric perfection by imitating the penitence of Amadís and those other knights who withdrew in madness and pain from the world of men to suffer in solitude when scorned by their ladies. In Quixote's case, he has imagined that his own lady love is the fabulous Dulcinea of Toboso—a conceit made all the more ridiculous by the fact that El Toboso, far from a fabled city worthy of a princess, is and was a tiny town in the region of Toledo whose greatest claim to fame was and always will be that Cervantes made it Dulcinea's supposed birthplace. When Sancho points out that, unlike those knights, Quixote has neither been scorned nor has he had any sign from Lady Dulcinea that she has betrayed him in any way (or any sign from her at all, we could add), Quixote responds, "Therein lies the virtue and the excellence of my enterprise, for a knight errant deserves neither glory nor thanks if he goes mad for a reason. The great achievement is to lose one's mind for no reason, and to let my lady know that if I can do this without cause, what should I not do if there were a cause?"[36]

Such an outright rejection of reality is too much even for Sancho, who angrily replies,

"By God, Señor Knight of the Sorrowful Face, but I lose my patience and can't bear some of the things your Grace says; because of them I even imagine that everything you tell me about chivalry, and winning kingdoms and empires, and giving me ínsulas and granting me other favors and honors, as is the custom of knights-errant, must be nothing but empty talk and lies."[37]

The time they spend together, however, is time in which the empathic power of character exerts its influence on them as well, for Sancho learns, bit by bit, to enter Quixote's world. Thus when, deep into the second volume, published in 1615, the knight insists at long last on a real encounter with his fabled beauty, Sancho is more than ready.

Caught up by an invented reply he has given his master from his nonexistent lady, Sancho decides to respond to Don Quixote's orders to present him in person to Dulcinea by insisting that a random peasant girl they run into by chance is in fact the knight's beloved, despite all appearances to the contrary. Knowing by now that the evil enchanter trump card works both ways, Sancho is prepared for Quixote's bewilderment when, far from a bejeweled and godly princess, "he could see nothing except a peasant girl, and one not especially attractive, since she was round-faced and snub-nosed." As Quixote kneels before her, "so astounded and amazed that he did not dare open his mouth," Sancho takes the lead for a change, taking on a courtly tone to plead for "the pillar and support of knight errantry on his knees in your subliminal presence." Upon hearing the girl's predictably rude response, Quixote again explains his disappointment by complaining how the "wicked enchanter who persueth me hath placed clouds and cataracts over my eyes, so that for them alone but not for others he hath changed and transformed thy peerless beauty and countenance into the figure of a poor peasant." The peasant girl, assuming this is all a joke played by the gentry on some country lass, informs him he can "tell that to my grandpa" and bounces off on her donkey after expertly vaulting over its rump and into the saddle.[38]

Like Don Quixote's fantasies of knights and ladies, the ideals of honor and blood purity propagated under the auspices of the Spanish state were fantasies that contrasted violently with the reality of a society where traditional elites maintained their material privileges at all costs. While the advantages of blood purity were touted in literature and on the stage, in fact allegations of Jewish blood seldom resulted in any material loss of status for the landed classes.[39] In the popular imagination fed by a culture industry seeped in stories of the violation and redemption of honor, this most important of imaginary attributes was anchored in an ideal of feminine purity that very few flesh-and-blood women could live up to, as Cervantes would experience firsthand through the wealth of worldly experiences collected by his sisters, Magdalena and Andrea, and later his daughter, Isabel, who were continually getting caught up in ill-advised dalliances with men who promised much but delivered little.

Holding real women up to ideal models engenders comedy in the world of *Don Quixote*, but it can engender tragedy in the real world, and Cervantes reflects on this as well. In the most famous of the various tales inserted into *Don Quixote*, "The Curious Impertinent," the protagonist, Anselmo, falls in love with and marries the beautiful Camila; but what he really falls in love with is an ideal image of what a woman should be.[40] What was desirable according to the myths propagated by popular culture of the time was a woman who, in the logic of Spanish honor code, was pure in every way.

The problem with purity as a virtue, however, is how to know if someone is really pure. As Anselmo tells his best friend, Lotario, beseeching him to test his wife by wooing her: "the desire which plagues me is my wondering if Camila, my wife, is as good and perfect as I think she is, and I cannot learn the truth except by testing her so that the test reveals the worth of her virtue, as the fire shows the worth of gold."[41] Against the desperate protestations of his good friend, Anselmo insists, with the result that Lotario and Camila fall in love and Anselmo's honor is destroyed in precisely the way he so feared. Like Don Quixote, Anselmo buys into a myth that is one of his society's fundamental illusions. By pushing the reality of his love to the extreme of the illusion, he forces it to fail, and ends up taking his own life. Cervantes has thus packaged as a fiction, within the comedy of Don Quixote's embrace of illusion, the tragedy of an embrace of illusion with real consequences.

This direct relation is made all the more clear by the fact that the story, which is being read out loud by fellow travelers at the inn where Quixote and Sancho are staying, is interrupted right at the point when the narrator announces that Anselmo's "reckless curiosity cost him his life," but before explaining how. Just as the reader and listeners are preparing for the story's denouement, Sancho bursts into the room from the garret he has been sharing with his master, beside himself with a tale of the knight's violent duel with a giant. It turns out that Quixote had been dreaming that he was engaged in righteous battle with an evil giant and had, while still asleep, taken his sword to some wine sacks that hung in his room, slashing them to pieces and soaking the room in red wine.

Upon seeing what he has done, Quixote—who believed the giant in question to be the scourge of one of his traveling companions, herself pretending to be the famous Princess Micomicona—kneels before the feigned princess and proclaims that "your noble and illustrious lady-ship may live in the certainty that from this day forth, this lowborn creature can do you no harm, and I, from this day forth, am released from the promise I made to you."[42] The parallel between the two story lines couldn't be more obvious: the knight's devotion to illusory ideals leads to comedy and spilled wine; but as for the illusions of honor and purity that animate the story of Anselmo and are sold as truths in the world beyond the pages of a book—the blood that they release may be dangerously real.

Cervantes may well have had his own sisters in mind as he composed these passages about the standards women were held up to, and the dangers to their reputations and persons when reality inevitably failed to reach them. Both Magdalena and Andrea had multiple relations with men of higher station who promised them marriage, a name, and a stable life, but then reneged on those promises. After one of these relations went sour, Magdalena even went so far as to change her name to Doña Magdalena Pimentel de Sotomayor, apparently in an effort to conceal her unmarried state.[43] Having lived through his own illusions and their bitter disappointment so many times, Cervantes felt profoundly for his sisters and other women like them, forced to deny their true desires and to conform to conventions and expectations that left them humiliated and exploited.

Only a short while after his exploits in the Sierra, Quixote and his fellow travelers happen upon a boy whom Quixote had earlier freed from an abusive master. Glad to have a living witness to the glories of knight-errantry, Quixote exhorts the young man to tell his companions about his liberation. But while corroborating his tale, the boy goes on to relate how his cruel master, once free from the influence of the well-armed knight, resumed the beating with even more ferocity than before, and he ends his tale pleading with Don Quixote to leave him out of any future fantasies: "For the love of God, Señor Knight Errant, if you ever run into me again, even if you see them chopping me to pieces, don't help me and don't come to my aid, but leave me alone with my misfortune; no matter how bad it is, it won't be worse than what will happen to me when I'm helped by your grace; and may God curse you and all the knights errant ever born in this world."[44]

In the chasm that opens up between the suffering and deeds of the hapless Don and his superhuman idols is distilled the essence of the modern age. When Cervantes invited a new generation of readers to follow his knight into the Sierra Morena, they discovered through their tears of laughter that they had entered a new world. For the writers and readers to come, the pages of a book could never again stand like foreign objects of wonder, to be admired from a distance. From now on, opening a book would mean stepping into a space more like one's own, a Sierra Morena next door instead of a mythical wood or a mystic crag, and even those places of mystery or magic, from Never Never Land to Hogwarts, would always be places in which other versions of our own selves would go for relief from the pressures, pain, or simply the boredom of our daily lives. Cervantes created this space when he put the space of readers into a book; when he made his own heroes not merely knights and squires but imitators of knights and squires who couldn't stop bickering about the rules of their own imitation; when he made real emotions shatter the molds of prior literary forms, allowing characters to spring forth; when he made his writing be about not only our dreams and desires, but also the pain caused when those dreams and desires dash against the rocky shores of reality.

FRESHLY MARRIED IN 1585, Cervantes began the year by bringing his new wife, Catalina, to Madrid to meet his aging parents. The encounter was a success, seeing as Rodrigo would list Catalina along with his wife, Leonor, as one of the executors of his will, even if there was very little to execute. The newfound trust ran both ways. Catalina's mother, also called Catalina, saw in her new son-in-law someone to administer her lands and serve as a father figure for her preadolescent sons, now that her own husband, Fernando de Salazar, was no longer there to raise them. It seemed that Cervantes's life was finally getting onto the right foot. He was a landowner now, married into a hidalgo family with a decent house, his land producing an abundance of olives and fruit. The illusion was not destined to last long.

Over the next year, Cervantes seems to have vacillated between the newfound cares of his country idyll and the life of a literary man at court. He was keeping up his reputation as a writer and traveling back and forth to Madrid with some frequency, signing in February of that year a contract for the publication of two of his *comedias*, *The Confusion* and *The Siege of Constantinople*, which earned him some forty ducats from Gaspar de Porres. April of the same year brought even more success with the publication of his first novel, *La Galatea*.

His reputation was growing, and his name was now in circulation as among the best writers in Spain. Unfortunately the novel would not bring him as much financial success as it did critical acclaim; its first run was just five hundred copies, and it would be reprinted just twice during his life. The second of those printings, in Paris in 1611, laid the groundwork for a respectable public in France, but by that time his name had already been made in Spain with the publication of *Don Quixote*. *La Galatea*'s real value lies in how it foreshadows the literary revolution Cervantes would inaugurate twenty years later. The subject matter was perhaps too tame; its targets of ridicule too limited and literary. But the promise of Esquivias and its inevitable disappointment laid the foundation for Cervantes's masterpiece. Its dried-out orchards and destitute nobles had found fertile soil in his imagination.

While on the surface this life had all the trappings of a pleasant and successful reward for the long-suffering man of action, in fact his worries were far from over. Back in Madrid, Ana Franca hadn't told her husband that the baby girl was not his, and Isabel herself would not know of her true parentage for many years. The year that had brought him the birth of his daughter, 1585, also saw the death of his father, and thus the need to help support his mother and sisters cannot have been far from his mind, either.

The loss of his father must have driven home the hollow imprint the man left behind him. Deaf in his later years and long since resigned to his inability to keep a family in anything like the lifestyle he had aspired to, Rodrigo had already rehearsed his demise on several occasions, pretending to be deceased so that his wife, Leonor, could make appeals on her sons' behalf enhanced by her widowed status. Even in death, Cervantes's father was withdrawn, unassuming, emphasizing in the testament he wrote five days before succumbing that at least his debts were cleared and that, while he did not remember how much and what articles came to him from his wife's dowry, her word should be believed and whatever owed to her paid from his possessions. An empty act of gallantry, naturally, as no possessions to speak of remained.[45]

While his father's death did little to change his fortunes, as neither did he have much to leave him nor, blessedly, did he pass on any debts, his absence gave Cervantes, along with his illegitimate daughter in Madrid, considerable responsibility for his mother and sisters in addition to the cares of his estate in Esquivias. Thus, already in the first year of his marriage, not only was Cervantes spending substantial time away from his wife and household to pursue his career as a writer in the big city, but he was also making trips to Seville, where in the spring of that year he signed a promissory note for a large amount of money. While Cervantes did manage to pay off that loan, he did so by borrowing again. As desirable as his life may have seemed from the outside, it was not sustainable. In February of the following year the execution of Scotland's Catholic Queen Mary by England's Protestant Elizabeth gave Philip the public excuse he had been waiting for, and preparations were begun for his invasion of the enemy island. The mobilization for the armada began in earnest, and Cervantes saw in the endeavor another chance at gainful employment. On April 28 he appeared before a notary in Toledo to give Catalina power of attorney over the lands he had just received from her family the prior summer, a necessary preparation for his planned departure for Seville to take up an assignment as a commissary agent for the armada.

Late in the afternoon of the following day, residents of the city of Cádiz looked over their stone ramparts in horror at the sight of Francis Drake's fleet entering the bay, guns ablaze. In a matter of hours Drake's ships had sunk dozens of Spanish ships, suffering no losses of their own. Back in Toledo, unaware of this decisive turn of events, Cervantes had already made his decision. He would not return to Esquivias, but would send the signed paperwork back to Catalina in the hands of a relative, himself heading south toward Seville. The time for pastoral was over. The time had come to sally forth once more.

7.

A Rogue's Gallery

It is recounted by Cide Hamete Benengeli, the Arabic and Manchegan author, in this most serious, high-sounding, detailed, sweet, and inventive history, that following the conversation between the famous Don Quixote of La Mancha and Sancho Panza, his squire, which is referred to at the end of chapter XXI, Don Quixote looked up and saw coming toward him on the same road he was traveling approximately twelve men on foot, strung together by their necks, like beads on a great iron chain, and all of them wearing manacles. Accompanying them were two men on horseback and two on foot; the ones on horseback had flintlocks, and those on foot carried javelins and swords; as soon as Sancho Panza saw them he said:

"This is a chain of galley slaves, people forced by the king to go to the galleys."

"What do you mean, forced?" asked Don Quixote. "Is it possible that the king forces anyone?"

"I'm not saying that," responded Sancho, "but these are people who, because of their crimes, have been condemned to serve the king in the galleys, by force."

"In short," replied Don Quixote, "for whatever reason, these people are being taken by force and not of their own free will."

"That's right," said Sancho.

"Well, in that case," said his master, "here it is fitting to put into practice my profession: to right wrongs and come to the aid of assistance of the wretched."

In 1604, the year Cervantes carried his manuscript to Francisco de Robles's shop in Valladolid, the bestselling book in Spain was the first-person account of a rogue, gambler, and thief by the name of Guzmán de Alfarache. Its author, Mateo Alemán, published the first part of the book in 1599, and it was so popular that it immediately began to spark imitations, including a sequel by a Valencian lawyer named Juan Martí, of which fourteen editions were printed before Alemán could come out with his own second part in 1604.[1] Here is how the title character narrates the final sentences of that second volume:

> In trying to blame nature, I will not be justified, for I had no less aptitude for good than inclination for evil. Mine was the fault, for nature has never done anything wrong; she has always been the mistress of truth and of good behavior, and never failed in what was necessary. But, because sin corrupts and my own sins were so numerous, I produced the cause of its effect, being the executioner of my own self.[2]

Guzmán de Alfarache was, by most standards we would recognize today, a work of fiction. Alemán was not the person narrating the book and made no attempt to hide the fact that he was not. Guzmán, however, was also not a character in the full sense we understand that word today. While he had a voice of his own and inhabited a richly described world, one does not get the sense that the reader is expected or able to enter into his perspective, to stand in his shoes. His purpose seems to be to remain someone else, someone whose misdeeds can thrill or repulse us, but whose life will always remain foreign to us.

What has been called the literature of roguery, or the *picaresque*, reached its acme in Europe at the end of the sixteenth century. In Spain the runaway success of *Guzmán de Alfarache* occurred simultaneously with the republication of the anonymous book that has been called the first picaresque novel, *Lazarillo de Tormes*.[3] *Lazarillo* had been published in 1554, but the censorship of the Inquisition ensured that it would be reprinted only once before the end of the century, and then in a highly abridged form.[4] Riding on the coattails of the *Guzmán*, however, the new edition of *Lazarillo* was an extraordinary success, and there were nine different editions in circulation by 1603.[5]

The rise of this genre devoted to the social outcast and criminal deviant dovetailed with an enormous rise in criminality in Spain's burgeoning urban centers. Books that had been severely restricted during the second half of the sixteenth century because of their unflinching look at social deviance were now spared and even encouraged by the royal censors.

The picaresque as typified by the *Guzmán* and its followers centered on a criminal life narrated by the criminal himself.[6] The picaro desires only freedom and the satisfaction of his basest desires, and has no scruples about how to achieve his goals. One can quickly see how the portrayal of a social outcast and his parasitic perspective on society would serve the regime's interest and help bolster the kind of image it wanted to project to the outside world. This image was of a religious, moral public being beset by parasitic outsiders, and whose sole protection was their loyalty to the Spanish crown and its laws. At the same time, the reading public and members of acceptable Spanish society were titillated by the possibility of peering into the rogue's world and having their own prejudices about his evil and sociopathic ways confirmed.

As Spain's population migrated toward the urban centers throughout the sixteenth century, criminality was indeed on the rise. Cities such as Madrid and Seville were crawling with gangs of thieves and swindlers and awash in illicit gambling houses and bordellos.[7] The government responded by expanding the legal system, and Spanish society was witness to a veritable explosion in litigation, both between individuals over economic claims and between the state and accused criminals.[8] Punishment was brutal, to be sure, but the bureaucratization of the legal system was also slowly moving Spain away from the traditional practices related to judging and sentencing and toward a society of control.[9] In traditional justice, those accused of crimes would often be required to undergo a trial by ordeal in which they would be submitted to some excruciating torture. The ability to withstand it would be seen as a sign from God of their innocence; the more likely and common outcome, that they would succumb to the pain, was taken as a sign of their guilt.

While in the sixteenth century the Inquisition still used such methods, the early modern state was adopting a legal system in which witnesses were deposed, statements taken, and sentences imposed in a more systematic, less arbitrary fashion.[10] The Inquisition, furthermore, was essentially an arm of the Spanish state, enforcing its ideology of monarchic Catholicism. The Spanish Church had been established already by the Catholic kings in order to ensure that religious obedience would not turn the faithful away from them to another earthly power they considered to be their rival, the papacy. The Inquisition was, to that end, concerned with policing the thoughts and beliefs of subjects far more than their actions. In fact, scholars have seen in the Inquisition a precursor to the mechanisms used under modern totalitarian regimes to control how and what their citizens think.[11]

Punishments, rather than resulting automatically in the maiming or death of the accused, as was still the case in the early sixteenth century, would more often than not involve jail time for lesser offenses, or to a period of time as a galley slave in the case of worse offenses. Philip himself was responsible for explicitly ordering that sentences for thievery be changed from flogging to time served in the galleys, and for reducing the minimum age requirement for galley slaves from twenty to seventeen years.[12] These changes had little to do with concern for human rights or the brutality of corporeal punishment, but were largely inspired by the enormous demand for slaves needed to power the Spanish navy's ships. Nevertheless, the overall effect was to contribute to the ever-increasing centralizing and bureaucratization of the Spanish state's power over individuals.

SITTING IN A DANK, stinking jail cell in Seville, choked by the smoke of oil lamps (when they were lit at all) and surrounded by an unwashed mass of society's dregs, Cervantes would spend months, perhaps up to half of the year between 1597 and 1598, savoring firsthand the perspectives of rogues and outcasts. Knowing the truth of his own story—a hero, abandoned by his country, forced to accept whatever demeaning labor came his way and then maligned, libeled, and imprisoned for his efforts—would give Cervantes a different kind of understanding of the lives of those who occupied society's bottom floors, and how they could contrast with the image painted of them by books and the stage. He would see in them the gamblers, tricksters, and hopeful social climbers who would populate his novels and tales, each and every one of them either battling against or profiting from the inability of others to see them for who they were. In this world, people lived or died by the sword of illusion, and Cervantes, from the depths of his disillusions, would learn to see that world clearly for the first time.

From the vantage of that cell in Seville, his life as a country squire a dozen years earlier must have looked like a different world. As a much older Cervantes would later reminisce, he stopped writing in those years because "my attention was elsewhere." In fact, that is an understatement. From 1587, when he published two poems glorifying the king's preparations for the Glorious Armada to be launched against England the following year, to that fabled year in 1605 when *Don Quixote* would be published, the world would hear barely a peep from the writer Miguel de Cervantes. That does not mean, however, that his life was quiet. On the contrary, if the years leading up to 1580 were those in which Cervantes discovered the world outside Spain, the next twenty years provided him his knowledge of the world within its borders.

Leaving Esquivias in Catalina's management, Cervantes would spend the following seven years working for the Spanish government as a commissary agent in charge of requisitioning goods, primarily grain and olive oil, from the farming communities in the regions of Seville and Córdoba. If he hoped to earn enough from this thankless job to pay back his debts, he was sorely disappointed. From the time of accepting the position in the early summer of 1587 to actually setting out on his first assignment, he had to spend three months of unemployment in Seville, where he could survive only by incurring even more debt. There he moved into an upscale boardinghouse run by his old friend from Córdoba, the highly successful but now retired actor Tomás Gutiérrez. Even taking into account that he occupied the humblest room in Tomás's residence, his lack of employment meant his tab was growing fast; one can only hope the extensive knowledge Cervantes's writings reveal of gambling means he occasionally left the tables in Tomas's parlors with heavier pockets than when he sat down.

After three months of waiting, he was finally granted his first commission: to go to the town of Écija to requisition grain for the armada. For far from receiving any portion of his salary in advance, he was to be granted a travel allowance of only thirteen reales a day to spend on food and lodging, with his salary to be paid as in arrears after each assignment. Even that miserly back pay was long in coming, as he would have to wait for a financially stressed treasury to deposit the funds not just for his salary, but also for the very grain and olive oil he was taking from the towns.

The townspeople, needless to say, were not overjoyed to see a commissary agent in their midst, especially as Écija had already given over its wares the previous year and had yet to see a *maravedí* (a fraction of a real) for its losses. In any community in Spain at the time, the Church both was a major landowner and held a good portion of the community's grain, and Écija was not an exception. Seeing that the townspeople had so little pricked Cervantes's deep-seated sense of justice, so he exercised his authority and took the required amount from the Church's supplies instead, which provoked his prompt excommunication at the hands of the local priest.

For a true believer, excommunication was no laughing matter, all the more so in a society like that of sixteenth-century Spain, where membership in the One True Faith was a legal requirement. But it was also not uncommon for the Church to take out its complaints against government overreach with the one weapon at its disposal; years later Cervantes would see enough humor in the event that he would have Don Quixote excommunicated for attacking a priest he had mistaken for a ghost. When the priest cordially informs him of his excommunication for "laying hands on this sacred body," Quixote replies that, to his recollection, "it was not my hand but this pike that landed on your sacred body."[13]

It would not be the last time, either. Before the end of the same year, Cervantes would again choose to requisition goods from the Church rather than take them from the people, this time in Castro del Río in the province of Córdoba, and would again be excommunicated for his troubles. In the end, both excommunications, subject to automatic appeal, were overturned and he was restored to the good graces of the Church. The legal challenges that emerged from the beleaguered townspeople when he did eventually requisition supplies, in contrast, were harder to shake off.

We have no reason to disbelieve Cervantes's protestations that "the aforesaid inquest is being carried out to the detriment of my honesty and the faithfulness with which I have carried out, and continue to carry out, my office."[14] Indeed, it seems that dishonesty was far from Cervantes's vice and that, on the contrary, he was unsuited for the complexities of what was essentially an impossible job. The crown was simply asking too much from a public that was already overburdened, and the inherent murkiness of the process of requisitioning goods for a massive war endeavor created too many opportunities for corruption for mistakes to be entirely avoided.

In fact, the paperwork Cervantes submitted to various and repeated inquests shows not only that he was honest but that, when he did make miscalculations, they tended not to be in his favor. In the end it was the very men to whom he was required to report who were accused of embezzlement, along with his own assistant. When he discovered the errors his assistant had made, Cervantes took full responsibility for them; but despite his best efforts to explain the mistakes, he was sentenced to jail time in Castro del Río, the same town responsible for his second excommunication. Though he was quickly cleared of those charges and released, the experience was the first of several descents into the prisons that would allow him to brush shoulders with an underworld of characters who would later populate his works.

DON QUIXOTE WAS PUBLISHED only a few years after *Guzmán de Alfarache*, but in the twenty-second chapter there is a clear reference to Alemán's success in creating a whole new genre of literature.[15] At the outset of that chapter, Don Quixote looks up to see "coming toward him on the same road he was traveling approximately twelve men on foot, strung together by their necks, like beads on a great iron chain, and all of them wearing manacles." When he asks Sancho what they are, Sancho replies, "This is a chain of galley slaves, people forced by the king to go to the galleys." "What do you mean, forced?" Quixote shoots back. "Is it possible that the king forces anyone?" When Sancho explains that the men have been condemned to the galleys, Quixote concludes that because "these people are being taken by force and not of their own free will . . . Here it is fitting to put into practice my profession: to right wrongs and come to the aid and assistance of the wretched."[16]

Sancho goes on to clarify that, as they are being punished for their crimes, it's not exactly accurate to say that the king is forcing or doing wrong to them, but Quixote ignores him and proceeds, upon receiving permission from the guards, to talk to several of the men. Each describes to him the crime, of greater or lesser severity, that led to his having been condemned to the galleys. The last one Quixote interrogates is a certain Ginés de Pasamonte—the picaro who will later show up in the guise of Master Pedro the puppet master—who, the guards tell him, is famous on account of the book he has written about his life. When Quixote asks if the book is finished, Ginés replies, "How can it be finished . . . if my life isn't finished yet?"[17]

Having completed his interrogation of the prisoners, Quixote decides that it is his duty to free them. But once he has attacked the guards and released their charges, he is rewarded for his mercy by being stoned by them before they run off in different directions. The other prisoners who tell their tales before being overshadowed by Ginés are a hodgepodge of minor, sad characters—an old man serving as a go-between who was suspected of sorcery; another who had stolen some laundry; one who failed to withstand a trial by ordeal; another who had sexual relations with a relative—but all of them were convicted on shady or suspect evidence. Only the literary character, only Ginés de Pasamonte, is an obvious villain; for only, Cervantes seems to be saying, a figment of the imagination would be so obviously guilty.

At the same time, it is precisely Ginés's awareness of the conventions he is supposed to match and his failure to fit into their mold that makes him come alive as a character. When Ginés appears as the last to be introduced among the prisoners on the chain gang, already he stands out for the way he is being handled by the authorities: he is double-chained, such that Quixote feels obliged to ask why "he wore so many more shackles than the others." The guards reply that he is a well-known rogue who has committed "more crimes than all the rest combined, and was so daring and such a great villain, that even though he was bound in that way, they still did not feel secure about him and were afraid he would escape."

When Ginés speaks, however, his character pulls itself even further out of the backdrop of expectations, for his language is personable and sincere, especially in contrast to the rough, mean language of his captors, who introduce him to Quixote as "the famous Ginés de Pasamonte, also known as Ginesillo de Parapilla." Their use of the nickname clearly marks Ginés as a classic rogue in the lineage of Lazarillo de Tormes—right down to the diminutive *-illo* appended to their names. But Ginés refuses to be branded:

> "Señor Commissary," the galley slave said, "just take it easy and let's not go around dropping all kinds of names and surnames. My name is Ginés, not Ginesillo, and my family is from Pasamonte, not Parapilla, as you've said: and if each man looks to his own affairs, he'll have plenty to tend to."
>
> "Keep a civil tongue," replied the commissary," you great thief, unless you want me to shut you up in a way you won't like."[18]

Hearing that Ginés has authored a book about his life, Quixote asks him if it is good, to which he replies, "It is so good that it is too bad for *Lazarillo de Tormes* and all the other books of that genre that have been or will be written. What I can tell your grace is that it deals with truths, and they are truths so appealing and entertaining that no lie can equal them." Quixote is impressed, and tells him "You seem clever," to which comes the response: "and unfortunate . . . because misfortunes always pursue the talented."[19]

Misfortunes pursue the talented. Is this Ginés speaking, or is it Cervantes himself, inserting himself and the truths of his travails into the persona of his miscast rogue? So often imprisoned and abused, his wit the excuse for further beatings even as his misfortunes fed his seemingly endless creativity, Cervantes could see himself in each and every rogue and criminal enslaved by the law; and the empathy that recognition ignited brought his characters to life.

If Cervantes explicitly makes his picaresque character the hero of a book in the episode with the galley slaves, elsewhere he communicates the artificial nature of the public's notion of criminality in other, subtler ways. In one of his most famous "exemplary tales," *Rinconete and Cortadillo*, Cervantes has his eponymous characters seek out their fortune in a society of thieves in Seville. Belying the reader's expectations, Cervantes does not depict a chaotic dearth of moral and civil codes; rather, the world of thieves and outsiders is a perfect inversion of acceptable society, with its own highly crafted rules of etiquette and reciprocity. Cervantes describes the lord of the thieves in these terms:

Then arrived the moment when Sir Monipodio descended, as eagerly awaited as he was well received by all that virtuous company. He seemed around forty five or forty six years old, tall of build and dark of face, with a uni-brow and thick, black beard; his eyes, deeply sunken. He came in shirtsleeves, through which a forest peaked: so rough and thick was the coating of hair on his chest.[20]

By describing the entrance of a grotesque, hirsute king of thieves in terms normally prescribed for royalty, Cervantes prompts his readers to think about how the sorts of behavior they use to tell commoners and nobility apart are themselves nothing but social conventions. He draws their attention to how deep-seated notions such as purity of blood and honor may be more like acts we put on for others than qualities we are born with. He exposes the prejudices and expectations of his readership regarding religion and race, the propriety of sexual roles, and the behavior of nobles and commoners.[21]

More important, since in Cervantes's stories about society's underbelly we are not dealing with social reality, but with illusions about social reality propagated by literature, his characters only start out as fitting representatives of the stereotypes expected of them, before decidedly failing to measure up. Thus the title characters, Rinconete and Cortadillo, are first presented as slumming privileged kids, with Rinconete referring to his father as a person of quality who works for the Holy Crusade. But right away an ironic twist emerges, for we learn that what a person of quality working for the Church may be doing is no less corrupt or criminal than his wayward son becoming a pickpocket. As Rinconete explains, "I'm saying he's a seller of papal bulls, or a *buldero*, as they are called. I went along with him for a few days and I learned the trade so that I wouldn't give advantage to the best seller out there. But preferring the cash from the bulls over the bulls themselves, I took a bag and ended up in Madrid with it."[22]

In similar ways, in another tale, *The Illustrious Kitchen Maid*, Cervantes confronts how popular notions of the roguish life are really just literary creations, and then proceeds to conjure palpable three-dimensional characters out of the failure of those notions. One of those characters is a bored young nobleman who deliberately abandons his privileged life in order to become a picaro:

So much did he revel in the life of liberty that amidst all the discomforts and miseries it brings he never missed the abundance of his father's house, nor did trudging on foot tire him, nor did cold offend him or heat annoy him. For him all the year's seasons were sweet and temperate spring; he slept as well on piles of corn as he would on cushions, and he was as comfy in a hayloft as between the finest Holland sheets. In short, he made such a fine *picaro* that he could have given lectures to the famous Alfarache.[23]

The young man, Diego de Carriazo, returns home after several summers spent in roguish pursuits at the tuna fisheries of Zahara, which as described in Cervantes's delightful hyperbole resembles a kind of cross between Las Vegas and Calcutta:

Don't call yourselves *picaros* if you haven't taken courses in the academy of the tuna fisheries! There, there you will find work together with laziness, clean filth, plump obesity, quick hunger, undisguised vice, gambling without end, brawls at every moment, occasional murders, obscenities at every step, dancing like at weddings, *seguidillas* you could publish.[24]

Carriazo is at his happiest in the fisheries, and when he returns he eventually convinces his friend Tomás, son of an equally privileged family, to pull a fast one on their tutor and escape with him to the fisheries. On the way, however, they are waylaid when Tomás falls desperately in love with a kitchen maid at an inn they stay at and both take up laborer jobs at the inn so that Tomás can remain close to her.

For all their time "slumming" among the common or even criminal elements, Tomás and Diego never cease to be privileged young men. Even when Diego is in actual danger of being judged and condemned for severely injuring another laborer with whom he gets into a fight, Tomás uses his money to grease the palms of local officials and ensure his eventual release. But they are not the only slumming hidalgos; even the kitchen maid of the title, Costanza, turns out to be as illustrious in lineage as she is in her bearing, the illegitimate child of a noblewoman impregnated by none other than Diego Carriazo's father, who shows up deus ex machina to recognize her and thus bestow on her the quality needed to become Tomás's wife. Can it have been too far from

Cervantes's mind that his own Constanza, his niece and Magdalena's daughter, was herself the unacknowledged daughter of a wayward hidalgo? Not only was Cervantes replacing caricatures with characters filled out by people he had met in his travels, but he was pulling in his own deceived and disillusioned family as well.

In Cervantes's tales, when scallywags and scullions turn out to be people of quality, these revelations undermine the very idea of a rapacious but alien underworld that was being spread by picaresque literature. Rogues are the projections of the fears and desires of an established social order; criminality and corruption are not something the rogues do, but rather something stitched into the very fabric of society, up to and including the highest echelons of political and ecclesiastic power. More to the point, precisely to the extent that Cervantes's rogues fail to comply with the flat, conventional portrayals of social outcasts that had become the norm, they are *humanized*; the reader is able to step into the space that separates them from those failed social expectations. Carriazo comes alive precisely because he is *not* a picaro; Costanza seems so real because she is *not* a kitchen maid. They are aware of their roles and their failure to fit them, and it is this awareness that animates them.[25]

The rampant disjunction between conventional roles and the people who fail to play them as expected becomes increasingly marked throughout Cervantes's career, achieving a kind of apogee in his posthumously published novel, *The Trials of Persiles and Sigismunda* (a book that for a long time rivaled its now more famous sibling in popularity).[26] The plot of that book revolves around the pilgrimage of a group of characters from their home in an unspecified northern country to Rome, center of the Holy Catholic faith that they, as minorities in their own land, have been forced to practice in secret. When one of the heroes of the novel, Periandro, finally arrives in the Holy City, Cervantes describes his reception as follows:

> Two of the Pope's guards just happened to be in the street—the ones they say can arrest people caught in the act—and since the shouting was about a thief they made use of their questionable authority and arrested Periandro. They reached into his jacket and took out the cross, slapping him around in the bargain; such is the payment the law makes to those just arrested, not even bothering to find out if they've committed a crime.[27]

When reading this passage it's hard not to reflect on Cervantes's own many brushes with the law and the times he spent in prison, almost certainly, from his perspective, without just cause. By using his own experiences on the outside of acceptable society to displace his characters—for example, making Catholics, who represented the mainstream of his own society, live in the margins in fear of being discovered—Cervantes brings them into relief much as he does when he confounds readers' expectations about how society's outsiders should behave.

That he goes even further in this regard than he does in *Don Quixote* helps explain the curious critical trajectory of Cervantes's last great novel, published the year after his death, about which he himself said, "It will either be the worst or best ever composed in our language; I must say I regret saying the worst, because in the opinion of my friends it is bound to reach the extremes of possible goodness."[28] As it happens, for about a hundred years after his death the *Persiles* was even more popular than the *Quixote*. But during the last several hundred years, that book slowly slipped into obscurity, as it was gradually pummeled by critics for its overly ornate style and unrealistic story, episodes, and characters. A new generation of critics, though, has begun to come to markedly different conclusions, however, and has seen in the *Persiles* a book that is in some ways even more daring and iconoclastic than his earlier works.[29]

IN 1593, CERVANTES LEARNED of the death of his mother, Leonor, and shortly thereafter the death of Catalina's uncle, the priest who had married them some ten years earlier and had taken over in Cervantes's absence the administration of his property in Esquivias. He was thus now thoroughly on his own, and fully responsible for the lives of Catalina and her brothers. By early 1594 the requisition work for the armada had wrapped up, and while he had not profited at all from the seven years he put into it, at least he had survived the various attacks on his virtue and absolved himself of any debts to the government. He thus made his way back to Madrid, where he met up with his wife and was reunited with his circle of friends.

It was through one of his Madrid circle that Cervantes immediately applied, on the strength of his résumé as a commissary agent, for the job of government tax collector. His financial needs ensured that he would take whatever post was available, so within only a few months he was again in Andalusia, this time in the province of Granada, where he began the unenviable assignment of collecting some two and a half million *maravedís'* worth of taxes, a task he spent the next several years working to complete. By 1595 he was back in the capital, having exchanged the money in his possession for a letter of credit from a banker in Seville.

While waiting in Madrid for the money, however, Cervantes learned that the banker, a scurrilous con man by the name of Simón Freire de Lima, had run off with all the accounts deposited with him. By the time Cervantes reached Seville he discovered that other creditors had beaten him to it and impounded all Freire's belongings, so he had to return to Madrid to request an order from the king that the treasury be given priority over all other creditors. This was granted, but even with the document in hand, Cervantes was unable to come up with the money, and in September of 1597 he was sent to Seville's royal prison, where he languished among the city's pickpockets and cutthroats until well into the following year, unable to convince the local authorities of his need to present his situation to the king, by whom he had been ordered to appear in Madrid in person.

Upon entering the prison for the first time, Cervantes would have felt as if he had been thrown back into the bagnio in Algiers. The architecture would have been frighteningly familiar: three stories of cells and larger rooms around a central patio with the prison's one drinking fountain. The prisoners were free to roam the grounds, shouting, fighting, sometimes killing, but also gambling, peddling contraband, and pimping prostitutes or frequenting them. And for those who couldn't afford a woman for the night, there were wild games of blind man's bluff played with real fisticuffs, or practical jokes such as the *mariposa*, in which a splint was tied to a sleeping man's fingers and set afire. The prison was a microcosm of the city, where everything was for sale, albeit for wildly inflated prices. Even the first set of doors to enter the premises, where almost two thousand men could be found at any one time, were referred to as the *puerta de oro*, or "golden gate," because it was there that those who could afford it would ensure that they lived in relative exclusion and luxury during their stay.[30]

The Cervantes who emerged in 1598 from months of imprisonment was a changed man. This was the man who would around that time start writing what would soon be published as *Don Quixote*, along with some of the stories he would later publish in his collection of *Exemplary Novellas*. Regardless of whether the writing began in prison or shortly thereafter, the experiences he accumulated there had an enormous impact on the period of creativity that was to follow; but those experiences influenced him in other ways as well. The man who emerged from that prison no longer believed in the ideals that Spanish society and its government had been promoting his entire life. While he had encountered many reasons to doubt the official story over the course of the previous twenty years, having been thrown in prison for doing his job for his government was the last straw.

The Cervantes who would, as would be expected from a poet of renown, publish an ode in honor of Philip II upon the king's death later that year, would no longer write the kind of laudatory verse he had produced for the death of Elizabeth of Valois thirty years earlier, or even for the Felicitous Armada ten years before. As we have seen, the poem published for Philip's death was a masterpiece of critical irony, depicting not the greatness of Philip, but a man pompously declaring the greatness of Philip, his speech then quickly seconded by a bully or rogue who declares it "true," accuses all who would question it as lying like dogs, and then furtively glances around before slipping away.[31]

It makes sense that Cervantes, while inspired by Alemán's remarkable success with the newly popular genre of the picaresque, would engage that genre in an entirely different way from those around him.[32] Cervantes, who had tried to live by the rules and follow the ideology of the Spanish state; who had been disappointed and rebuffed at every turn; who had spent five years among the infidels and come to know their ways; who had learned the techniques of the theater and used them to analyze how humans bought into illusions and worked to keep them alive; and who had now lived on the other side of the law whose abuses he had experienced for himself—this Cervantes understood that the picaro, like every other category his society promulgated for understanding the world, was a farce, an invention, an illusion. Using the techniques of the stage, he would start to create characters whose startling realism, ironic awareness,

and vivid emotion burst forth from their inability to recognize themselves in that farce.

In the last and most complicated of his exemplary tales, actually
one story nested within another, Cervantes has one of the characters
from one story, who himself matches the most common perceptions
of a picaro, supplement that story by telling another story, one he
says his interlocutor will scarcely believe, and one that may well have
been the result of a syphilitic hallucination. That tale, which becomes
the extraordinary *Dogs' Colloquy*, recounts a conversation between two
dogs that the teller claims to have overheard one night while recovering from syphilis in a hospital.[33] By placing the entire story in the
mouths of dogs—who, themselves surprised at their sudden gift of
speech, resolve to make good use of it and engage in the pleasures of
discussion for as long as they can—Cervantes nudges his readers to
reflect on the very kinds of illusions that picaresque literature depends
on and reinforces.

As he does in so many other cases, in *The Deceitful Marriage* and
the *Dogs' Colloquy*, Cervantes essentially begins by taking a genre, in
this case the picaresque that achieved such success with the *Guzmán*,
and invades it like a parasite. *The Deceitful Marriage* begins with a sick
solider named Campuzano barely staying on his feet as he leaves the
Hospital of the Resurrection in Valladolid, just down the street from
Juan de Navas's house in the Rastro de Carneros. There he bumps into
an old friend named Peralta, who invites him to his house for a meal to
catch up on old times. Campuzano tells him the story of how he
arrived in this sad state: how he met the beguiling and wealthy
Estefanía; how he wooed her and eventually won her over; how he
married her, combined his wealth with hers in a great trunk, and
moved into her stately house, marveling at his good fortune.

He then describes how in the midst of their happy idyll they are
surprised by some visitors, who themselves seem astonished and quite
angry to find them in the house. Estefanía hurriedly tells him that the
woman is a dear friend, that she has promised this friend to pretend
that the house is hers so she can convince the man who is accompanying her to marry her, and that Campuzano should trust her and leave
the house to them for some days. Of course by now we realize that it
is Campuzano who has been conned and that the visiting woman is
the house's real owner. When he finds out and tries to track Estefanía

down, it is too late; she has run off with the goods. But we are in for another twist: the trickster has also been tricked, for Campuzano's gold was fake all along.

Cervantes's tale would already be a masterpiece of storytelling, beautifully structured around the interplay of desires and hidden intentions that all good fiction to come will adopt. But it is in what comes next that his real genius is deployed. Estefanía serves her revenge up hot, in the form of a syphilitic infection that leaves Campuzano sweating in the hospital for the next few weeks. On the second-to-last night there, he overhears a conversation that he writes down word for word, and offers to let Peralta read it. He warns him, though, that he will not believe who it was who was speaking; and indeed Peralta does not, for the conversation purportedly took place between two dogs, named Cipión and Berganza. Nevertheless, Peralta agrees to read the story, provided, as he adds, "that you not tire yourself out anymore trying to persuade me that you heard dogs talking, for being written and noted by the good wit of the soldier, I already judge it to be good."[34]

Berganza's story begins exactly like any number of picaresque novels, with the narrator recounting a rough and even bestial upbringing—the hitch being, of course, that it is an actual beast that is telling his own story! In other words, Cervantes puts the first-person story—usually told by a man, and normally intended to show how some men are just like animals and hence worthy of being excluded from human society—in the mouth of an animal, and then has it be overheard by a criminal human and written down in the form of a story, which is being read and enjoyed by the criminal's old friend, but not believed as true. To make the point even clearer, the dogs begin their colloquy by noting with some surprise that not only are they speaking, but they are speaking reasonably—which, they reason, is impossible, since the definition of man is a rational animal, and that of a beast, an irrational one.

To make matters worse, once the dog Berganza has gotten started on his long-winded tale, his companion, Cipión, can't seem to stop interrupting him and giving him tips on how best to tell the tale, pointing out, for example, that some stories carry themselves on their content alone while others are in need of a good bit of rhetorical ornamentation. The implication is clear: Berganza's story, sounding for all the world like the beginning of a picaresque narrative about a rogue's real-life adventures, really needs some attention to literary form before being presentable as a tale.

At the end of the story, after Berganza has led us through his life and many masters, each representing different slices of Spanish social life, Peralta finishes reading and Campuzano awakes from his nap. Peralta then declares that "although this colloquy is made up and never occurred, it seems to me that it is so well composed that the soldier should pass on to the second one."[35] To which Campuzano replies that he will start at once on writing it and not enter into arguments anymore about whether the dogs were real. Thus the final lesson of his exemplary tales—the book in whose preface Cervantes famously wrote that they are united by a mystery and that the careful reader is sure to reap some benefit from them if he reads them as a whole—is that the benefit of fiction comes to those who learn not to subject it to the standard of truth and falsity that we apply to statements about the world. We ask of fiction not whether it is true, but what would it be like for us if it were true. For fiction is not a picture of the world; it is a picture of how we, and others, picture the world; the truths it tells are not the factual ones of history, or the more philosophical ones of poetry, but the subjective truths that can be revealed only when we suspend our disbelief and imagine ourselves as someone completely different.

IN THE SPRING OF 1609 the racial policies of the Spanish regime, which had in some ways begun with the taking of Granada and the subsequent expulsion and forced conversion of the Jews in 1492, reached their logical culmination. After years of unrest and repression, Philip III's government decreed that all remaining Moriscos had to wrap up their affairs and depart from Spanish land. Tellingly, the decree Philip III approved on April 9 of that year came on the same day as the signing of the Twelve Years' Truce, the agreement that ended Spain's long and failed attempt at military dominance of the Netherlands. The decline of real influence was, yet again, masked by the drive to purity.

There can be little doubt of the popularity of this move among the Christian population at large. Blame for years of economic and social distress had been deftly hoisted upon the Moriscos, who tended to stand out anyway as a result of their different dress and practices. They were also widely suspected of sympathizing with the Turkish Empire and of abetting the Barbary pirates as they raided Andalusian seashore villages in search of captives to take back to Algiers as slaves. Between the time of the decree and 1614, the government systematically carried out the expulsion, forcing some two hundred seventy thousand of the estimated three hundred thousand remaining Moriscos to leave their homes and lives behind them and to embark for North Africa. Of these, countless would die, whether of hunger and exposure or by violence at the hands of unwelcoming natives.

In Cervantes's treatment of the Moriscos, and of racial and religious Others in general, and specifically in his references to the expulsion in the second part of *Don Quixote*, we see both the full expression of his changed attitudes and its manifestation in the new literary form he uses to represent the event. In that book the travelers meet up with Ricote, a Morisco from Sancho Panza's village, and a man Sancho knows well. After the two stay up late sharing wine and stories, Ricote says about the expulsion decree, speaking, as the narrator tells us, "in pure Castilian," that "it was and is reasonable for us to be chastised with the punishment of exile: lenient and mild, according to some, but for us it was the most terrible one we could have received. No matter where we are we weep for Spain, for, after all, we were born here and it is our native country."[36]

Not content with this wrenching description of exile, Cervantes returns the word to Ricote some eleven chapters later. There Ricote comments on the specific actions of Don Bernardino de Velasco, Philip's appointed deputy in the expulsion of the Moriscos, about whom he says,

Although it is true that he mixes mercy with justice, he sees that the entire body of our nation is contaminated and rotten, and he burns it with a cautery rather than soothing it with an ointment; and so, with prudence, sagacity, diligence, and the fear he imposes, he has borne on his strong shoulders the weight of this great plan, and put it into effect, and our schemes, strategies, pleas and deceptions have not been able to blind the eyes of Argus, which are always alert so that none of our people can stay behind or be concealed, like a hidden root that in times to come will send out shoots and bear poison fruits in Spain, which is clean now, and rid of the fears caused by our numbers. What a heroic decision by the great Felipe III, and what unparalleled wisdom to have entrusted its execution to Don Bernardino de Velasco.[37]

If the use of metaphors of disease and purgation to deal with minority populations makes us cringe in an age that has witnessed the atrocities of the Nazis and that continues to live through episodes of "ethnic cleansing," the parallel is entirely justified.[38] The Jewish intellectual and critic Walter Benjamin, who was persecuted by the Nazis and committed suicide while trying to escape Nazi-occupied France, cited in Cervantes's creation "the magic of true critique [that] appears precisely when all counterfeit comes into contact with the light and melts away."[39]

Cervantes was using the powerful vitality of his new form of writing to invite his readers to experience the world through the eyes of others, and then allowing that perspective to draw attention to the hypocritical policies of the early modern Spanish state. This was the surprising verdict of someone who was simultaneously a great reader of literature and himself a fascist ideologue: Ernesto Giménez Caballero, who aspired to be Francisco Franco's cultural minister. Prior to the war that brought Franco to power, Giménez Caballero published a book called *Genius of Spain: Exaltations for a National and World Uprising*, in which he lambasts *Don Quixote* as a dangerous book, "the spiritual equivalent of the fall of the Spanish Empire."[40]

The reasons he gives are extraordinary in their insight and honesty: an empire requires blind pride, and Cervantes's irony was his "weapon against stupor." Essential to Cervantes's irony is something Giménez Caballero astutely recognizes as "excessive orthodoxy."[41] The fascist ideologue saw in Ricote's support of Spain's genocidal attack on his own people a subversion that generations of professional critics of the novel failed to see: in appearing to agree so fervently with the state's ideology, Cervantes deliberately pushed his agreement too far, opening a space in which the brutality and absurdity of that ideology could show through.

BY APRIL OF 1598, Cervantes was finally out of jail, still living in Seville. The preface to the famous book he most likely began during that imprisonment makes sardonic reference to its being "begotten in a prison, where every discomfort has its place and every mournful sound makes its home,"[42] and with little else to occupy his time other than avoiding the occasional calls to present himself in Madrid before the Ministry of Taxation, Cervantes spent at least until the summer of 1600 in the southern capital, working on his masterpiece and gathering with writers at the local literary salons. In May of the same year, Ana Franca de Rojas died and his daughter, Isabel, was taken into the care of a local attorney. Within a short time an arrangement was made for her to live and apprentice as a seamstress with Miguel's sister Andrea in Madrid; the contract for that arrangement lists her name as Saavedra and her grandfather as Juan de Cervantes, in recognition of her true identity.

The summer of 1600 saw Seville fall under the influence of the black plague, which killed at least eight thousand people that year. But death hit closer to home for Cervantes in the form of news that, on July 2, his brother Rodrigo fell in action on the fields of Flanders. The next year, Cervantes was reunited with his wife, Catalina, in Esquivias at the baptism of a niece of hers, for whom he became the godfather. After so many years the couple seems to have begun to draw closer, and later that year he moved his writing endeavors and his family back to Madrid.

In the same year, news began to spread of the impending move of the court from Madrid to Valladolid. While the new king Philip III cited his poor health and the desire to avoid Madrid's winters, it was well known that his favorite, the Duke of Lerma, who in fact held the keys to power in the government, wanted to move the young sovereign out from under the influence of his grandmother, the Empress Margarita, a nun at the Carmelite convent in Madrid who was deeply suspicious of the duke's influence on her grandson. The transfer of the court came as a huge blow to Madrid, and a boon to Valladolid, whose city council enriched the Duke of Lerma by some four hundred thousand reales to help seal the deal. Many of those whose sources of livelihood were to be found in the former capital, including Cervantes's sisters, followed the king to Valladolid in short order. Andrea and Magdalena moved there in 1603, bringing with them Isabel and Andrea's daughter, Constanza.

Francisco de Robles, son of Blas de Robles, the publisher who brought out Cervantes's first novel twenty years earlier, also opened up shop in the new capital, and it was to him that Cervantes brought his manuscript on that summer day in 1604.

8.

The Fictional World

They spent a good part of the night in these and other similar conversations, and although Don Juan wanted Don Quixote to read more of the book in order to hear his comments, he would not be persuaded, saying he considered that he had read it, and confirmed that all of it was foolish, and if it happened to come to the attention of the author that he had held it in his hands, he did not want him to celebrate the idea that Don Quixote had read it, for one's thoughts must eschew obscene and indecent things, as must one's eyes. They asked him where he had decided to travel. He responded to Zaragoza, to take part in the jousts for the suit of armor that are held in the city every year. Don Juan told him that in the new history, the account of how Don Quixote, or whoever he was, ran at the ring was lacking in invention, poor in letters, and very poor in liveries, though rich in stupidities.

"For this very reason," responded Don Quixote, "I shall not set foot in Zaragoza, and in this way I shall proclaim the lies of this modern historian to the world, and then people will see that I am not the Don Quixote he says I am."

In the introduction to his now classic study *The Western Canon*, the critic and literary historian Harold Bloom writes, "Art is perfectly useless, according to the sublime Oscar Wilde, who was right about everything. He also told us that all bad poetry is sincere. Had I the power to do so, I would command that these words be engraved above every gate at every university, so that each student might ponder the splendor of the insight."[1]

Bloom's words, far from a denigration of poetry, are his version of a spirited defense of it. Unlike Aristotle, Horace, and all their premodern followers, though, Bloom rejects the idea that literature is or need be in any sort of imitative relation with truth. Thus, while Aristotle defended poetry as representing something more universal than historical truth, and Horace believed poetry could and should incite us to moral truths, Bloom (along with Wilde and the Romantics who came before them) finds the value of great literature and art elsewhere. For while he vehemently denies that it is or should be "a program for social salvation,"[2] without the great literature that composes what he calls the Western Canon, Bloom writes, "we cease to think."[3]

Bloom's defense of poetry and his dismissal of the Horatian mandate to delight *while* instructing is built on an understanding of literature that is specific to the modern age, and that arose to prominence in the century after Cervantes's great creation. Wilde's insight that all bad poetry is sincere, or (in his actual words), "all bad poetry springs from genuine feeling,"[4] implicitly locates the source of good poetry not in insincerity or artifice per se, but in another idea of truth from either the historically accurate or morally beneficial versions that animated classic and Renaissance poetic theory.[5] As the critic Lionel Trilling explained it, in making his statement about bad poetry and genuine feeling, Wilde "does not mean that most genuine feeling is dull feeling, or even that genuine feeling needs the mediation of artifice if it is to be made into good poetry. He means that the direct conscious confrontation of experience and the direct expression of it do not necessarily yield the truth and indeed that they are likely to pervert it."[6] To quote another of Wilde's dictums, "Man is least himself when he talks in his own person. Give him a mask and he will tell you the truth."[7]

This idea of what truth is and how man can best come to know it bears witness to a world that was thoroughly schooled in Cervantes's invention of fiction. The characters that populate our fictions are the masks we put on to tell ourselves the truth. The truths we seek in fiction are thus not truths about the physical world or the facts of history; they are the truths of who we are, which we can discover solely by imagining ourselves otherwise.

As the practice of fiction spread, this basic function of literary character blossomed into an understanding of human knowledge for which the imagination was no longer an impediment, but rather a necessity. A mere hundred years after the publication of *Don Quixote*, the great German thinker and mathematician Gottfried Leibniz, who, along with Sir Isaac Newton, invented calculus, could argue that, as Bloom would later claim, literature indeed teaches us to think:

> If someone looks attentively at more pictures of plants and animals than another person, and at more diagrams of machines and descriptions and depictions of houses and fortresses, and if he reads more imaginative novels and listens to more strange stories, then he can be said to have more knowledge than the other, even if there is not a word of truth in all that he has seen and heard . . . Provided that he takes nothing in these stories and pictures to be true which really is not so, and that these impressions do not prevent him in other contexts from distinguishing the real from the imaginary, the existent from the possible.[8]

In the modern world, the world that had learned to read fiction, thinkers such as Leibniz could start to envision how works of imagination could benefit knowledge as opposed to detract from it, not because such works necessarily pointed to a greater or more general truth, as in Aristotle's defense of poetry, but because they saw them as essential to how we think. We think by connecting and relating ideas to one another; by entertaining and rejecting hypotheticals; by learning to distinguish the real from the imaginary, the existent from the possible, yes, but *from the vantage of imaginary and possible worlds*, not from a preordained and given reality.[9] In the modern world, fiction can help us find truth by creating the space in which we learn to tease apart the real from the imaginary—a space that Don Quixote mapped for us when he failed to do just that.

IN JANUARY OF 1605, Cervantes published *Don Quixote*, and its rapid success brought him fame throughout Spain. By February, shipments of the book were leaving for the New World, and when international dignitaries, including England's Lord Howard of Effingham, descended on the new capital Valladolid to celebrate the birth of the future king Philip IV on Good Friday, Sancho and Quixote were featured among the costumed characters who thronged around his retinue. Included in the many gifts presented to Lord Howard on this festive occasion was a copy of *Don Quixote*, already in its second edition. By three years before the second part was published, *Don Quixote* had been translated into French, English, Italian, and German, and its author was renowned throughout Europe.

In the years after his death, that reputation exploded as his work was rapidly translated and spread around the world. A litany of the greatest writers of modern times have singled him out as having beaten the trail for all writing to follow: Fielding, Flaubert, Schiller, Goethe, and Kundera, to name only a few, have all sung his praises; William Faulkner claimed he reread *Don Quixote* at least once a year.[10] To be sure, Cervantes's direct influence on the history of literature is unparalleled, but his indirect influence on intellectual history in general is simply immeasurable. His books were to be found on the shelves of every intellectual in early modern Europe, and many in the Americas as well, and would eventually be adapted for readers of all ages.

In 1787, Thomas Jefferson wrote to a nephew about the Spanish language that he should "bestow great attention on this and endeavor to acquire an accurate knowledge of it. Our future connection with Spain and Spanish America will render that language a valuable acquisition." While he no doubt meant his admonitions about geopolitics, Jefferson's interest in Spanish culture came from his fascination with *Don Quixote*, a copy of which he had borrowed from John Cabot in advance of a sea voyage to France in 1784, and used alongside a Spanish dictionary to master the language during the nineteen-day journey. This was noted by John Quincy Adams in a journal entry he jotted down after a dinner with Jefferson in 1804, although Adams then adds, "but Mr. Jefferson tells large stories."[11]

Being a famous author didn't stop Cervantes's ill fortune, however, or even prevent him from having further scrapes with the law. Late in the evening of July 27, 1605, Cervantes was awoken by voices from the upstairs apartment. His neighbor, a young man named Luis de Garibay ran downstairs to tell him that he had heard raised voices and the clash of swords outside their house. Cervantes rushed down to find a nobleman by the name of Gaspar de Ezpeleta lying in the

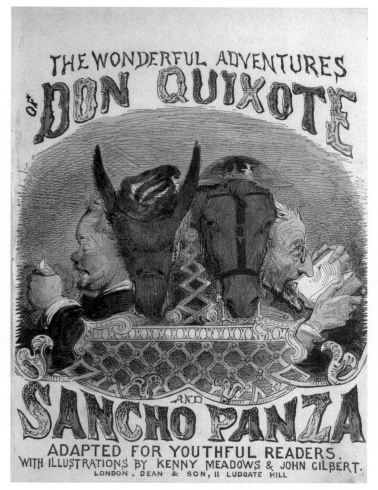

Sir Marvellous Crackjoke, with illustrations by Kenny Meadows & John Gilbert, *The Wonderful Adventures of Don Quixote and Sancho Panza Adapted for Youthful Readers*. London: Dean & Son, 1872. Half-title page. George Peabody Library, the Sheridan Libraries, Johns Hopkins University

street, bleeding profusely. He carried him in to the apartment, where the entire household was now awake and abuzz, and Magdalena at once began to care for him. Soon they were joined by a surgeon and a priest, the first to tend to his wounds, the second to his soul. Unfortunately, Ezpeleta ended up needing the extreme unction more than the surgeon's attention, for the stab wounds to his stomach and thigh were too deep to mend, and by the morning of the twenty-ninth he was dead.

The local magistrate charged with solving the case questioned all the residents of the building, and when a gossipy neighbor mentioned that men were visiting the Cervantes residence, which consisted mostly of women, at all hours of the day and night, the entire family was hauled in and detained for two days. In what was certainly a bitter irony for him, this last stay in prison would be behind the same walls that once housed his grandfather and his father. After their release, Cervantes had to face the dishonor that accrues to men whose daughters or sisters are perceived to be involved in illicit affairs. Specifically the magistrate cited suspicions that Isabel was the concubine of a local treasury official named Simón Méndez. Even after the family was cleared of all charges, Méndez was barred from returning to the residence on the Calle del Rastro.[12]

Undoubtedly, Cervantes felt some relief when it was announced that the court would return to Madrid the following year, as the industrious Duke of Lerma had found ways to profit even more from moving back than from remaining in Valladolid. Andrea and Magdalena followed in short order, while Cervantes and Catalina retired to Esquivias for some time before joining them in Madrid. There the first order of business was marrying Isabel to Diego Sainz del Águila as a safeguard against further perception of dishonor. Predictably, perhaps, the attempt was futile, as Isabel was soon pregnant with the child of a nobleman named Juan de Urbina, who was decidedly not her husband. Diego would die the next year, and Isabel and her baby daughter moved into a house belonging to Urbina on Madrid's Pasaje del Comercio.[13]

While the success of *Don Quixote* finally allowed him to repay some of the debts incurred during his years in captivity, Cervantes was soon borrowing again, this time from his publisher, Francisco Robles. Even more irritating from his perspective, his literary peers continued to condescend to him, and he even suffered the ultimate indignity of having his most famous characters stolen. In 1614, before he finished writing his own sequel to his great novel, someone hiding behind the pseudonym Alonso Fernández de Avellaneda published a continuation of the adventures of Don Quixote and Sancho Panza, adding insult to the theft by using the book's prologue to excoriate the aging warrior and author.[14] Cervantes is, the author writes, as old as the Castle of San Cervantes and, because of his years, so malcontent that everything and everyone annoys him, and for that reason he has so few friends that, when he wants to adorn his books with sonnets of praise he has to "godfather" them, as he himself says . . . because he can't find a prominent name in Spain that wouldn't be ashamed to have him pronounce his name . . . let him be content with his Galatea and his plays in prose, which is what most of his novellas are, and stop tiring us![15]

Cervantes's response was nothing short of ingenious. If the so-called Avellaneda dared to step into Cervantes's fictional world, he would use that world against him. Sure enough, rather than simply engage the author in the tit-for-tat roasting that the literati of the age exulted in, in the second book of the *Quixote*, which he hastened to publish in the wake of the plagiarist's salvo, Cervantes has his fictional characters discuss how the enormous fame and appeal of Don Quixote and Sancho has led to their being impersonated by pitiful mimics who fail even to come close to the brilliance of the originals. When, to Quixote's and Sancho's great astonishment, a guest at an inn where they are staying proposes to continue reading "the second part of *Don Quixote of La Mancha*," another responds immediately, "Why does your grace want us to read this nonsense? Whoever has read the first part of the history of Don Quixote of La Mancha cannot possibly derive any pleasure from reading this second part."

In a coup de grace, Cervantes lets Quixote himself react to the fact that Avellaneda's apocryphal duo opted to go to Zaragoza by deciding not to go to Zaragoza but to Barcelona instead: "For this very reason . . . I shall not set foot in Zaragoza, and in this way I shall proclaim the lies of this modern historian to the world, and then people will see that I am not the Don Quixote he says I am."[16] In other words, Cervantes defends his claim on fiction by using fiction to do what fiction does best: put a frame around a picture of reality that suspends the question of whether it is true or not. Instead of insulting Avellaneda and thereby validating him, Cervantes turns him and his cardboard cutouts into the playthings of his own characters, thereby making them come alive all the more.

* * *

Partial map of Spain featuring those areas visited by Don Quixote and Sancho Panza on their travels. Taken from *El Ingenioso hidalgo Don Quixote de la Mancha*. Madrid: Joaquin Ibarra, 1780. George Peabody Library, the Sheridan Libraries, Johns Hopkins University

AS WE SAW AT THE OUTSET of this book, the period in European history known as the late Middle Ages witnessed an extraordinary explosion of individuals' understanding of their relation to their communities and to the whole of the world. Rather than conceiving of their identities and place in society as direct expressions of the world as ordained by God, thinkers, artists, and writers began to understand each person's perception of the world as communicating a specific perspective; ascertaining the truth became less and less a question of aligning oneself with a tradition of textual commentary and instead began to involve defending a subjective interpretation of events. Recognizing the inherent danger for established orders in such a proliferation of subjective interpretations, emerging modern states such as Spain established institutions dedicated to ensuring not only that people obeyed authority in their actions, but also that they conformed to authority's dictates in their beliefs, and even in their very perceptions of reality.[17]

As a direct consequence of these efforts, intellectuals of the time turned to the classical discussion of history and poetry that had filtered

down through the translations of Arab scholars, and began to dissem-
inate a new interpretation of Aristotle's theory of poetry as conveying a
different order of truth. According to this interpretation, history and
poetry were both concerned with relating the truth, but while history
conveyed the truth of events, or verisimilitude, poetry existed to convey
the truths of morality, or decorum.[18] To put it another way, poetic texts
would have to portray humans as they ought to behave, speak, and
believe, and failure to do so would result in censure and even punishment for the authors. Presented with the challenge of portraying the
world according to the dictates of a society whose version of the truth
he had once accepted but now knew to be false, Cervantes developed a
brilliant solution. He would present in perfect verisimilitude conflict-
ing portrayals of the world *and* the attempts of individuals to choose
between them.[19] In this way he could undermine the state's version of
reality while claiming with complete deniability that he was teaching
by example.

By opening the space of fiction, Cervantes contravened the state's
control over imaginative expressions of individual subjectivity.[20] The
space he opened, while ostensibly offering moral truths, in fact taught
its readers to suspend judgments of truth or falsity, since they simply
could not apply to the complex structure Cervantes had developed.
And in the suspension of that judgment, readers would learn not to
subject the expressions of their imagination to the controls of the
state, but rather to subject the reality they had come to believe to the
questioning of their own judgment, exactly as the readers at the inn
had subjected Avellaneda's characters to *their* own judgment.[21] While
Cervantes could have no knowledge of the afterlife of his invention,
this suspension of judgment and the concept of reality it produced
would have a pivotal impact on the development of modern intellectual history.

Whether we think of it explicitly or not, most of us, if asked, would
define "reality" as being what happens independently of what we may
think. While we accept that different people have different ways of
seeing the world, we mostly assume that the world itself exists in a
certain way regardless of our subjective take on it. As obvious as this
idea may seem to us, it is not universal, and has not always existed.
That is not to say that, at other times, people took for granted that
there was no objective reality, and that everyone simply had his or her

own version. Rather, the very distinction between objective reality and subjective versions of that reality is itself historically and culturally specific, and not one that every culture at every time has had at its disposal.

While there have been (and are) cultures that didn't begin with that basic distinction, in Western culture it has been enormously influential. The political organization of modern states, be they monarchic, totalitarian, or democratic, is based on this notion of reality. What are known as the scientific revolution and the secular worldview also share this model, as do most of the major movements in intellectual history since the seventeenth century. It is not a coincidence that the English term *reality* as well as its cognates in the other European languages entered into common usage only from the middle of the sixteenth into the early seventeenth century.[22] (In the case of Spain, the first recorded usage was two years after book one of *Don Quixote* was published.)[23] And it was not until René Descartes wrote his *Meditations* at the end of the 1630s that a rigorous distinction between how things *appear* to be to a person's senses and how they in fact *are* in themselves entered the philosophical lexicon.

Prior to the sixteenth century, Europeans did not have much use for the notion of an objective reality that can be interpreted differently by different people. People saw themselves as very much part of one world, and the world itself as the expression of both God's will and the interaction of people and communities with it. The cultural, political, and scientific influences that brought about this sea change in worldviews were innumerable and highly complex, but art and literature played key roles in reflecting and propagating new beliefs and perceptions. And among all the events that participated in that process, none was so reflective of the changing times or more instrumental in propagating the new worldview than the emergence of fiction.

In a famous episode of Cervantes's great novel, Don Quixote and his squire, Sancho, encounter a barber from whom the Don had previously stolen a bowl, convinced that it was the famous magical helmet of Mambrino. Sancho had also taken advantage of the fight to steal the man's packsaddle, and when the barber accuses them of theft before a group of fellow travelers, Quixote responds by declaring him under the sway of an enchantment, saying,

"Now your grace may clearly and plainly see the error of this good squire, for he calls a basin what was, is, and will be the helmet of Mambrino, which I took from him in righteous combat, thereby becoming its lawful and legitimate owner! I shall not intervene in the matter of the packsaddle, but I can say that my squire, Sancho, asked me permission to remove the trappings from the steed of this vanquished coward; I granted it, he took them, and with regard to those trappings being transformed into a packsaddle, I can give only the ordinary explanation: these are the kinds of trans-formations seen in matters of chivalry. To confirm this, Sancho my son, run and bring here the helmet that this good man claims is a basin."

"By God Señor," said Sancho, "if this is the only proof we have of what your grace has said, then the helmet of Malino is as much a basin as this good man's trappings are a packsaddle!"

But Don Quixote insists, and when Sancho returns with what is clearly a basin, the Don holds it up in triumph, crying, "Just look, your graces; how does this squire presume to say that this is a basin and not the helmet I say it is? I swear by the order of chivalry which I profess that this helmet is the same one I took from him, and nothing has been added to it or taken away."[24]

When the barber turns to the other travelers to verify his version of the story, they decide to play a trick on him and pretend that they, too, see a helmet and not a basin. There is no question that this is a joke, and that in reality the packsaddle and the basin have never been anything but what they are. In a great comic moment, Quixote admits that the packsaddle "looks like a saddle to me . . . but I have already said I shall not intervene in that."[25] And it is vital that the basic assumption of what is real *not* be in question, because the characters can argue about the nature of their perceptions insofar as we, the readers, have a concept of reality that is independent of their various reports. For *Don Quixote* does not just feature scenes that depend on this concept; rather, the entire plot and structure of the novel exist to explore its many ramifications. Cervantes's fiction actually helped its readers formulate the modern idea of reality (what happens indepen-dent of what we think), and that idea in turn became central to all modern thought, and to all fiction written in his wake.

Popularly known as the father of modern philosophy, the French thinker and mathematician René Descartes won that title ostensibly by rejecting traditional modes of intellectual inquiry associated largely with commentary on prior texts, and replacing them with the first attempt at a radical questioning of what he could possibly know and be certain of.[26] He recorded the drama of this attempt autobiographically in the first of his six *Meditations*, in which he describes the strenuous process of sloughing off received ideas and subjecting to doubt everything he thinks he knows. He finds it tough going, and repeatedly realizes that he has fallen back on some "long standing opinions" that "take advantage of his credulity." His last-ditch effort to subject all possible knowledge to doubt comes in the form of a figure he calls an evil genius or demon, in Latin a *genius malignus*, "supremely powerful and clever, who has directed his entire effort at deceiving me. I will regard the heavens, the air, the earth, colors, shapes, sounds, and all external things as nothing but the bedeviling hoaxes of my dreams, with which he lays snares for my credulity."[27]

This device leads him at the outset of the second meditation to the distinction that still bears his name, the dualism between what can be doubted (namely, the accuracy of my knowledge about the extended world) and what cannot be (the fact that there is something that is doing the doubting, that is thinking, having that knowledge, true or false, about the extended world: "And let him do his best at deception, he will never bring it about that I am nothing so long as I shall think that I am something."[28] The distinction Descartes's experiment engendered is basic to all modern thought. It animates the entire history of modern philosophy from Immanuel Kant to current debates about the mind-body problem. But far more crucially, it infiltrates, in a variety of guises, modern science and political discourse as well: in the form of the researcher who strives to derive reliable laws from the messy influx of experimental data, necessarily minimizing human error and bias as he goes; in the idea of an abstract citizen who stands on equal footing with all other members of the same state, in patent contradiction to the blatant, real inequalities that beset the people living under the aegis of that sovereign power.

We see this dualism in the great Romantic thinkers, in Friedrich Schelling's dichotomy between the ideal and the real that he sees as structuring our understanding of the world, and in Friedrich Schlegel's notion of Romantic irony as the very paradox of self-consciousness, falling into *mise en abyme* as it tries to represent itself in its very subjectivity. Georg Wilhelm Friedrich Hegel perhaps takes it the farthest, making him for some the *non plus ultra* of modern philosophy (and for others its impenetrable nadir). His *Phenomenology of Spirit*—a book of such suggestive power that it paved the way for Karl Marx and Friedrich Engles's scientific materialism, Alexandre Kojève's vision of postwar European universalism, and Francis Fukuyama's argument for neoliberalism as the natural end of history—is in some ways nothing other than the drama of the soul's struggle to know the world, now projected onto a vast history of consciousness. And although divided by substantial philosophical and poetic differences, one thing these thinkers shared (apart from the name Friedrich and a fascination with the mind-body problem) was having identified *Don Quixote*, as a foundational text of the modern world and a source and inspiration for their own work.

Friedrich Schiller, a poet of the Sturm and Drang movement, purchased a copy of Friedrich Justin Bertuch's 1775 translation of *Don Quixote* in 1794, and in his *On Naïve and Sentimental Poetry*, published the following year, already singled out Cervantes as the epitome of the sentimental poet. Ludwig Tieck, one of the founders of the Romantic movement and author of the celebrated translation of *Don Quixote* into German, related in a letter to Johann Wolfgang von Goethe how he and Schiller had discussed *Don Quixote* and other works of Spanish literature during the summer of 1799 while he was at work on his translation, praising them as "spiritually rich material" for Schiller's own "romantic and fantastic tendencies."[29] (Tieck, it should be noted, was also one of the few poets at the time not to be named Friedrich, an oversight quickly corrected in his family when his brother, the sculptor Friedrich Tieck, came along three years after his birth.)

Schlegel, the Romantics' primary theorist, called *Don Quixote* "the Greatest Romantic Novel" and saw in it a model for his notion of irony.[30] As he wrote, "He who is capable of studying and relishing Cervantes aright, well knows that mirth and seriousness, wit and poetry, are mingled with success elsewhere unparalleled in this rich picture of life."[31] For the archetypical Romantic philosopher Schelling, the novel was "a mythical saga symbolizing the inevitable struggle between the ideal and the real, a conflict typical of our world, which has lost the identity between the two."[32] Hegel, for his part, situated Romanticism in the past as, in fact, the last age propitious to artistic production at all. For him, Cervantes was remarkable for having written the last Romantic work, and as such occupied a transitional moment between the Romantic period and Hegel's own present, a time, Hegel wrote, that "is in its general state unfavorable to art."[33]

For Hegel, his age was unfavorable to art because culture had become reflective, and the objects of people's desires and judgments had been transformed into general principles, duties, rights, and laws, abstractions that form the basis of social life. But art, Hegel argued, no longer functioned in such an environment because it belonged to a time or a culture in which the human spirit had not yet abstracted itself from its immersion in the living world, and in which individuals were not capable of detaching themselves from their physical environments and conceiving of themselves as the ideal citizens of a universal state.

For Hegel, *Don Quixote* was a kind of border work between two ages, retaining, on the one hand, all the characteristics that Hegel found so delightful in romantic art (Quixote's noble character, the interpolated tales), and on the other hand, tolling their death knells via the mockery of its very own contents.[34] Romantic art died with *Quixote* because, quite simply, its time had come, and because the modern individual was at heart ironic, divided at his core into an actor and the characters he portrays, into a perceiver and the vast world of the senses that he knows he is perceiving, and whose reality he strives to get right.

Given the inheritance of this idea from Descartes through to the nineteenth century, it would not be an exaggeration to claim that modern intellectual history was born of the speculation that *I can be wrong about everything I know while still being me;*[35] the possibility that everything about my world could be a show, put on for my benefit; that the people I engage with could be part of it; that everything could appear to be perfectly real and perfectly natural, but that it could all be false.[36] While there is no *philosophical* formulation prior to Descartes of this idea that has proven so influential for modern thought,[37] there is a *literary* one. In fact, it is the idea that animates the entirety of Cervantes's great novel.[38]

In the roughly four hundred years since Cervantes published *Don Quixote* and Descartes published his *Meditations*, a few scholars have noted the similarities between Descartes's evil genie and the enchanter

who bedevils Don Quixote's world, popping up as the perfect rational-
ization for every instance when Quixote's assertions are disproven,
when reality fails to deliver on his illusory expectations.[39] Descartes
alludes to having read *Don Quixote* in his *Discourse on Method*, where he
warns readers of falling under the influence of "fables, tales of chivalry,
and even of the most faithful histories . . . lest they conceive
of plans that surpass their abilities."[40] The first French translations of
Don Quixote were published in 1614 and 1618, and the two books were
translated anew by François de Rosset and published in 1639, two years
before Descartes published his *Meditations*.[41] But there is no need to
yearn for greater evidence of a direct influence; by that time every intellectual in Europe was aware of Cervantes's creation; his influence was
impossible to avoid.[42]

This is not merely an issue of noting the presence of a similar figure
in two books. While the influence of witches was widely acknowledged
as a potentially vexing obstacle for determining responsibility in the
popular consciousness of the time,[43] the idea of an enchanter dedicated
to making the entire world appear differently to me from how it does
to everyone else is brilliant and outrageous hyperbole, and was as much
at the core of Cervantes's artistic innovation as it was central to
Descartes's project and the subsequent course of philosophy.[44] Here's
how Don Quixote formulates the function of the *encantador maligno* in
a moment of frustration at his and Sancho's earlier disagreements over
whether what Quixote wears on his head is in fact the fabled helmet of
Mambrino or merely a well-used barber's basin:

"Well, Sancho, by the same oath you swore before, I swear to you,"
said Don Quixote,

> that you have the dimmest wits that any squire in the world has or
> ever had. Is it possible that in all the time you have traveled with me
> you have not yet noticed that all things having to do with knights
> errant appear to be chimerical, foolish, senseless, and turned inside
> out? And not because they really are, but because hordes of enchanters
> always walk among us and alter and change everything and turn
> things into whatever they please, according to whether they wish to
> favor us or destroy us; and so what seems to you a barber's basin
> seems to me the helmet of Mambrino, and will seem another thing to
> someone else.[45]

In fact, the translation I have been using dissimulates an even more revealing coincidence with Descartes's thought. What Edith Grossman renders as "chimerical" was, in the original Spanish, a noun, *quimera*.[46] This would be of no importance were it not for the fact that thirty-six years later, as Descartes puzzled over how to salvage the possibility of certain knowledge from the hypothetical possibility that his perception of the world was manipulated by a great deceiver, he found solace in this argument: "Now as far as ideas are concerned, if they are considered alone and in their own right, without being referred to something else, they cannot, properly speaking, be false. For whether it is a she-goat or a chimera that I am imagining, it is no less true that I imagine the one than the other."[47]

While we are free to remain entirely skeptical as to the coincidence of that mystical beast's appearance in both these foundational modern works—especially given that chimeras had been used metaphorically since the late sixteenth century to signify unreal products of the imagination—the point remains that Descartes is seeking his philosophical support in exactly the same place *Don Quixote* situates the reader's own ground: as long as we know that what things appear to be is secondary to our knowledge that they appear at all, or that things can appear in various ways to various people, then we have the security of our own existence intact. The hordes of enchanters that turn things into whatever they please are unable to turn you, me, or someone else (that is, those to whom the world appears in one way or the other) into something other than what we are. It is for that very reason that we persist through the changes around us to argue our positions; we can disagree on the variety of our perceptions only if we are secure in the identity of the self who perceives. Modern philosophy sought to determine the truth of that self's perceptions; modern psychology sought to understand its desires; and modern political thought sought to grasp the relation of the abstract citizen to the body politic. But it was fiction that taught us to think about ourselves this way in the first place.

IN 1995, UNESCO declared April 23 the International Day of the Book, at least partly in recognition of the almost simultaneous deaths in 1616 of two of the greatest writers of all time. That the deaths of

William Shakespeare and Miguel de Cervantes neither coincided (the former died some ten days after the latter, but England at the time had not yet adopted the Gregorian calendar used today) nor actually fell on April 23 (Cervantes probably died the previous day and was buried on the date later etched into posterity) bestows on that date a fitting irony. The Day of the Book celebrates those who write fiction, the glorious art of facts that aren't, histories that didn't happen, and lies that reveal the truths papered over by the habits of everyday life.[48]

Both Cervantes and his greatest character die quietly in their beds, surrounded by their loved ones. But whereas the Knight of the Mournful Countenance admits defeat and renounces fantasy for a death of stolid virtue, his author's mighty imagination lived on in ways no one could have predicted, and that few even grasp today. That reputation was sealed in the last years of his life, as Cervantes—now back in Madrid, first in a house on the Calle León, then in what he would call "my humble cottage" in the Calle de las Huertas—raced against his failing health to produce and publish his final works. He continued to suffer losses along with the physical pains of his failing body; Andrea's death in 1609 was followed by that of Magdalena in January 1611, in the house on the Calle León, her passing marked by a pauper's funeral and the austere rites of her religious order.[49]

Under duress from his publisher and the surprise appearance of Avellaneda's theft, Cervantes toiled through his pain and in February 1615 put the final words down on the second part of *Don Quixote*. Approbation from his friend Márquez-Torres followed in March, and shortly thereafter Cervantes secured a publisher for his collection of plays, which would come out later the same year. In fact the plays, printed on cheap paper by a back-alley publisher, would beat *Don Quixote*'s sequel to the bookstores. By the time the great novel came off the press in November 1615, Cervantes and Catalina had moved one last time, and were now installed on the ground floor of a stately house owned by a royal scribe named Gabriel Martínez, from which Miguel could look out his window into the little courtyard where the actors of Madrid gathered to exchange the latest gossip. The house was located at the corner of the Calle León and the Calle de Francos; the latter is now called the Calle de Cervantes.[50]

For the last five months of his life the now-famous-but-still-impoverished writer spent his days in that room, working away at his final novel, perhaps exchanging quips with the actors outside or reading them snippets from the growing book. The dropsy likely caused by his failing heart was wracking him with thirst and had swollen his legs beyond recognition, such that he would have had to limp to Mass at the Trinitarian convent, supported by Catalina for the few short strides separating the convent from Martínez's house.[51] On April 2, when he professed his faith and donned the habit of the Tertiary Order of St. Francis, the swelling was such that the monks were able to dress him only in the cassock, "yoked and hooded, with a cord that hung to his knees, for the breeches would not cover him."[52]

On April 18, 1616, Cervantes was given his last rites surrounded by Catalina, their maid, his niece Constanza, although not his daughter, Isabel, whose acrimony toward her natural father and his family would remain unabated until her own death almost forty years later. On April 19, Cervantes fought through his agony to write a dedication to the Count of Lemos for the front matter of his last novel, *Persiles and Sigismunda*, which would be published the next year to great acclaim. To the sponsor he had always hoped for but found too late, but really to the world and posterity, he wrote these words: "With my foot already placed in the stirrup, and full of fear in the face of death, great lord, I write this. Yesterday they gave me extreme unction, and today I write this; time is short, my anguish grows, my hopes diminish; and yet, despite all this, I carry my life on with the desire I have to keep living."[53]

Desire against reality. The theme that resonates throughout his greatest creations comes to the fore in his last statement to the world. Critics have made much of the fact that Don Quixote renounces his madness on his deathbed, cursing the passion for books of chivalry that drove him out of his sanity, and embracing his real name, Alonso Quixano the Good. They have insisted that this ending, along with Cervantes's apparent protestations that his sole purpose in writing the book was to skewer the romances of chivalry, should put to rest any suspicions that *Don Quixote* can mean anything other than that. But these critics fail to get the joke. It is as if they really believe that the only alternative to their reduction of the extraordinary wealth of the world's first and greatest work of fiction would be to interpret it as expressing the opposing thesis, that somehow we, Cervantes's readers then and now, *should be* emulating the tales of chivalry.

But the meaning of *Don Quixote* cannot be either Cervantes's distaste for *or* his love of the tales of chivalry; indeed, asking what *Don Quixote means*, as if such a shorthand answer could ever be given, already misses the boat entirely. If we really want to know, let us attend to the ending our author composed a year or so before coming to the end of his own story. Approaching their village in the twilight hours of their adventure together, the heroes pause on a hillside overlooking their home; "when he saw it, Sancho dropped to his knees and said":

> "Open your eyes, my beloved country, and see that your son Sancho Panza has come back to you, if not very rich, at least well flogged. Open your arms and receive as well your son Don Quixote, who, though he returns conquered by another, returns the conqueror of himself; and, as he has told me, that is the greatest conquest anyone can desire."[54]

To conquer oneself; to rein in the force of desire, the pull of illusion—for this, more than the imminence of death, is what Quixote fears and foresees, crying, *"malum signum,"* as he enters the village. For passing two boys in the street, he overhears their patter and misinterprets the sentence "You won't see it in all the days of your life," as referring to Dulcinea: "Don't you see that if you apply those words to my intention it signifies that I am not to see Dulcinea again?"[55]

As he has learned to do, Sancho hastens to reassure his friend; strangely, though, this time his down-to-earth realism in the face of Quixote's superstitions is intended to save his illusions, not dispel them. He gathers from under his donkey the terrified hare whose flight from a pack of dogs Don Quixote first took as an evil omen and carefully hands it to his master, saying,

> "Your grace is a puzzle . . . Let's suppose that this hare is Dulcinea of Toboso and these greyhounds chasing her are the wicked enchanters who changed her into a peasant; she flees, I catch her and turn her over to your grace, who holds her and cares for her: what kind of sign is that? What kind of evil omen can you find here?"[56]

How far we have come since Sancho sought to set a windmill-battered Quixote aright in his saddle and straight in his interpretation of reality! For Sancho, over the course of the journeys and travails imposed on him, has learned to love not only Quixote the man, but also the world Quixote has dreamed for himself. If he followed the errant knight out of a fool's wish to govern an *insula*, his desire to shelter his master's illusions at the twilight of their adventures seems born of wiser sentiments, almost noble.

A few days later, Alonso Quixano, having fallen ill and now under the loving care of his niece and housekeeper, loudly declares that he is cured of his illusions, renounces the tales of chivalry, and calls for a confessor and a scribe to take down his will. Immediately, those around him, especially Sansón Carrasco and Sancho Panza, begin to protest that he is wrong, and how can he say such things,

> when we have news of the disenchantment of Lady Dulcinea? And now that we are on the point of becoming like shepherds and spending our lives in song, like princes, now your grace wishes to become a hermit? For God's sake, be quiet, come to your senses, and tell us no more tales![57]

While the knight urges reason, his companions know such realism is madness, they realize that he is giving up the essence of who he is and has become. Even as reality tightens its noose, the urge to be free of it reasserts itself.

The narrator, our supposed ventriloquist of Cide Hamete, then tells us that the news of his impending death

> put terrible pressure on the already full eyes of his housekeeper, his niece, and his good squire, Sancho Panza, forcing tears from their eyes and a thousand deep sighs from their bosoms, because the truth is, as has already been said, that whether Don Quixote was simply Alonso Quixano, or whether he was Don Quixote of La Mancha, he always had a gentle disposition and was kind in his treatment of others, and for that reason he was dearly loved not only by those in his household, but by everyone who knew him.[58]

Just as one character, Don Quixote, had espoused and emulated the tales of chivalry, another character, Alonso Quixano, abjures them. Deciding that one is right and the other wrong is exactly what

Cervantes's book doesn't allow us to do, for the space it opens, the space of fiction, is one in which exactly those questions can never be resolved.[59] Because that space does not refer to the reality in question, to that place where the books of chivalry either are evil or are harmless fun; the space of fiction refers to that place where such debates take place and where we are called to make a judgment, about them and ourselves. Whether Quixote was Quixano or Quixano Quixote, he was, Cervantes seems to be telling his present-day interpreters, still good, one way or the other.

So, with a last good-humored wink to his leisurely readers, and to the listeners around the dying embers of the tavern's hearth, now sitting riveted to their benches, ignoring the innkeeper's plaintive requests that they clear out, Cervantes brings his tale to a close. He has the priest draw up a document stating for posterity, just in case any future Avellanedas are tempted to revive him, that "Alonso Quixano the Good, commonly known as Don Quixote, had passed from this life and had died a natural death."[60] Then, for good measure, Cervantes adds something to ensure that he and only he could ever be recognized as Quixote's author. Except he doesn't name himself as that author, but someone else: the fictional Arab historian Cide Hamete Benengeli, whose ode to his own pen ends the book: "For me alone was Don Quixote born, and I for him; he knew how to act, and I to write; the two of us alone are one . . ."[61] So, dear reader, if you really want to believe, as the author writes one last time, that "my only desire has been to have people reject and despise the false and nonsensical books of chivalry,"[62] by all means, be my guest. After all, it's Cide Hamete who told you so himself, and he always speaks the truth.[63]

As a young man, Cervantes bought into the religious and political doctrines of his day. He dueled for honor, risked his life for his country, spent long years in captivity, and returned fueled with hope for a comfortable and honorable old age. These hopes were dashed as he found that, in the eyes of his society and his government, he was not much more than an aging cripple whom they would rather be rid of than reward. His early attempts at prose and theater showed sparks of literary genius and critical wit, but it was only as his life progressed and his hopes and plans turned to naught that the real genius we now recognize came alive, that Cervantes became, as it were, Cervantes.

In the decade lasting from the publication of *Don Quixote* to his death in 1616, in novels, collections of stories, a mock-epic poem, and a series of plays and theatrical interludes he published in written form instead of seeing them performed, Cervantes pushed the envelope of every literary genre, parodying established styles and conventions along the way. Armed with a style in which he had bundled everything he learned from his years at war, from the theater, his travels, and the mean streets of Spain, Italy, and Algiers, he responded to the despair of his failed expectations with the equally caustic and generous wit of his fiction, turning the world and all its false promises into the canvas for his newfound prose, and instilling his characters with an emotional depth and reality that had never been seen before.

The man who lay dying, his legs swollen from dropsy, meant those words he wrote in his dedication to the Count of Lemos, the patron he had so longed for but found too late. His writing conveyed neither flights of fancy nor the impassive portrayal of reality; instead, in a crescendo of vivid characters able to connect with readers across chasms of culture and time, it revealed the achingly tragic and yet mordantly funny battle to the death between reality and our immortal desire to transcend it.

ACKNOWLEDGMENTS

This book would not have been possible without my many teachers, colleagues, and students in the fields of golden age Spanish literature and history, Spanish literature, and comparative literature, both those who came before me and those who continue to produce such vibrant and compelling research today. More scholars are listed in the bibliography than I have space to be thankful for here, but those with whom I have been in personal contact, who have reacted to my blog posts, who have read and commented on the manuscript, or who have engaged with me at lectures I have given include: Ellen Anderson, Marina Brownlee, Susan Byrne, David Castillo, Moisés Castillo, Bob Davidson, Edward Friedman, Charles Ganelin, Francisco Gómez Martos, Eduardo González, Hans Ulrich Gumbrecht, Carlos Gutiérrez, Richard Kagan, Alison Maginn, Carmen Moreno-Nuño, Bradley Nelson, Gabriel Paquette, Andrés Perez-Simón, Harry Sieber, Nicholas Spadaccini, and Diana de Armas Wilson. I am especially grateful to Troy Tower for his proofreading prowess, and my dear friend María Antonia Garcés deserves special mention here for having exhaustively read the manuscript, spotting many errors and providing priceless feedback. To Lauren Schnaper and James Carleton, I give my heartfelt thanks for their gift of a beautiful nineteenth-century English edition of the *Quixote*, just as I do to John O'Neill for his gift of the 1605 and 1615 facsimile editions. I am also deeply grateful to my agents, Michael Carlisle and Lauren Smythe, and to my UK editor, Bill Swainson, for their enthusiasm, support, and inspiring feedback. My U.S. editor, Anton Mueller, oversaw the transformation of the manuscript through three revisions; without his patient reading and insightful feedback, this would have been a much different book, and a much inferior one. To Paul Espinosa and Earle Havens of the George Peabody Library and the Special Collections of the Sheridan Libraries at Johns Hopkins University, I owe thanks for their extraordinary knowledge and assistance in accessing the great literary treasures we keep in Baltimore. Finally, my greatest thanks go to Bernadette Wegenstein, my wife, collaborator, and partner in all life's challenges, who read and commented extensively on countless versions of these pages, and who supported me in innumerable ways from its inception to its completion.

To these friends and scholars, and to all those who came before me whose insights and research allowed this book to take shape, I offer my heartfelt thanks—all the while accepting full responsibility for any mistakes or misinterpretations I may have engendered along the way.

A NOTE ON THE SOURCES

The literature on Cervantes is vast and far more than any one individual can master. It follows that the works I list in the bibliography
are a very select group, corresponding to my judgment of what is most
important and most useful for this project. As far as the biographies
are concerned, there are, again, many, spanning as far back as the first
century after Cervantes's death up to as recently as this century.
I make no claim in this book to revealing anything new about
Cervantes's life; nor am I able to judge the likelihood of one or another
speculation about episodes in his life. This is not a biography in any
traditional sense, as I am not trying to retell the life of a great man;
rather, I am using the story of his life as we know it to try to answer
the question of what his contribution to cultural and intellectual
history was, and how he came to be the one to make it. Consequently,
my approach to the biographical sources has been cumulative. When
describing a period or set of episodes from his life, I try to limit myself
to what most scholars accept as likely and simply to pass over what
would require too much speculation. In each case, I consulted all the
biographical sources I list here, and chose details that the majority
agree on. For this reason, I cite biographical sources only in those
cases where I judge one particular source to have been especially
informative for my purposes, or if I am quoting directly from that
text.

As I am not making any claim to have produced original knowledge
about his life, the reader should assume that all facts concerning the
life of Cervantes were taken from one or more of the books authored
by Astrana Marín, Byron, Canavaggio, McCrory, or McKendrick. As a
general guide to these sources, I would add the following: Astrana
Marín is exhaustive, but also highly speculative and hagiographic;
Byron's is detailed and literary in its style, and includes a great deal of
speculation as well; Canavaggio's offers a good number of correctives

regarding the excesses of prior biographers; McCrory's is concise and restrained, agreeing with much of what Canavaggio offers but doing so more selectively; and McKendrick's, published prior to Canavaggio's work, is the statement of a Cambridge literature professor, beautifully written, but mostly a forcefully argued volley in favor of a very limited, to my mind, interpretation of Cervantes's literary worth. All other works I have referenced appear in the notes cited by author surname and with full citations in the bibliography.

For *Don Quixote* itself, I decided to take my quotations from Edith Grossman's beautiful 2003 translation, in part so that those who cannot enjoy the original may easily find the passages I comment on. These quotations are referenced as *DQ* followed by the page number. In other cases, I have chosen published translations where I felt the quality was sufficient, checking them against the original Spanish, or have translated the texts myself in all cases where existing translations struck me as dated, inaccurate, or otherwise wanting. The notes refer to which edition is being cited; the full citation for both translations and originals can be found in the bibliography.

NOTES

Introduction

1 Cervantes, *Don Quixote*, 19. Hereafter cited as *DQ*.

2 Ibid., 21.

3 Ibid.

4 Ibid., 35.

5 Ibid., 58.

6 Ibid., 59.

7 Ibid., 60.

8 Ibid., 678–79.

9 Erich Auerbach, *Mimesis: The Representation of Reality in Western Literature* (Princeton, NJ: Princeton University Press, 1953), 347.

10 Fitzgerald, 30–31.

11 ". . . aut prodesse volunt aut delectare poetae, aut simil et iucunda et idonea dicere vitae . . .": Horace, *Satires*, 94, verses 333–34. Horace's influence on Renaissance letters was most directly felt through Robortello's 1548 paraphrase along with Aristotle's *Poetics*. See Anthony Grafton, Glenn Most, and Salvatore Settis, *The Classical Tradition*, 456.

12 Jackson, ed., 314.

13 As John Gardner puts it, "an important part of what interests us in good fiction is our sense, as we read, that the writer's imitation of reality's process . . . is accurate; that is, our feeling that the work, even if it contains fabulous elements, is in some deep way 'true to life'" (51).

14 As I explain in what follows, characterization is central to my stipulated definition of fiction. Thus my argument is in no way in conflict with Mark Payne's 2007 work positing Theocritus as the inventor of fiction. As he writes in that book, "the presence of the bucolic characters is not like our access to the interiority of characters in the modern novel. He goes on to clarify that what is at stake in the modern novel is "empathy, or identification with characters," precisely what I am arguing is key to our experience of fiction.

15 I should make clear at this point that by insisting on the empathic dimensions of Cervantes's creation of character, I am not thereby arguing with those proponents of "empathy theory" that reading novels and identifying with the characters in them automatically makes us into better people, lays the groundwork for human

rights, or, in Martha Nussbaum's words, leads us to "attribute importance to the material conditions of happiness while respecting human freedom" (90). As Suzanne Keen asks, "how can we know that readers' passionate involvement with fictional others didn't inspire a desire to collect and control people they did not personally know?" (xx). My argument about empathy is, in fact reversed, namely, it was Cervantes's experience of the falsity of popular representations that endowed him with an empathy for his fellows that was in turn projected into his characters. We expect believable characterization in part because of Cervantes's empathy; it does not necessarily follow that all modern novels thereby invoke empathy or marshal it in socially beneficial ways.

16 As Celenza writes, "After the industrial revolution and the development of large sovereign states with equally large and ever-expanding governments, the modern world puts the institutions of government far away from most of us. In Machiavelli's Florence, however, a citizen was likely to see and know those who governed, to be enmeshed in an extended web of kinship ties with some of them—or to feel resentment at not being part of whatever larger kinship group did hold power. There was no mass transit, no mass circulation of ideas through newspapers, and no significant novels with long arcs of character development, through which one could learn about the emotions—and the common humanity—of people one had never met" (23).

17 I should note that, although I am focusing on different aspects of the modern world from those that lie at the heart of Stephen Greenblatt's compelling book, *The Swerve: How the World Became Modern*, the two theses are entirely compatible. Greenblatt emphasizes the rational worldview as being the essence of the modern, and finds a potent influence for it in the rediscovery in the early sixteenth century of Lucretius' great poem *De rerum natura, On the Nature of Things*, a work that posits "a universe formed of the clash of atoms in an infinite void" (8). The dissemination of that text after its recovery by the humanist scholar and book hunter Poggio Bracciolini was a vital chapter in the cultivation of a spirit of open inquiry in the sixteenth century that, as we will see, most certainly influenced Cervantes and his great creation.

18 Elliott, 319–20.

19 Shakespeare, *As You Like it*, 2.7.

20 See the article by Carlos Wesley, "The Joy of Reading Don Quixote." This is a speculative and ultimately unprovable claim, but one that I believe has a rational basis. There is a raging debate on the Internet about such competing claims, and *Don Quixote* is not listed by such sources as the *Huffington Post* when it publishes similar lists, but the main arguments marshaled in favor have merit: first, that *Don Quixote* has been in circulation with countless translations and editions for more than four hundred years, far longer than any of its closest competitors; and second, recent editions and translations have continually and repeatedly achieved bestseller status. The edition released after the quadricentennial of the publication of *Don Quixote* in Spain sold six hundred thousand copies in less than two months. The United States has seen three editions since the turn of the millennium alone.

The truth is, though, that we cannot know how many copies have been made, sold, or, much less, read in the four hundred years since *Don Quixote* was first published; its influence has been, in every sense of the word, immeasurable.

21 Some of the books that most influenced Cervantes were themselves already international bestsellers, even if they did not endure to the same extent or have quite the influence that *Don Quixote* would. Principal among these was Ariosto's great poem *Orlando furioso*, which enjoyed enormous popularity in Spain and was an important item in Cervantes's own literary world. See Javitch, *Proclaiming a Classic*. Steven Moore, at the outset of his *The Novel: An Alternative History*, has a very nice summary of what Cervantes must have read (1).

22 See note 20 in this chapter.

23 Bloom, "Introduction," xxii.

24 Parr and Vollendorf, 1.

25 Quoted in Kamen, *Empire*, xxv.

1. Poetry and History

1 The rival is Lope de Vega, who borrowed Cervantes's glasses at a literary event. Canavaggio, *Cervantes*, 245–46.

2 Ibid., 199.

3 See Francisco Rico, *El texto del Quijote*, 100–101 and 108–9 for a reproduction of the jail letter. For more on the complex and involved process of bringing a book to print in the sixteenth and seventeenth centuries, see Fernando Bouza Alvarez, *Dásele licencia*.

4 Sieber, "The Romance of Chivalry," 213–14; Nalle, 67–69.

5 *DQ*, 20.

6 Ibid., 43.

7 Ibid., 52.

8 Standage, 50.

9 Kagan, *Clio and the Crown*, 188–89.

10 *Index*, 9, my translation.

11 The anecdote is recorded in Márquez Torres's official approbation of the second part of *Don Quixote* (Cervantes, *Don Quijote*, 2:21, my translation). Some scholars have suggested that Cervantes, taking advantage of his friendship with the censor, actually wrote most of the approbation himself, and thus likely made up the anecdote about the Frenchmen. See Ferrer-Chivite, 555.

12 Aristotle, 68–69.

13 As Amélie Rorty writes, "Aristotle's characterization of tragedy is, perhaps, all too familiar, so familiar that we misread him, replacing his intentions with ours" (1).

14 Aristotle, 63.

15 As Rorty explains, "'Flaw' misleadingly suggests that hamartia is built into the protagonist's character" (10). In fact, the term is associated with archery, and specifically with "missing the mark." Thanks to Christopher Celenza for noting this etymology.

16 Jones, 16.

17 "For Tragedy is an imitation, not of men, but of an action and of life, and life consists in action, and its end is a mode of action, not a quality. Now character determines men's qualities, but it is by their actions that they are happy or the reverse. Dramatic action, therefore, is not with a view to the representation of character: character comes in as subsidiary to the actions" (Aristotle, 62).

18 Frye, 305.

19 *DQ*, 64.

20 Ibid., 68.

21 Ibid.

22 Borges, 450, my translation.

23 Cervantes, *Novelas ejemplares*, 1:52, my translation. Hereafter cited as *NE*.

24 *NE*, 1:52.

25 Ibid., 1:53.

26 Ibid., 1:51.

27 Cascardi also reads the novellas' exemplarity as initiating a break with the past, and aligns the move with Descartes, as I do in what follows. See "Cervantes's Exemplary Subjects," especially 57.

28 *Viaje del Parnaso*, 253. Hereafter cited as *VP*. The Spanish reads, "Yo he abierto en mis Novelas un camino/Por do la lengua castellana puede/Mostrar con propiedad un desatino."

29 As E. C. Riley points out, the very idea "that it might be important to seek a distinction between what was and was not verifiable fact gained ground slowly in the sixteenth century" (E. C. Riley, 164). Fiction as we understand it today, of course, presupposes such a distinction implicitly.

30 Branca, 5.

31 Boccaccio wrote stories that were *novelle*, "news," in the sense of departing from the everyday. In the words of the Boccaccio scholar P. M. Forni, "The colloquial segments, connecting fictional events with the extratextual world, and situating them within the sphere of the ordinary, not only project the light of verisimilitude on the stories and color them realistically, but assume a significant function in the texture of narrative discourse as well" (45).

32 Boccaccio, *Decameron*, 808–9, my translation.

33 As Forcione adds, unlike in a tale such as Cervantes's *La gitanilla*, "the Boccaccian tale only exceptionally does anything to bring indeterminacy to its fictional world or to disorient the reader and trouble his anticipation and suspense as he moves toward the climactic point and an apprehension of the themes implicit in the action" (Forcione, *Cervantes and the Humanist Vision*, 32).

34 *DQ*, 548.

35 Ibid., 660.

36 Ibid., 649–50; translation slightly modified.

37 Canavaggio, *Cervantes*, 217.

38 *DQ*, 117.

39 Rabelais, *Les cinq livres*, 39; translation from Rabelais, *Gargantua and Pantagruel*, 52.

40 *DQ*, 148.

41 Landy, 3.

42 Cercas, *Anatomy of a Moment*.

43 Bakhtin, 32.

44 Several biographers note that the notion of the novel's immediate overwhelming success may be somewhat overblown, and that other books at the time went to more editions sooner than *Don Quixote*, which is certainly true. But no book had the sustained and international success that it did.

45 See Roger Chartier's fascinating study *Cardenio Between Cervantes and Shakespeare*, as well as Barbara Fuchs's article "Beyond the Missing *Cardenio*" and the corresponding chapters in her book *The Poetics of Piracy*.

46 Fernández de Avellaneda, 198, my translation.

2. Open and Closed

1 Griffin, 26.

2 Johnson, *Quest*, 4.

3 Elliott, 161.

4 Erasmus, x.

5 Hopkins, 51.

6 Erasmus, 4.

7 Ibid., 14.

8 *DQ*, 6.

9 Ibid., 4.

10 Byron, 418.

11 *Obras completes de Miguel de Cervantes*, 11:988, my translation. Hereafter cited as *OC*.

12 *OC*, 2:996.

13 Ibid., 2:993.

14 Byron, 71.

15 *OC*, 528; my translation.

16 See Gil Pujol's excellent article. See also Rodríguez Salgado's essay on multiple identities in sixteenth-century Spain.

17 Kamen, *Empire*, 332.

18 *DQ*, 835. As Grossman's notes on the passage point out, the literary scholar Martín de Riquer argues that the phrase could have meant simply, "Attack, Spain!" But Sancho's question clearly indicates that the other meaning was a possibility as well.

19 Elliott, 221–23. As Kamen points out, however, there was a great deal of controversy surrounding the original laws, and they were initially suspended before being ratified only nine years later. Even then, it was hard to enforce them, and "by the 1570s, ironically, the demands for proofs of purity had come to a virtual stop" (*Inquisition*, 238–39).

20 Elliott, 153.

21 Ibid., 161.

22 Quoted in ibid., 222.

23 Calderón, *El alcalde de Zalamea*, 1:857. See also Castillo and Egginton, "All the King's Subjects."

24 The connotations of blood purity advanced and spread with the Spanish conquest of the Americas, as Moisés Castillo has shown, leading to prejudices against those who would return having made their wealth in the New World and even to suspicions of Jewish blood as a result (*Indios*, 21).

25 While connected at base, there were in fact two different sets of issues and policies for *conversos* and Moriscos. The Morisco problem was exacerbated in 1568–1570 with the rebellion of the Alpujarras, but even toward the end of his reign, Philip II did not dare to expel the Moriscos. This had to wait until his son Philip III's reign. See a summary of these debates in Bernabé Pons, as well as in the books by Carrasco and Harvey.

26 Byron, 28–29.

27 Ibid., 34.

28 McKendrick, 16

29 Canavaggio, *Cervantes*, 23.

30 *NE*, 2:301.

31 Astrana Marín, 1:82.

32 *NE*, 2:316.

33 Byron, 43.

34 McCrory, 39.

35 Picón, see intro.

36 *OC*, 2:156.

37 Gonzalo, "El erasmismo en España," 99. According to Vilanova, Erasmus's greatest influence on Spanish literature was through his satire (8).

38 Elliott, 161. As Forcione writes, Cervantes remained "committed to the Erasmists' fundamental optimistic assumptions concerning man's social and ethical nature and the value of education in molding the crowd of beasts into the civilized community of humanity" (*Cervantes and the Mystery of Lawlessness*, 153).

39 *Obras de Cervantes*, 532; this translation is quoted from Canavaggio, *Cervantes*, 181. Astrana Marín explains that the poem was never published by Cervantes but was copied down by one Francisco Ariño, who was present when Cervantes recited it before a gathering of friends (Astrana Marín, 5:321). Cervantes himself clearly liked the poem, giving it pride of place among his poetic works during the literary reminiscence that occupies part of his *Journey to Parnassus* (*VP*, 254).

3. Soldier of Misfortune

1 See Daniel Javitch's *Proclaiming a Classic*, in which he describes the remarkable success of the *Orlando* and the 113 printings that made it, by 1580, the defining work of literature of the sixteenth century.

2 Tasso, *La Gerusalemme liberata*, 12; translation, slightly modified, from Tasso, *Jerusalem Delivered*, 14–15.

3 *DQ*, 126.

4 Ibid., 129.

5 Ibid., 60.

6 The line comes from Mercury, who is speaking to Cervantes and recalling his bravery as a soldier (*VP*, 222).

7 McCrory, 51.

8 See Hugh Bicheno's *Crescent and Cross: The Battle of Lepanto, 1571.*

9 Byron, 108.

10 Ibid., 111.

11 Quoted in ibid., 116.

12 Ibid., 121.

13 Ibid., 125–26.

14 Parker, *Europe in Crisis*, 52.

15 Ibid.

16 *DQ*, 329. As Stephen Rupp puts it, "the play of rhetorical structures and techniques allows Cervantes to construct a complex discourse that adapts a conventional theme to issues of the conduct and ethos of armed conflict in his own time" (34).

17 *DQ*, 331.

18 As Anthony J. Cascardi writes, "Cervantes wrote under conditions that required indirect and oblique approaches to nearly all controversial matters" (*Cervantes, Literature and the Discourse of Politics*, 198).

19 *DQ*, 332.

20 Ibid., 332–33.

21 Susan Byrne, "Cervantes's Reason of State," address delivered at the Thirteenth Annual Cervantes Symposium at the Instituto Cervantes, Chicago, IL, April 26, 2013. For more on the concept of reason of state in early modern state, see Francisco Tomás y Valiente, "La monarquía española del siglo XVII: El absolu tismo combatido," and José A. Fernández-Santamaría, *Razón de estado y política en el pensamiento español del barroco (1595–1640)*, esp. 35–37, where he describes how Spanish intellectuals distinguished between true and false uses of the concept.

22 *DQ*, 459–60.

23 Ibid., 460.

24 As Cascardi writes in reference to this episode, "Given its position at the very opening of Part II, this passage reminds us that the quixotic project to restore knight errantry is, in fact, the comic transposition of an underlying political project that has both theoretical and practical dimensions" ("Cervantes and Descartes on the Dream Argument," 50).

25 Although, Kagan shows that under Philip the interest in an official history "that defended his policies and, most importantly, Spain's right to imperium in . . . both the Old World and New" grew (*Clio and the Crown*, 95). Kagan's book is the most authoritative study of the role and function of "official history" in early modern Spain.

26 Kagan, *Clio and the Crown*, 189–90.

27 Quoted in Castillo, *Baroque Horrors*, 137. It is Castillo's insight that Aznar's attempt to place Spain at the crossroads of the contemporary "war on terror" is a straightforward continuation of the project of "historians working under the auspices of the emerging absolutist monarchy . . . to establish the existence of an ancestral Spain going all the way back to the biblical time of Noah and his direct line of descendants" (139).

28 "The first way of all in which a ruler can do good to his subjects is to secure and preserve the rights of each by the exercise of justice; and this is without doubt the foundation of internal peace and concord" (Botero, 16).

29 See Tomás y Valiente, and Fernández-Santamaría, esp. 35–37.

30 See note 21. The two editions are available online at: http://books.google.com /books/about/Diez_Libros_de_la_Razon_de_Estado.html?id=sBo8AAAAcAAJ; http://books.google.com/books/about/Diez_Libros_de_la_Razon_de_Estado .html?id=Wn5LAAAAcAAJ.

31 Susan Byrne has traced the movement of this concept in juridical circles in Spain, and has pointed out the ways that Cervantes uses juridical concepts propagated by legal theorists of the time, such as Jerónimo Castillo de Bobadilla, although very much against the grain. As she writes, "Cervantes's criticism of that system is stinging and mordant, albeit hidden behind the mask of a 'fictional' narrative. The practical jurist sought stability in a chaotic environment, without concern for the attendant perversion of laws and ideals that this would entail. The creative writer highlighted those same processual perversions, and also appropriated many other literal legal details not found in manuals like those of Castillo de Bobadilla, but only in the laws themselves and in the jurists' glosses" (42). In a 1614 manual, a chapter heading reading "Artifice of reason of state as used by the Romans, more powerful than arms for attracting subjects," continues, "the Spaniards also knew the art of adulation and pleasing in order to win goodwill, it being in their natures to be welcoming of foreigners, hosting them with great love" (Aldrete, my translation).

32 *DQ*, 464–65.

33 Ibid., 466.

34 *NE*, 2:45.

35 Ibid., 2:56.

36 Ibid., 2:74.

37 As María Antonia Garcés tells me, the story may well have been composed shortly after Rodrigo's death, which seems to be alluded to in the story. Tomás is referred to as having been stricken with *alferecía*, and Rodrigo's rank was *alférez*, a junior officer.

38 Kamen, *Empire*, 185.

39 See Garcés's account in *Cervantes en Argel*, 358–59.

40 Parker, *Europe in Crisis*, 51–52. In Braudel's words, "The cost of war in the Mediterranean was so great that bankruptcy often followed. Philip II's expenditure was phenomenal. In 1571 it was estimated at Madrid that the maintenance of the allied fleet (belonging to Venice, the Pope and Spain) comprising 200 galleys,

100 roundships and 50,000 soldiers, would cost over four million ducats a year. Floating cities, such war fleets devoured money and supplies" (604).

41 Kamen, *Empire*, 187.

42 Botero quoted in Parker, *The Army of Flanders*, 14.

43 *VP*, 305–6, my translation. Herrero García argues that there is little evidence for believing that Cervantes is referring to a real son here (*VP*, 888). To my mind, the character seems quite meaningless if not, but unless some document emerges to settle the case, we cannot know either way.

44 Cervantes, *Los tratos de Argel*, OC, 11:15.

4. A Captive Imagination

1 McCrory, 79–80.

2 Byron, 189.

3 McCrory, 76.

4 Cervantes, *Los tratos de Argel*, OC, 2:13.

5 Garcés, *Cervantes in Algiers*, 47. This book is the definitive study of Cervantes's time in captivity and was the principal resource for the writing of this chapter. See also the revised and expanded Spanish edition.

6 De Sosa reports this number. See also Robert Davis's book *Christian Slaves, Muslim Masters*, xviii–xix.

7 See Braudel, 624–50.

8 I chose to use the term *class* for purposes of readability in this book, despite its being anachronistic. Spanish society was really one divided by orders or estates rather than classes, a much more modern term of analysis.

9 See Garcés's edition of Wilson's translation of de Sosa's work, *An Early Modern Dialogue with Islam*.

10 Garcés, 98.

11 Ibid., 191–201. Again, credit is due to Garcés for her intricate analysis of what this name must have meant to Cervantes. I am indebted to her for the discussion that follows.

12 *OC*, 22.

13 *DQ*, 344. Garcés advances a very plausible theory that Hasan was actually accepting bribes in order not to punish Cervantes. See *Cervantes en Argel*, OC, 2:118–21.

14 These arguments are laid out in detail in Egginton, "Affective Disorder."

15 Ledoux, 114.

16 Vesely, 110.

17 Radice, 41; Orgel and Strong, 63–64.

18 As Panofsky explains, Dürer insisted on the limits of theoretical rules in humans' attempts to represent "the infinite complexity of God's creation." He felt that human theory was "sorely limited, not only by the inequality of individual gifts and tastes, but also by the finiteness of human reason as such: 'For, the lie is inherent in our very cognition'" (*Life and Art*, 12).

19 As Stoichita writes in reference to another Dürer painting, "He is in the image, and yet he is not" (205).

20 Foucault, *Order*, 4. As the Spanish historian José Antonio Maravall puts it, "We thus have to recognize Velázquez as one of the founders of modern culture" (*Velázquez*, 148, my translation).

21 ". . . as though the painter could not at the same time be seen on the picture where he is represented and also see that upon which he is representing something. He rules at the threshold of those two incompatible visibilities" (Foucault, *Order*, 4).

22 Stoichita also sees Velazquéz's *Las meninas* in a similar light, in which the painting splits itself into "a figure who was both but not entirely—'spectator' and 'author'" (255).

23 "Don Quixote is the first modern work of literature," Foucault writes, "because in it we see the cruel reason of identities and differences makes endless sport of signs and similitudes; because in it language breaks off its old kinship with things and enters into that lonely sovereignty from which it will appear, in its separate state, only as literature" (*Order*, 48–49).

24 "It must represent; but that representation, in turn, must be represented within it" (Foucault, *Order*, 64). The German philosopher Martin Heidegger, writing some years before Foucault published his book, made a similar observation in an influential essay explaining the emergence of what Germans call *die Neuzeit*, the "new time" or "modernity." In that essay, which he called "The Age of the World Picture," Heidegger argues that our very idea of worldview is culturally and historically specific; the problem with modern thought is that, having adopted an understanding of knowledge in which the world is packaged into specific world-views or world pictures, it forgets that it is part of the world it is thinking. Nevertheless, and just as with Foucault, this does not mean that the subject who is responsible for the representation in question is not part of the picture. On the contrary, as Heidegger puts it, "wherever this happens, 'man gets into the picture' in precedence over whatever is" (*The Question Concerning Technology*, 131).

25 Garcés, *Cervantes in Algiers*, 233.

26 Knausgaard, 97.

27 See especially Garcés, *Cervantes in Algiers.*, 191–201. Garcés argues that Saavedra and Aurelio represent a split or traumatized subject in Cervantes's play (195–96), and that, moreover, by writing continuously about these events from different perspectives, Cervantes was able to "work through" in some ways the effects of the trauma of his captivity.

28 Cervantes, *Los baños de Argel*, OC, 2:443 (my emphasis).

29 Fiction entails the liar's paradox, in that the reader must simultaneously believe and disbelieve what is being read in order to understand it. Lucian of Samosata played with this idea already in the second century, when he wrote a "True History" that acknowledged that the only truth it told was that it was a lie. Cervantes may have had Lucian in mind, and was also very aware of the liar's paradox, which he has Sancho "solve" when he becomes governor of Barataria.

30 See Kidd and Castano.

31 *DQ*, 333.

32 Ibid., 363.

33 One of the reasons critics have cited for crediting Cervantes with the creation of the modern novel is the conflict in *Don Quixote* between the individual and society. Don Quixote, like Robinson Crusoe, Faust, and Don Juan, represents one of the great myths of modern individualism, and helped change the way people think about themselves in relation to their communities (Ian Watt, *Myths of Modern Individualism*). Some specialists of Spanish literature and history have rejected this claim, insisting that categories such as the individual and society are modern ideas that Cervantes could not possibly have conceptualized the way we do today. But what they have not considered is the extent to which ideas that would later become the centerpiece of the Enlightenment (such as freedom of conscience) or of the Romantic age (such as the struggle of individual creativity against drab conformism) might have been cultivated and spread by works of imagination such as those of Cervantes, whose novel was inspirational to not only all the writers who would follow in his wake, but also many of the most important philosophers and political thinkers of the modern age.

34 *DQ*, 365.

35 Hemingway, *The Sun Also Rises*, 247.

5. All the World's a Stage

1 Garcés, *Cervantes in Algiers*, 136.

2 My thanks to Gabriel Paquette for these details.

3 McCrory, 103.

4 I owe this connection to an unpublished paper by María Antonia Garcés, for which I am grateful to her for sharing. The letter was first discovered around 1863, and then was lost again some ten years later, only to be rediscovered in 2005 by José Luis Gonzalo Sánchez-Molero. He documents this discovery in the article listed in the bibliography.

5 McCrory, 149–51.

6 Quoted in Canavaggio, *Cervantes*, 102–3.

7 Lope was only a budding playwright at the time Cervantes published *La Galatea*, and would suffer his own vicissitudes, including exile from Madrid and sailing with the ill-fated armada of 1588, before hitting his stride in the 1590s.

8 Prologue, *OC*, 2:158.

9 See Lope, *Arte nuevo*.

10 *DQ*, 418.

11 Quoted in Canavaggio, *Cervantes*, 203.

12 See my *How the World Became a Stage*, 60–66, along with Ronald Surtz's classics study, *The Birth of a Theater*.

13 Gabrielle Ponce argues convincingly that Cervantes's use of allegorical figures was influenced by how Gian Giorgio Trissino deployed the chorus in his tragedy the *Sofonisba* (722).

14 *OC*, 2:151.
15 Díez-Borque, *El teatro*, 23.
16 Díez-Borque, *Sociedad y teatro*, 217.
17 Ibid., 27, 22.
18 Maravall, *Teatro*, 54.
19 *La estrella de Sevilla*, in Alpern, ed., *Diez comedias*, 1:743.
20 See Castillo and Egginton, "All the King's Subjects."
21 See Thomas O'Connor's article on metatheater, which I discuss later in this chapter.
22 A sermon delivered for Philip at his death in 1598 expressed the spirit of his rule in these words: "The eminent power that a king has, derives from God and is communicated by Him. Those who resist and rebel against the king, resist God and break God's established order." Quoted in Parker, *Europe in Crisis*, 32. It is vital to note that the absolutism is a troubled term in Spanish political history, as the power of the monarchy was in fact far more contested than in its French manifestation. See in particular the excellent books by Tomás y Valiente and Juan Carlos Rodríguez.
23 *La estrella de Sevilla*, Alpern, ed., 1:659.
24 *DQ*, 527.
25 Lope, *Comedias*, 248.
26 Ibid., 275.
27 *DQ*, 632.
28 Ibid., 634.
29 *VP*, 314.
30 Nicholas Spadaccini's influential article "Writing for Reading" makes this argument: "Cervantes's reluctance to write plays for an undiscriminating 'mass' audience that has been coopted ideologically by one of the vehicles of official culture (Lope's *comedia nueva*) compels him to redirect his own theater toward the private sphere of reading" (164). See Cory Reed's article "Cervantes and the Novelization of Drama" (66), for a counterargument.
31 Even if not intended to be read instead of seen, his theater is written, no doubt, in a spirit of protest against the popular style of drama at the time. See Sevilla Arroyo's introduction to *Los bagnios de Argel* for an in-depth discussion.
32 For Canavaggio, the metatheatrical aspect of Cervantes's theatrical writings "establishes the essential coherence of Cervantine dramaturgy" (*Cervantes entre vida y creación*, 151; see also 148).
33 The original can be found in *La entretenida*, *OC*, 2:725–820. For quotes from *The Diversion*, I've used John O'Neill's impressive translation for the online Out of the Wings project. The play is cited by act and scene number.
34 Cervantes, *The Diversion*, 1.1.
35 Ibid., 1.5.
36 Ibid., 1.3.
37 In this regard my view departs only slightly from the influential interpretation of Edward Friedman, who writes about this play that "the group failure in *La entretenida* results from the negation of the true self, as seen from various

perspectives. The characters cannot fulfill these goals because the goals are misdirected and because the assumed roles are inauthentic" (113). My only rejoinder would be to emphasize that Cervantes conceives of the true self as the self whom one composes for oneself. Here I am in agreement with Nicholas Spadaccini and Jenaro Taléns, who make the argument in their important book *Through the Shattering Glass: Cervantes and the Self-Made World* that one should "characterize Cervantes's universe as metadiscursive," and that his writings "aim, simultaneously, toward the production of a new image of the world and toward a dialogue with the very discourses that have constructed the world the way we actually know it" (168–69). I strenuously disagree, as does Friedman, with Thomas O'Connor's contention that "Spain's dramatists were stressing man's theatrical or dramatic nature only by emphasizing his acceptance of the notion that life is a dream and the world, a stage, and the falsity that this notion implies" (286–87). For the dramatists of early modern Spain, the idea of life as a dream or the world as a stage was pervasive; the question was how they interpreted it in their work.

38 The greatest student of Cervantes's theater, Jean Canavaggio, saw in *The Diversion* both the "revenge of life on literature" and the "revenge of creative invention on inventive imitation." He also saw *Pedro de Urdemalas* as the next step in this trajectory (*Cervantes dramaturge*, 121, my translations).

39 Cervantes, *The Diversion*, 3.7.

40 The play is usually interpreted as being about the art of theater, a kind of instruction manual for actors. As Casalduero puts it, it is in the actor that one finds "in their potentiality all the possible forms of man" (*Forma y sentido*, 179).

41 *OC*, 2:908, my emphasis.

42 The sobering reality of social mobility at the time is extensively documented by José Antonio Maravall in his *Poder, honor y élites*.

43 *OC*, 2:912.

44 See Stephen Orgel's classic study *Impersonations: The Performance of Gender in Shakespeare's England*.

45 Byron, 294.

6. Of Shepherds, Knights, and Ladies

1 After several ill-fated attempts to produce a translation myself that would not sound too ridiculous, I found RoseAnna M. Mueller's elegant translation (Montemayor, *The Diana*, 52).

2 López Estrada provides us with the most definitive understanding of the history and reception of pastoral novels in Spain. As he explains, their popularity exploded after Spaniards living in Italy encountered the work of the Neapolitan writer Jacopo Sannazaro, especially his *Arcadia*, which was translated into Spanish in Cervantes's birth year, 1547, and which exercised enormous influence on the Spanish poet Garcilaso (145–51).

3 Sieber, "The Romance of Chivalry," 213–14; Nalle, 67–69.

4 *DQ*, 267.

5 Ibid., 52. The words are those of the priest, who is referring explicitly to Cervantes, "a good friend of mine for many years, and I know that he is better versed in misfortunes than in verses. His book has a certain creativity; it proposes something and concludes nothing. We have to wait for the second part he has promised; perhaps with that addition it will achieve the mercy denied to it now; in the meantime, keep it locked away in your house my good friend" (52). The second part of *La Galatea* never did appear.

6 Cervantes, *La Galatea*, 338. My translation and emphasis. Henceforth cited as *G*.

7 Montemayor, *Los siete*, 167. See Mary Gaylord's excellent study of *La Galatea*, "The Language of Limits and the Limits of Language" (258), to which I am indebted for my interpretation.

8 As Gaylord puts it, "Cervantes here makes the central issue of pastoral art not sentiment but the way sentiment can be expressed" (258).

9 *G*, 168.

10 Gaylord, 266.

11 *DQ*, 19.

12 Byron, 302.

13 Ibid., 299.

14 Guevara, chapter 5, first lines.

15 Quoted in Harry Levin, xv.

16 Ibid., xvi.

17 Sieber, "The Romance of Chivalry," 214.

18 Castro, *Pensamiento*, 37.

19 See ibid., 36.

20 As Pilar García Carcedo puts it, Cervantes uses the contrast between real and idyllic shepherds to "overcome the very lack of verisimilitude of the genre, carrying out a degradation of the utopic isolation by way of the invasion of quotidian reality" (19, my translation).

21 *G*, 601.

22 This is also Byron's claim, and for these lines I have quoted his translation (174).

23 *G*, 501.

24 Ibid., 609–10.

25 Márquez Villanueva, 26.

26 This strikes me as being in concert with Cascardi's argument for "Cervantes's literary investigation of the foundations of political thought," in which context Don Quixote's speech to the goatherds, which I analyze in what follows, serves two purposes: "to debunk the power of myth as 'mere' fantasy that cannot possibly say anything meaningful about the world," and "to offer an alternative to political theory in the form of a vision that derives its force from the essence of fantasy, i.e., from its ability to negate one world and hypothesize another" (*Cervantes, Literature, and the Discourse of Politics*, 77).

27 *DQ*, 75.

28 Ibid., 76.

29 Ibid., 76–77.

30 Ibid., 78.

31 Ibid., 85.

32 Ibid., 100.

33 Ibid., 101.

34 All translations from Rodríguez de Montalvo are mine.

35 Rodríguez de Montalvo, 2:414.

36 *DQ*, 194.

37 Ibid., 194–95.

38 Ibid., 518.

39 See Maravall, *Poder*, in which he shows that honor really only accrued according to social rank, and that all other manifestations were "induced, secondary, subaltern" (43).

40 One of the persistent criticisms of Cervantes's great novel has been the presence in it of what have come to be known as the intercalated tales: stories the protagonists tell or read to one another that are recounted in full within the framework of the novel but that seem to have little or no relation to the work itself. Nabokov, who elsewhere had words of praise for Cervantes's creation, excoriated *Don Quixote* in his lectures on the history of the novel delivered at Harvard University in 1951 for the lack of unity and coherence introduced by the presence of these tales. The criticism was far from new; in fact, Cervantes himself prefigured it some three hundred fifty years earlier in the book's second part, when he had Don Quixote criticize the inclusion of intercalated tales in the first part. Speaking of the narrator Cide Hamete, Cervantes writes in the second book that "he said that to have his mind, his hand, and his pen always fixed on writing about a single subject and peaking though the mouths of so few persons was an insupportable hardship whose outcome did not redound to the benefit of the author; in order to overcome this difficulty, in the first part he has used the device of some novels" (*DQ*, 737). Nabokov writes about the claim that "Don Quixote has been called the greatest novel ever written," that "this is of course nonsense. As a matter of fact, it is not even one of the greatest novels of the world . . ." He goes on to call it a "very patchy haphazard tale, which is saved from falling apart only by its creator's wonderful artistic intuition that has his Don Quixote go into action at the right moments of the story" (27–28). René Girard also reflects on this tradition, pointing out that "the unity of the masterpiece seems somewhat compromised" (52), while going on to argue against that impression in much the same vein as I do here. As we've seen, the unifying theme of all Cervantes's writing is how we imitate models while thinking we're doing what we want. In this regard, Don Quixote is not just a figure to ridicule; rather, he is us. And the proof of this comes in how the "realistic" portrayals of the intercalated tales relate to Don Quixote's impossibly fantastic role models.

41 *DQ*, 275.

42 Ibid., 307.

43 Mancing, 132.

44 *DQ*, 266.

45 Byron, 307.

7. A Rogue's Gallery

1 Sieber, *Picaresque*, 24.

2 Alemán, 288–89.

3 Sieber, *Picaresque*, 9.

4 Castro, *Pensamiento*, 234. See also Francisco Rico's excellent analysis of the publication history of *Lazarillo* in his *The Spanish Picaresque*, especially 56–57. The *Index* made its rules explicit in this regard: rule VI of the 1667 *Index* "prohibits all books in vulgate dealing with disputes and controversies having to do with religion, between Catholics, and Heretics of our time." But not "prohibited are books dealing with ways of living well, contemplating, confessing, and such arguments, in vulgate" (*Index*, 9, my translation).

5 Sieber, *Picaresque*, 11.

6 Ibid., 25.

7 As García Santo-Tomás points out, urban expansion was extreme, with Seville's population actually tripling between 1534 and 1561 (31).

8 See Kagan, *Lawsuits and Litigants*, 5–10.

9 The French historian Michel Foucault would associate this shift with the emergence of the modern age, albeit, in his telling, this did not happen until the nineteenth century (*Discipline*, 78). See González Echevarría's discussion as well (27). See also Usunáriz Garayoa, who argues for the emergence of a disciplinary society reflected in all aspects of social life.

10 It is important to note that in Spain the rise of the modern state was a gradual and fitful process, one that involved the co-optation and political incorporation of a variety of other loci of power. See Fernández Albaladejo's excellent study, in particular 241–45.

11 González Echevarría, 25. For a particularly nuanced exposition of the relations between the Inquisition and the Spanish government, see Bethencourt, especially 354–63.

12 Gonzalez Echevarría, 8.

13 Canavaggio comments on the connection (*Cervantes*, 146).

14 Ibid., 151.

15 Sieber argues that for this reason Cervantes is the first to recognize the picaresque as a literary genre (*Picaresque*, 10).

16 *DQ*, 163.

17 Ibid., 169

18 Ibid., 168.

19 Ibid.

20 *NE*, 1:211.

21 According to the *Diccionario de Autoridades*, the word *monipodio* referred to a contract or agreement among persons conspiring to commit some wrong.

Monipodio at one point orders Rinconete to read from his "memory book," which is a list of all the sorts of crime they are in essence contracted to commit as a part of his guild. As Bouza points out, one of those crimes is publishing libels, a sly remark on Cervantes's part on the very common practice among writers of slandering one another in their verses, as often occurred between Lope and him, for example. See Bouza, *Corre manuscrito*, 112–13. As Baena points out, there can be no doubt that "Monipodio's microcosm projects the macrocosm with an exactitude only found in accounting books" ("Los naipes," 119).

22 *NE*, 1:195.

23 Ibid., 2:139.

24 Ibid., 2:141.

25 Like Robert Alter, I see an intimate connection between what he calls self-aware fiction, on the basis of which he grants Cervantes the status as the creator of the first novel, and the emergence of psychologically realistic, "three-dimensional" characters (*Partial Magic*, 2–8).

26 A 1741 translation begins with an "extract from Mr. Bayle's General Historical Dictionary" pointing out that "this Performance is of a better Invention, more artificial Contrivance and of a more sublime Stile than that of *Don Quixote de la Mancha*."

27 Cervantes, *Trials*, 327.

28 *DQ*, 454.

29 These critics, some of whose books and articles on the *Persiles* can be found in the works cited hereafter, include Michael Armstrong-Roche, Julio Baena, David Castillo, William Childers, Diana de Armas Wilson, and Barbara Fuchs. Childers, for example, writes, against the more canonical critique associated with Alban Forcione's classic study, *Cervantes's Christian Romance*, that the *Persiles* is a transnational romance, by which he means that it "situates Spain in the broader context of early modern Europe, demonstrating the permeability of the borders defining the territory of the Habsburg monarchy, as well as the imagined community to which all 'Spaniards' belonged" (Childers, 124). In Baena's estimation, while he finds much to criticize in the novel, he nevertheless finds it exemplary of what he terms the "'rebel' Spanish Baroque," in opposition to the "'official' Spanish Baroque" (*El círcolo y la flecha*, 98). See Castillo's excellent discussion in his review of Baena's book.

30 Byron, 387–89.

31 See also McCrory's commentary, 172.

32 Cervantes's take on the genre is notably different from that of Alemán and his followers, even the great satirist Francisco de Quevedo. As Américo Castro put it, Cervantes made use of the figure of the picaro, but he subordinated it to his complex vision of the world. As others have noted, for Cervantes the subject of the picaresque novel would "never be allowed to exist by itself without a larger context. It had to be contained within a fictional framework and its fictional nature had to be constantly pointed out to his readers" (*Picaresque*, 25). Or, as Alban Forcione writes, focusing on the last and most obviously picaresque of Cervantes's

Exemplary Novellas, the tale "transcends the literature of delinquency which attained such popularity in Spain of Philip III . . . only after thoroughly assimilating it in a critical dialogue" (*Cervantes and the Mystery of Lawlessness*, 15). What all these scholars are noticing is Cervantes's tendency to focus his vision not on an aspect of the world, but on how the world is being portrayed in books, in conversations, or in the popular consciousness at large. This is why Sieber is entirely right when he says that Cervantes placed the picaresque within a fictional framework and then constantly pointed out its fictional nature to his readers.

33 As Sieber points out, "Cervantes places several allusions in their conversation to contemporary picaresque narratives—primarily to the *Guzmán*—humorously undercutting the picaresque novel's claim to portray accurately the human experience of a rogue or to stand as an autonomous art form" (*Picaresque*, 26).

34 *NE*, 2:294.

35 Ibid., 2:359.

36 *DQ*, 813. Canavaggio comments on this passage and draws a similar conclusion (*Cervantes*, 239).

37 *DQ*, 891–92. Castillo cites this passage in particular as an example of excessive orthodoxy, and argues against John J. Allen's contention that he is unable "to find any clues of irony in this text." Castillo, "Don Quixote and Political Satire," quoting Allen, *Don Quixote: Hero or Fool*, 103.

38 This has been thoroughly demonstrated by Caroll Johnson. As he writes, "One of these 'final solutions' involved the deportation of the Moriscos to Newfoundland, where they would perish in the harsh climate," or "'castrating the male adults and children, and the women as well,' as Don Martín de Salvatierra, bishop of Segorbe, noted forcefully but redundantly'" (*Cervantes and Material World*, 53).

39 Castillo, *A(wry)*, 86.

40 Ibid. His comment should remind us of Joseph Goebbels's reluctant admiration for Sergei Eisenstein's *Battleship Potemkin*, a film he called "The greatest propaganda film ever."

41 Castillo, "Don Quixote and Political Satire."

42 *DQ*, 3.

8. The Fictional World

1 Bloom, *Western Canon*, 16.

2 Ibid., 29.

3 Ibid., 41.

4 Trilling, 119.

5 But are we overplaying our hand when we repeat that fiction prior to the modern age had to conform to moral standards? Certainly it's a stretch to claim that everything from the bawdy tales of Chaucer and the eschatological humor of Rabelais to the ribald comedies of Pietro Aretino all concerned themselves to any serious extent with Horatian instruction in their urge to delight. Joshua Landy

skewers such pompous critical certainty in an imagined dialogue with one Dame Erica Auerbach, "a graduate student who knows her literary history," about competing interpretations of Chaucer's "The Nun's Priest's Tale." But as Landy himself clarifies, "Dame Erica is right about one thing: medieval audiences expected the stories they heard to have easily detachable, easily assumable morals. And the Nun's Priest obliges his (and by extension Chaucer's) audience. He just obliges a little too much ... 'The Nun's Priest's Tale' is, in fact, a parody of didacticism, a story that reminds us how extraordinarily easy it is to draw edifying lessons from any narrative" (27). Landy's contention, then, is not that medieval readers would not have read his texts against the backdrop of an implicit moral standard, but that *we* should not do so. It is not a historical claim at all, but rather a methodological one, one about the value of reading fictions—and specifically certain kinds of fiction, such as those of Chaucer—in a way that does not depend on that reading providing any kind of moral dividend. In this way he is defending literature while implicitly accepting Wilde's and Bloom's admonitions that art can be (at least morally) useless, that while sincerity may well engender bad poetry, literature remains somehow necessary for thinking.

6 Trilling, 119.

7 Ibid.; Wilde, 389.

8 Leibniz, 355.

9 In this sense, I would argue that the "account of the process of reading and entering a story" that the cognitive scientist Jerome Bruner sought in his influential book *Actual Minds, Possible Worlds*, is itself dependent on a modern conception of literature (4).

10 *Don Quixote* was Flaubert's first and favorite novel, as Soledad Fox states at the outset of her book dedicated to comparing the two great novelists' signature creations, Don Quixote and Madame Bovary (vii). Faulkner's claim is cited by Moore (7). I should add that I am intentionally mentioning only international authors here; to list Cervantes's influence on Spanish and Latin American literature would be a never-ending exercise.

11 All these quotations are taken from the Web-based research resource "Spanish Language: Thomas Jefferson's Monticello." My heartfelt thanks to Carlos Gutiérrez for alerting me to this connection.

12 Byron, 447–51.

13 Ibid., 454–55.

14 There have been many hypotheses as to the identity of Avellaneda. Martín de Riquer proposed (and wrote a book defending) the thesis that Avellaneda was in fact one Gerónimo de Passamonte, a former comrade in arms of Cervantes who had been the model for the picaro Ginés de Passamonte, just described. The apocryphal *Quixote* and insulting prologue would have been Gerónimo's revenge for the insult of Cervantes's depiction (160). Suarez Figaredo lists several dozen suspects (25).

15 Fernández de Avellaneda, 198–99, my translation.

16 *DQ*, 847–49.

17 In this claim I am following a group of scholars whose work has been enormously influential to me, starting with that of my former adviser, the literary theorist and historian Hans Ulrich Gumbrecht (esp. 94–118), and including, among others, Luiz Costa Lima and Howard Bloch. See the works cited in the bibliography for their key contributions in this regard, but one succinct statement comes from the outset of Costa Lima's classic *Control of the Imaginary*: "To the extent that the notion that truth has been inscribed by the Divinity in the things of the world and therefore revealed itself in unequivocal signs was abandoned, phenomena were increasingly allowed multiple meanings; and it was the subject who was responsible for apprehending the correct one" (5).

18 Costa Lima, *Control of the Imaginary*, 17.

19 "If few heroes of literature are at once so substantial and so elusive, in such a life-like way, the effect owes a great deal to the fact that Cervantes, as an integral part of his representation, has occasional recourse to, and repeatedly reminds us of, other points of view than that of the immediate narrator" (Riley, *Cervantes's Theory of the Novel*, 219).

20 Costa Lima, *Control of the Imaginary*, 15. As he makes explicit in his sequel to that book, *The Dark Side of Reason*, "Modern fiction, as it appeared in the seventeenth century with the publication of the first part of *Don Quixote* (1605), had an inevitable oblique character; this was so because explicit thematization was then impossible. The conception of human nature in terms of a constancy that explained the makeup of human society, the impossibility of conceiving difference, and the existence of control mechanisms for regulating fiction—that is, for justifying and providing an evaluation criterion for texts that were neither true nor false—these were the variables that produced this result" (314). Gumbrecht's crucial treatment of Cervantes appears in *Eine Geschichte der Spanischen Literatur*, 294–301.

21 As Iser puts it, fiction "turns into a judgment that human beings make about themselves" (86).

22 The following analysis first appeared in my article "Cervantes, Romantic Irony, and the Making of Reality."

23 Corominas, 494.

24 *DQ*, 390.

25 Ibid., 392.

26 See Bernard Williams, *Descartes: The Project of Pure Enquiry*, 27.

27 Descartes, *Meditations on Philosophy*, 62.

28 Ibid., 64.

29 Quoted in Altmann, "Schiller *Meditations on Philosophy*, 62. und Cervantes." Tieck would also say of Cervantes, "That great inventor pointed readers and authors the way to real life, and his great genius showed how the common and small could take on the shimmer and color of the wondrous" (quoted in Lussky, *Tieck's Romantic Irony*, 122, my translation).

30 Strohschneider-Kohrs, *Die Romantische Ironie*, 79.

31 Schlegel, *Lectures*, 2:114.

32 Bergel, "Cervantes in Germany," 322.

33 Hegel, *Ästhetik*, 49.

34 Ibid., 657.

35 It is crucial to note immediately that, while this dialectic appears to have profound similarities to the Platonic problem laid out in the Allegory of the Cave, it is essentially different. The denizens of Plato's cave are bound with their heads facing a wall, where the shadows cast by a fire behind them are the only images they see. The philosopher who escapes the cave is momentarily blinded by the sun before returning to the cave and facing persecution from his fellows for the truths he attempts to impart. Plato's allegory—along with his theory that the True and the Beautiful exist in a heaven of pure forms that are then expressed in transient, degenerate forms in temporal life—concerns the superiority of a contemplative life and the desirability of philosopher kings, but does not envision the kind of dualism Descartes assumes. His vision does not take that first, irrevocable step that Descartes's does when he subjects all existence to doubt and reveals thereby the independence of a thinking thing. See Michael Williams's article "Descartes's Transformation of the Skeptical Tradition."

36 Bernard Williams explicitly credits the genie argument with this decisive step, one from doubting individual perceptive judgments to "hyperbolic doubt," i.e., "the collective hypothesis that they may all be false," and calls it "a new step, marked by a new development" (*Descartes: The Project of Pure Enquiry*, 56).

37 In recent years, psychiatrists have begun to identify a new condition they are calling *Truman Show* syndrome, after the 1998 Jim Carrey movie about a man whose life is the subject of a television show without his being aware of it. The symptom of this syndrome is the patient's persistent belief, against all evidence to the contrary, that his or her life is the subject of a reality TV show, that his or her actions are being filmed twenty-four hours a day, and that his or her friends, relatives, and even closest family members are part of the cast, all of whom are in the know and all of whom are conspiring to keep the patient in the dark about the true nature of his or her existence.

38 See Bernstein, *Philosophy of the Novel*, who makes this argument in inverse form: "I wish to displace *Don Quixote* as the founding moment of the novel, and to replace it with Descartes' *Discourse*" (153). Blaise Pascal called Descartes's philosophy "nature's novel, similar in ways to *Don Quixote*" ("Pensées sur la religion et sur quelques autres sujets," 203). As Popkin writes, "The next level, the demon hypothesis, is much more effective in revealing the uncertainty of all that we think we know. This possibility discloses the full force of skepticism in the most striking fashion, and unveils a basis for doubting apparently never dreamed of before" (*The History of Scepticism from Erasmus to Spinoza*, 178).

39 See Cascardi's article "Cervantes and Descartes on the Dream Argument," which argues for the difference in approaches that the two display, but remains focused on the status of dreams in both texts. Nadler's article "Descartes et

Cervantes: Le malin gènie et la folie de Don Quichotte" makes the connection most directly.

40 Quoted in Nadler, "Descartes et Cervantes: Le malin gènie et la folie de Don Quichotte," 607.

41 Ibid., 608.

42 As Esther Crooks demonstrated, Cervantes's work was ubiquitous in France in the early seventeenth century, reaching even those who could not read or did not have the book, via his direct influence on numerous playwrights (*The Influence of Cervantes in France in the Seventeenth Century*, 198–99).

43 Walter Stephens quotes the fifteenth-century inquisitor Jean Vineti, for instance, who discusses how demons can cause illusions in two different ways: "One way is from within, for the demon can change a man's imagination [*fantasia*] and also his bodily senses so that something will be seen as other than it is . . . The other way is from without since he can form and configure a body so that, by assuming it, he will appear visibly within it" (quoted in *Demon Lovers*, 291).

44 While initially entertaining the hypothesis that the introduction of the genie "supports no additional doubts beyond those that Descartes has already engendered prior to introducing it," Frankfurt concludes that God and the demon are, in the logic of Descartes's argument, one and the same being, whose purpose is "to provide a basis for doubts that had not previously been entertained at all" (*Demons, Dreamers, and Madmen*, 85–87).

45 *DQ*, 195.

46 Cervantes, *Don Quijote*, 1:305.

47 Descartes, 72.

48 It should go without saying that my thesis in this book is in no way intended to deny Shakespeare's extraordinary importance. Indeed, the innovations of character that I attribute to Cervantes can easily be seen in Shakespeare's immortal inventions. The point is that Cervantes, while nowhere near the playwright that Shakespeare was, imported the architecture of characters into his prose, hence creating a more potent vehicle for influencing culture and thought. For a powerful argument for Shakespeare's centrality to intellectual history, see Harold Bloom's *Shakespeare: The Invention of the Human*.

49 Byron, 478.

50 Ibid., 508.

51 We can only speculate as to the exact cause of his death, but Cervantes is quite specific about the symptoms. Dropsy was the name for what might have been edema, or the swelling of the lower limbs as a result of congestive heart failure.

52 Byron, 509–10.

53 Cervantes, *Persiles*, my translation.

54 *DQ*, 928.

55 Ibid., 929.

56 Ibid.

57 *DQ*, 936.

58 Ibid.

59 I take this to be Ortega y Gassett's point when he writes that "Cervantes was put on this earth to place our spirits beyond that dualism" (55, my translation).

60 *DQ*, 938.

61 Ibid., 939.

62 Ibid., 940.

63 As Ellen Anderson writes, "What he does not reject is Cide Hamete's book, contained in Cervantes's book, a true story of what he was but is no longer" (186).

BIBLIOGRAPHY

Aldrete, Bernardo. *Varias antiguedades de España Africa y Otras Provincias*. Amberes: Juan Hafrey, 1614. Print.

Alemán, Mateo. *Guzmán de Alfarache II: Edición y notas de Samuel Gili y Gaya*. Madrid: Espasa-Calpe, 1963. Print.

Allen, John J. *Don Quixote: Hero or Fool?* Gainesville: University of Florida Press, 1969. Print.

Alpern, Hymen. *Diez comedias del Siglo de Oro: An Annotated Omnibus of Ten Complete Plays by the Most Representative Spanish Dramatists of the Golden Age*. 2nd ed. New York: Harper and Row, 1968. Print.

Alter, Robert. *Partial Magic: The Novel as Self-Conscious Genre*. Berkeley: University of California Press, 1975. Print.

Althusser, Louis. *Lenin and Philosophy and Other Essays*. Trans. Ben Brewster. New York: Monthly Review Press, 2001. Print.

Altmann, Werner. "Schiller und Cervantes." *Dialnet*, n.p., n.d. Accessed June 21, 2013, at dialnet.unirioja.es/descarga/articulo/2881767.pdf.

Anderson, Benedict R. O. *Imagined Communities: Reflections on the Origin and Spread of Nationalism*. Rev. and extended ed. London: Verso, 1991. Print.

Anderson, Ellen M. "Dreaming a True Story: The Disenchantment of the Hero in Don Quixote, Part 2." In *Essays on Life Writing: From Genre to Critical Practice*. Ed. Marlene Kadar. Toronto: University of Toronto Press, 1992, 171–89. Print.

Ardilla, J. A. G., ed. *The Cervantean Heritage: Reception and Influence of Cervantes in Britain*. Leeds: Legenda, 2009. Print.

Aristotle. *Poetics*. Trans. S. H. Butcher. New York: Hill and Wang, 1961. Print.

Armstrong-Roche, Michael. *Cervantes's Epic Novel: Empire, Religion, and the Dream Life of Heroes in* Persiles. Toronto: University of Toronto Press, 2009. Print.

Astrana Marín, Luis. *Vida ejemplar y heroica de Miguel de Cervantes Saavedra*. 7 vols. Madrid: Reus, 1948–58. Print.

Auerbach, Erich. *Mimesis: The Representation of Reality in Western Literature*. Princeton, NJ: Princeton University Press, 1953. Print.

Austin, J. L. *How to Do Things with Words*. Cambridge, MA: Harvard University Press, 1962. Print.

Baena, Julio. *El círculo y la flecha: principio y fin, triunfo y fracaso del* Persiles. Chapel Hill: University of North Carolina Press, 1996. Print.

———. "Los naipes de Rincon(et)es cortad(ill)os: Hacia una lectura marginal de las *Novelas ejemplares*." In Julio Baena, ed. *Novelas ejemplares: Las grietas de la ejemplaridad*. Madrid: Juan de la Cuesta, 2008, 111–26. Print.

Bakhtin, M. M., and Michael Holquist. *The Dialogic Imagination: Four Essays*. Austin: University of Texas Press, 1981. Print.

Baretti, Joseph. *Tolondron: Speeches to John Bowle about his Edition of* Don Quixote, *Together with Some Account of Spanish Literature*. London: R. Faulder, 1786. Print.

Bergel, Lienhard. "Cervantes in Germany." In *Cervantes Across the Ages*. Ed. Ángel Flores and M. J. Bernadete. New York: Dryden Press, 1947. Print.

Bernabé Pons, Luis F. *Los Moriscos: Conflicto, expulsión y diaspora*. Madrid: Catarata, 2009. Print.

Bernstein, J. M. *The Philosophy of the Novel*. Minneapolis: University of Minnesota Press, 1984. Print.

Bertrand, Jean-Jacques Achilles. *Cervantes et le Romantisme Allemand*. Paris: Félix Alcan, 1914. Print.

Bethencourt, Francisco. *The Inquisition: A Global History, 1478–1834*. Cambridge, UK: Cambridge University Press, 2009. Print.

Bicheno, Hugh. *Crescent and Cross: The Battle of Lepanto, 1571*. London: Phoenix, 2005. Print.

Bloch, R. Howard. *Medieval French Literature and Law*. Berkeley: University of California Press, 1977. Print.

Bloom, Harold. "Introduction: Don Quixote, Sancho Panza, and Miguel de Cervantes Saavedra." In *Don Quixote*. Trans. Edith Grossman. New York: Ecco, 2003. Print.

———. *Shakespeare: The Invention of the Human*. New York: Riverhead, 1999. Print.

———. *The Western Canon: The Books and School of the Ages*. New York: Harcourt Brace, 1994. Print.

Boccaccio, Giovanni. *Decameron*. Torino: Giulio Einaudi, 1992. Print.

Boccaccio, Giovanni, and Charles Grosvenor Osgood, trans. *Boccaccio on Poetry; Being the Preface and the Fourteenth and Fifteenth Books of Boccaccio's Genealogia Deorum Gentilium in an English Version with Introductory Essay and Commentary*. New York: Liberal Arts Press, 1956. Print.

Borges, Jorge Luis. *Obras completas*. Vol. 1. Buenos Aires: Emecé, 1996. Print.

Botero, Giovanni, and P. J. Waley, trans. *The Reason of State: The Greatness of Cities*. London: Routledge, 1956. Print.

Bouza Alvarez, Fernando J. *Communication, Knowledge, and Memory in Early Modern Spain*. Philadelphia: University of Pennsylvania Press, 2004. Print.

———. *Corre manuscrito: Una historia cultural del Siglo de Oro*. Madrid: Marcial Pons, Historia, 2001. Print.

———. *«Dásele licencia y privilegio». Don Quijote y la aprobación de libros en el Siglo de Oro*. Madrid: Akal, 2012. Print.

Branca, Vittore. *Giovanni Boccaccio, profilo biografico*. Firenze: Sansoni Editori, 1977. Print.

Braudel, Fernand. *The Mediterranean and the Mediterranean World in the Age of Philip II*. New York: Harper and Row, 1972. Print.

Bruner, Jerome. *Actual Minds, Possible Worlds*. Cambridge, MA: Harvard University Press, 1986. Print.

Byrne, Susan. *Law and History in Cervantes's* Don Quixote. Toronto: University of Toronto Press, 2012. Print.

Byron, William. *Cervantes: A Biography*. New York: Paragon, 1988. Print.

Calderón de la Barca, Pedro, and Gabriel Mas. *El alcalde de Zalamea*. Madrid: Cátedra, 2008. Print.

Canavaggio, Jean. *Cervantes*. Trans. J. R. Jones. New York: W. W. Norton, 1990. Print.

———. *Cervantes dramaturge: Un théâtre à naître*. Paris: Presses Universitaires de France, 1977. Print.

———. *Cervantes entre vida y creación*. Alcalá de Henares: Biblioteca de Estudios Cervantinos, 2000. Print.

Carrasco, Rafael. *Deportados en nombre de Dios*. Barcelona: Destino, 2009. Print.

Casalduero, Joaquín. *Forma y sentido del teatro de Cervantes*. Madrid: Aguilar, 1951. Print.

Cascardi, Anthony J. "Cervantes and Descartes on the Dream Argument." *Cervantes* 4, no. 2 (1984): 109–22. Print.

———. *Cervantes, Literature, and the Discourse of Politics*. Toronto: University of Toronto Press, 2012. Print.

———. "Cervantes's Exemplary Subjects." In *Cervantes's Exemplary Novels and the Adventure of Writing*. Ed. Michael Nerlich and Nicholas Spadaccini. Santa Fe, NM: The Prisma Institute, 1989, 49–72. Print.

Castillo, David R. *(A)wry Views: Anamorphosis, Cervantes, and the Early Picaresque*. West Lafayette, IN: Purdue University Press, 2001. Print.

———. *Baroque Horrors: Roots of the Fantastic in the Age of Curiosities*. Ann Arbor: University of Michigan Press, 2010. Print.

———. "Don Quixote and Political Satire: Cervantine Lessons from Sacha Baron Cohen and Stephen Colbert." In James Parr and Lisa Vollendorf, eds. *Approaches to Teaching* Don Quixote. New York: MLA, 2014. Print.

———. "Julio Baena: *El círculo y la flecha: Principio y fin, triunfo y fracaso del* Persiles." Review. Chapel Hill: University of North Carolina Press, 1996, 165 pp. *Revista Cervantes* 17, no. 2 (Fall 1997): n.p. Accessed June 25, 2013, at http://www.cervantes-virtual.com/obra-visor/cervantes-bulletin-of-the-cervantes-society-of-america--48/html/02790320-82b2-11df-acc7-002185ce6064_29.html.

———. "The Literary Classic in Today's Classroom: *Don Quixote* and Road Movies." Hispanic Literature and the Question of a Liberal Education. *Hispanic Issues Online* 8 (2011): 26–41, at http://hispanicissues.umn.edu/assets/doc/02_castillo-hlqle.pdf.

Castillo, David, and William Egginton. "All the King's Subjects: Honor in Early Modernity." *Romance Language Annual* 6 (1995): 422–27. Print.

———. "The Perspectival Imaginary and the Symbolization of Power in Early Modern Europe." *Indiana Journal of Hispanic Literatures* 8 (1997): 75–94. Print.

Castillo, Julián del. *Historia de los reyes godos que vinieron de la Scythia de Europa contra el Imperio Romano, y a España: Con sucession dellos, hasta los catolicos reyes Don Fernando y Doña Isabela*. Madrid: Luis Sánchez, 1624. Print.

Castillo, Moisés R. *Indios en escena: Le representación del amerindio en el teatro del Siglo de Oro*. West Lafayette, IN: Perdue University Press, 2009. Print.

Castro, Américo. *El pensamiento de Cervantes*. Madrid: Editorial Hernando, 1925. Print.

Celenza, Christopher. *Machiavelli: A Portrait*. Cambridge, MA: Harvard University Press, 2014. Print.

Cercas, Javier. *Anatomy of a Moment*. Trans. Anne McLean. London: Bloomsbury, 2011. Print.

Cervantes Saavedra, Miguel de. *Don Quixote*. Trans. Edith Grossman. New York: Ecco, 2003. Print.

———. *El ingenioso hidalgo Don Quijote de La Mancha*. Ed. John Jay Allen. Madrid: Cátedra, 1994. Print.

———. *Entremeses*. Ed. Nicholas Spadaccini. Madrid: Cátedra, 1982. Print.

———. *Información de Miguel de Cervantes de lo que ha servido á S.M. y de lo que ha hecho estando captivo en Argel: Documentos*. Ed. Pedro Lanzas. Madrid: J. Esteban, 1981. Print.

———. "La entretenida." Ed. John O'Neill. N.p., n.d. Accessed May 17, 2013, at http://entretenida.outofthewings.org/index.html.

———. *La Galatea*. Ed. Francisco Estrada. 2nd ed. Madrid: Cátedra, 1999. Print.

———. *Los trabajos de Persiles y Sigismunda*. Ed. Carlos Muñoz. Madrid: Cátedra, 1997. Print.

———. *Novelas ejemplares*. Ed. Harry Sieber. Madrid: Cátedra, 1990. Print.

———. *Obras completas de Miguel de Cervantes*. Vols. 1–3. Madrid: Turner, 1993. Print.

———. *Obras de Cervantes*. Novísima Edición. Madrid: Gaspar y Roig, 1866. Print.

———. *Persiles and Sigismunda, A Celebrated Novel Intermixed with a Great Variety of Delightful Histories and Entertaining Adventures Written in Spanish by Michael De Cervantes Saavedra, Author of Don Quixote*. Translated into English from the Original. London: C. Ward and R. Chandler, 1741. Print.

———. *The Trials of Persiles and Sigismunda: A Northern Story*. Trans. Cecilia Richmond Weller and Clark A. Colahan. Berkeley: University of California Press, 1989. Print.

———. *Viaje del Parnaso*. Ed. Miguel Herrero García. Madrid: Instituto Miguel de Cervantes, 1983. Print.

Chartier, Roger. *Cardenio Between Cervantes and Shakespeare: The Story of a Lost Play*. Trans. Janet Lloyd. Cambridge, MA: Polity Press, 2013. Print.

Childers, William. *Transnational Cervantes*. Toronto: University of Toronto Press, 2006. Print.

Close, Anthony J. *Cervantes*: Don Quixote. Cambridge, UK: Cambridge University Press, 1990. Print.

———. *The Romantic Approach to 'Don Quixote.'* Cambridge, UK: Cambridge University Press, 1978. Print.

Coleridge, Samuel Taylor. *Samuel Taylor Coleridge*. Ed. H. J. Jackson. Oxford: Oxford University Press, 1985. Print.

Corominas, Joan. *Breve diccionario etimológico de la lengua castellana*. Madrid: Gredos, 1998. Print.

Costa Lima, Luiz. *Control of the Imaginary: Reason and Imagination in Modern Times.* Minneapolis: University of Minnesota Press, 1988. Print.

———. *The Dark Side of Reason: Fictionality and Power.* Stanford, CA: Stanford University Press, 1992. Print.

Crooks, Esther J. *The Influence of Cervantes in France in the Seventeenth Century.* Baltimore, MD: Johns Hopkins University Press, 1931. Print.

Davis, Robert C. *Christian Slaves, Muslim Masters: White Slavery in the Mediterranean, the Barbary Coast, and Italy, 1500–1800.* New York: Palgrave Macmillan, 2004. Print.

Descartes, René. *Meditations on First Philosophy*, 4th ed. Trans. Donald Cress. New York: Hackett, 1998. Print.

Díez Borque, José María. *El teatro en el siglo XVII.* Madrid: Taurus, 1988. Print.

———. *Sociedad y teatro en la España de Lope de Vega.* Barcelona: A. Bosch, 1978. Print.

Dowd, Maureen. "The Oscar for Best Fabrication," *New York Times*, Feb. 16, 2013, n.p. Accessed June 5, 2013, http://www.nytimes.com/2013/02/17/opinion/sunday /dowd-the-oscar-for-best-fabrication.html?_r=0.

Eco, Umberto. "C'era una volta Churchill." *L'Espresso*, n.p., n.d. Accessed Apr. 16, 2013, at http://espresso.repubblica.it/dettaglio/cera-una-volta-churchill/2007409//1.

Egginton, William. "Affective Disorder," *Diacritics* 40, no. 2 (2012 [appeared 2013]): 24–43. Print.

———. "Cervantes, Romantic Irony, and the Making of Reality." *MLN* 117, no. 5 (2002): 1040–68. Print.

———. *How the World Became a Stage Presence, Theatricality, and the Question of Modernity.* Albany: State University of New York Press, 2003. Print.

Elliott, John Huxtable. *Imperial Spain.* London: Penguin Books, 2002. Print.

Erasmus, Desiderius. *The Praise of Folly.* Trans. Clarence H. Miller. New Haven, CT: Yale University Press, 1979. Print.

Farrell, John. *Paranoia and Modernity: Cervantes to Rousseau.* Ithaca, NY, and London: Cornell University Press, 2006. Print.

Fernández Albaladejo, Pablo. *Fragmentos de monarquía: Trabajos de historia política.* Madrid: Alianza, 1992. Print.

Fernández de Avellaneda, Alonso. *El ingenioso hidalgo Don Quijote de La Mancha.* Madrid: Biblioteca Nueva, 2000. Print.

Fernández-Santamaría, José A. *Razón de estado y política en el pensamiento español del barroco (1595–1640).* Madrid: Centro de Estudios Constitucionales, 1986. Print.

Ferrer-Chivite, Manuel. "Cervantes, Avellaneda y la Aprobación de Márquez Torres." *AISO* (1999): 552–61. Accessed at Centro Virtual Cervantes, Mar. 20, 2013, cvc. cervantes.es.

Fitzgerald, F. Scott. *The Great Gatsby.* New York: Everyman's Library, 1991. Print.

Forcione, Alban K. *Cervantes and the Humanist Vision: A Study of Four Exemplary Novels.* Princeton, NJ: Princeton University Press, 1982. Print.

———. *Cervantes and the Mystery of Lawlessness: A Study of* El casamiento engañoso *and* El coloquio de los perros. Princeton, NJ: Princeton University Press, 1984. Print.

———. *Cervantes's Christian Romance: A Study of* Persiles y Sigismunda. Princeton, NJ: Princeton University Press, 1972. Print.

Forni, Pier Massimo. *Adventures in Speech Rhetoric and Narration in Boccaccio's Decameron*. Philadelphia: University of Pennsylvania Press, 1996. Print.

Foucault, Michel. *Discipline and Punish: The Birth of the Prison*. New York: Vintage Books, 1979. Print.

———. *The Order of Things: An Archaeology of the Human Sciences*. New York: Pantheon Books, 1970. Print.

Fox, Soledad. *Flaubert and* Don Quijote*: The Influence of Cervantes on* Madame Bovary. Brighton, UK: Sussex Academic Press, 2008. Print.

Frank, Thomas. *What's the Matter with Kansas? How Conservatives Won the Heart of America*. New York: Metropolitan Books, 2004. Print.

Frankfurt, Harry G. *Demons, Dreamers, and Madmen; The Defense of Reason in Descartes's Meditations*. Indianapolis, IN: Bobbs-Merrill, 1970. Print.

Franklin, Julian H. *Jean Bodin and the Rise of Absolutist Theory*. Cambridge, UK: Cambridge University Press, 1973. Print.

Freud, Sigmund. *The Standard Edition of the Complete Psychological Works of Sigmund Freud*. Ed. James Strachey, Anna Freud, Carrie Lee Rothgeb, and Angela Richards. 24 vols. London: Hogarth Press, 1953–74. Print.

Friedman, Edward H. *The Unifying Concept: Approaches to the Structure of Cervantes's Comedias*. York, SC: Spanish Literature Publications Co., 1981. Print.

Frye, Northrop. *The Anatomy of Criticism, Four Essays*. Princeton, NJ: Princeton University Press, 1957. Print.

Fuchs, Barbara. "Beyond the Missing Cardenio: Anglo-Spanish Relations in Early Modern Drama." *Journal of Medieval and Early Modern Studies* 39, no. 1 (2009): 143–59. Print.

———. *Passing for Spain: Cervantes and the Fictions of Identity*. Urbana: University of Illinois Press, 2003. Print.

———. *The Poetics of Piracy: Emulating Spain in English Literature*. Philadelphia: University of Pennsylvania Press, 2013. Print.

Galilei, Galileo. *Dialogue Concerning the Two Chief World Systems, Ptolemaic and Copernican*. Ed. Stillman Drake. New York: Modern Library, 2001. Print.

Garcés, María Antonia. *Cervantes en Argel: Historia de un cautivo*. Madrid: Gredos, 2005. Print.

———. *Cervantes in Algiers: a Captive's Tale*. Nashville, TN: Vanderbilt University Press, 2002. Print.

García Carcedo, Pilar. *La Arcadia en el* Quijote*: Originalidad en el tratamiento de los seis episodios pastoriles*. Bilbao: Beitia, 1996. Print.

García Santo-Tomás, Enrique. *Modernidad bajo sospecha: Salas Barbadillo y la cultura material del siglo XVII*. Madrid: CSDIC, 2008. Print.

Gardner, John. *The Art of Fiction*. New York: Vintage, 1991. Print.

Gaylord, Mary. "The Language of Limits and the Limits of Language: The Crisis of Poetry in La Galatea." *MLN* 97, no. 2 (1982): 254–71. Print.

Gilman, Ernest B. *The Curious Perspective: Literary and Pictorial Wit in the Seventeenth Century*. New Haven, CT: Yale University Press, 1978. Print.

Gil Pujol, Javier. "Un rey, una fe, muchas naciones: patria y nación en la España de los siglos XVI y XVII." In *La monarquía de las naciones: Patria, nación, y naturaleza en la Monarquía de España*. Ed. Antonio Álvarez-Ossorio Alvariño and Bernardo J. García García. Madrid: Fundación Carlos Amberes, 2004, 39–76. Print.

Girard, René. *Deceit, Desire, and the Novel: Self and Other in Literary Structure*. Baltimore, MD: Johns Hopkins University Press, 1976. Print.

Goffman, Erving. *Frame Analysis*. Cambridge, MA: Harvard University Press. 1974. Print.

González Echevarría, Roberto. *Love and the Law in Cervantes*. New Haven, CT: Yale University Press, 2005. Print.

Gonzalo Sánchez-Molero, José Luis. "El erasmismo en España: La utopía de una Edad de Oro." In *Erasmo en España: La recepción del humanismo en el primer renacimiento español*. Salamanca: Sociedad Estatal para la Acción Cultural Exterior, 2003, 96–111. Print.

———. "La 'Epístola a Mateo Vázquez,' redescubierta y reivindicada." *Cervantes: Bulletin of the Cervantes Society of America* 27, no. 2 (2007): 181–211. Print.

Grafton, Anthony, Glenn Most, and Salvatore Settis. *The Classical Tradition*. Cambridge, MA: Harvard University Press, 2010. Print.

Greenblatt, Stephen. *The Swerve: How the World Became Modern*. New York: W. W. Norton, 2011. Print.

Griffin, Clive. *Oficiales de imprenta, herejía e inquisición en la España del siglo XVI*. Madrid: Ollero y Ramos, 2009. Print.

Guevara, Antonio de. "Menosprecio de corte y alabanza de aldea (1539)." Proyecto Filosofía en español, n.p., n.d. Accessed June 3, 2013, at http://www.filosofia.org/cla/gue/gueca.htm.

Gumbrecht, Hans Ulrich. *Eine Geschichte der Spanischen Literatur*. Frankfurt: Suhrkamp Verlag, 1990. Print.

Harvey, L. P. *Muslims in Spain: 1500–1614*. Chicago, IL: University of Chicago Press, 2005. Print.

Hegel, Georg Wilhelm Friedrich. *Vorlesungen über die Ästhetik*. Stuttgart: Reclam, 1971. Print.

Heidegger, Martin. *The Question Concerning Technology, and Other Essays*. New York: Harper and Row, 1977. Print.

Hermenegildo, Alfredo. *La "Numancia" de Cervantes*. Madrid: Sociedad General Española de Librería, 1976. Print.

Hobbes, Thomas. *Leviathan: Parts One and Two*. New York: Liberal Arts Press, 1958. Print.

Hopkins, Jasper. *Nicholas of Cusa. On Learned Ignorance: A Translation and an Appraisal of De docta ignorantia*. Minneapolis, MN: A. J. Benning Press, 1981. Print.

Horace. *Satires, Epistles, and Ars Poetica*. Ed. W. Brownrigg Smith. London: Crosby Lockwood & Co. 1878. Print.

Huebener, Theodore. "Goethe and Cervantes." *Hispania* 33, no. 2 (1950): 113–15. Print.

Hutchins, Robert Maynard, ed. *Machiavelli/Hobbes*. Vol. 23 in *Great Books of the Western World* series. Chicago, IL: Encyclopedia Britannica, 1952. Print.

Index Librorum Prohibitorum. (General Inquisitor: Antonio Sotomaior) Madrid: 1667. Print.

Iser, Wolfgang. *The Fictive and the Imaginary: Charting Literary Anthropology.* Baltimore, MD: Johns Hopkins University Press, 1993. Print.

Javitch, Daniel. *Proclaiming a Classic: The Canonization of the "Orlando Furioso."* Princeton, NJ: Princeton University Press, 1991. Print.

Johnson, Carroll B. *Cervantes and the Material World.* Urbana: University of Illinois Press, 2000. Print.

———. *Don Quixote: The Quest for Modern Fiction.* 1990. Reprint. Long Grove, IL: Waveland Press, 2000. Print.

Jones, John. *On Aristotle and Greek Tragedy.* New York: Oxford University Press, 1962. Print.

Kagan, Richard L. *Clio and the Crown: The Politics of History in Medieval and Early Modern Spain.* Baltimore, MD: Johns Hopkins University Press, 2009. Print.

———. *Lawsuits and Litigants in Castile, 1500–1700.* Chapel Hill: University of North Carolina Press, 1981. Print.

Kahn, Aaron M. *The Ambivalence of Imperial Discourse: Cervantes's La Numancia Within the 'Lost Generation' of Spanish Drama (1570–90).* Oxford: Peter Lang, 2008. Print.

Kamen, Henry. *Empire: How Spain Became a World Power, 1492–1763.* New York: HarperCollins, 2003. Print.

———. *The Spanish Inquisition: A Historical Revision.* New Haven, CT: Yale University Press, 1999. Print.

Keen, Suzanne. *Empathy and the Novel.* Oxford: Oxford University Press, 2007. Print.

Kidd, David Comer, and Emanuele Castano. "Reading Literary Fiction Improves Theory of Mind." *Science,* October 3, 2013: Vol. 342 no. 6156 pp. 377–80. Accessed April 17, 2015 at http://www.sciencemag.org/content/342/6156/377.full.

Knausgaard, Karl Ove. "I Am Someone, Look at Me." *T, the New York Times Style Magazine,* June 15, 2014, 94–97. Print.

Landy, Joshua. *How to Do Things with Fictions.* New York: Oxford University Press, 2012. Print.

Ledoux, Joseph. *The Emotional Brain: The Mysterious Underpinnings of Emotional Life.* New York: Simon and Schuster, 1996. Print.

Leibniz, G. W. *New Essays on Human Understanding.* Trans. and ed. by Peter Remnant and Jonathan Bennett. Cambridge, UK: Cambridge University Press, 1982. Print.

Levin, Harry. *The Myth of the Golden Age in the Renaissance.* Bloomington: Indiana University Press, 1969. Print.

López de Hoyos, Juan. *Real aparato, y suntuoso recibimiento con que Madrid (como casa y morada de su M.) recibio a la serenísima reyna D. Ana de A.* Madrid: ABACO, 1976. Print.

López Estrada, Francisco. *Los libros de pastores en la literatura española.* Madrid: Editorial Gredos, 1974. Print.

López Pinciano, Alonso. *Philosophia Antigua Poética.* Madrid: Instituto Cervantes, 1953. Print.

Lukács, Georg. *The Theory of the Novel*. Trans. Anna Bostock. Cambridge, MA: MIT Press, 1973. Print.

Lussky, Alfred Edwin. *Tieck's Romantic Irony: With Special Emphasis upon the Influence of Cervantes, Sterne, and Goethe*. Chapel Hill: University of North Carolina Press, 1932. Print.

Mancing, Howard. *The Cervantes Encyclopedia: A–K*. Westport, CT: Greenwood Press, 2003. Print.

Maravall, José Antonio. *Culture of the Baroque: Analysis of a Historical Structure*. Minneapolis: University of Minnesota Press, 1986. Print.

———. *Poder, honor y élites en el siglo XVII*. 1st ed. Madrid: Siglo Veintiuno de España. 1979. Print.

———. *Teatro y literatura en la sociedad barroca*. Madrid: Seminarios y Ediciones, 1972. Print.

———. *Velázquez y el espíritu de la modernidad*. Madrid: Alianza Editorial, 1987. Print.

Márquez Villanueva, Francisco. *"Menosprecio de corte y alabanza de aldea" (Valladolid, 1539) y el tema áulico en la obra de Fray Antonio de Guevara*. Santander: Universidad de Cantabria, 1998. Print.

Maslin Nir, Sarah. "Colbert's Super-Pac Raises More than $1 Million." Jan. 31, 2012, n.p. Accessed June 17, 2013, at http://thecaucus.blogs.nytimes.com/2012/01/31/colberts-super-pac-raises-more-than-1-million-dollars.

McCrory, Donald. *No Ordinary Man: The Life and Times of Miguel de Cervantes*. London: P. Owen, 2002. Print.

McKendrick, Melveena. *Cervantes*. Boston: Little, Brown, 1980. Print.

Montemayor, Jorge de. *Los siete libros de la Diana*. Ed. Francisco López Estrada. Madrid: Espasa Calpe, 1993. Print.

———. *The Diana*. Trans. and ed. RoseAnna M. Mueller. Lewiston, NY: E. Mellen Press, 1989. Print.

Moore, Steven. *The Novel: An Alternative History. 1600–1800*. New York/London: Bloomsbury, 2013. Print.

Nabokov, Vladimir. *Lectures on Don Quixote*. Ed. Fredson Bowers. San Diego, CA: Harcourt Brace Jovanovich, 1983. Print.

Nadler, Steven. "Descartes et Cervantes: Le malin génie et la folie de Don Quichotte." *Laval Théologique et Philosophique* 53, no. 3 (1997): 605–16. Print.

Nalle, Sara T. "Literacy and Culture in Early Modern Castile." *Past and Present* 125 (1989): 65–96. Print.

North, John David. *The Ambassadors' Secret: Holbein and the World of the Renaissance*. Rev. ed. New York: Hambledon and London, 2004. Print.

Nussbaum, Martha. *Cultivating Humanity*. Cambridge, MA: Harvard University Press, 1998. Print.

O'Connor, Thomas. "Is the Spanish *Comedia* a Metatheater?" *Hispanic Review* 43 (1975): 275–89. Print.

Orgel, Stephen. *Impersonations: The Performance of Gender in Shakespeare's England*. Cambridge, UK: Cambridge University Press, 1996. Print.

Orgel, Stephen, and Roy C. Strong. *Inigo Jones, the Theatre of the Stuart Court: Including the Complete Designs for Productions at Court for the Most Part in the Collection of the Duke of Devonshire Together with Their Texts and Historical Documentation*. London: Sotheby Parke-Bernet, 1973. Print.

Orr, H. Allen. "Awaiting a New Darwin." *New York Review of Books*, Feb. 7, 2013, n.p. Accessed June 17, 2013, at http://www.nybooks.com/articles/archives/2013/feb/07/awaiting-new-darwin/?pagination=false.

Ortega y Gasset, José. *Meditaciones del Quijote*. Madrid: Publicaciones de la Residencia de Estudiantes, 1914. Print.

Panofsky, Erwin. *The Life and Art of Albrecht Dürer*. Princeton, NJ: Princeton University Press, 1955. Print.

———. *Perspective as Symbolic Form*. New York: Zone Books, 1991. Print.

Parker, Geoffrey. *The Army of Flanders and the Spanish Road, 1567–1659: The Logistics of Spanish Victory and Defeat in the Low Countries' Wars*. Cambridge, UK: Cambridge University Press, 1972. Print.

———. *Europe in Crisis, 1598–1648*. 2nd ed. Oxford: Blackwell, 2001. Print.

Parr, James, and Lisa Vollendorf. "Introduction." *Approaches to Teaching Don Quixote*. New York: MLA, 2014, 1–32. Print.

Pascal, Blaise. "Pensées sur la religion et sur quelques autres sujets." N.d., n.p. Accessed June 8, 2013, www.ub.uni-freiburg.de/fileadmin/ub/referate/04/pascal/pensees.pdf.

Payne, Mark. *Theocritus and the Invention of Fiction*. Cambridge, UK: Cambridge University Press, 2007. Print.

Peterson, Mark A. *Galileo's Muse: Renaissance Mathematics and the Arts*. Cambridge, MA: Harvard University Press, 2011. Print.

Picón, V., A. Cascón, P. Flores, C. Gallardo, A. Sierra, and E. Torrego. "Introducción." *Teatro escolar latino del siglo XVI: La obra de Pedro Pablo de Acevedo*. Madrid: Ediciones Clásicas—UAM Ediciones, 1997, iv. Print.

Plato. *Complete Works*. Ed. John M. Cooper. Indianapolis, IN: Hackett Publishing, 1997. Print.

Ponce Hegenauer, Gabrielle Piedad. "Trissinian Tragedy, Cervantes, and *La Numancia*: Anonymous Traditions and Canonized Authors." *MLN* 126, no. 4 (2011): 709–37. Print.

Popkin, Richard, H. *The History of Scepticism from Erasmus to Spinoza*. Berkeley: University of California Press, 1979. Print.

Rabelais, François. *Gargantua and Pantagruel*. New York: Penguin, 1955. Print.

———. *Les cinq livres*. Paris: Librairie Générale Française, 1994. Print.

Radice, Mark A. *Opera in Context Essays on Historical Staging from the Late Renaissance to the Time of Puccini*. Portland, OR: Amadeus Press, 1998. Print.

Reed, Cory. "Cervantes and the Novelization of Drama." *Cervantes* 11, no. 1 (1991): 61–86. Print.

Rico, Francisco. *El texto del "Quijote": Preliminares a una ecdótica del Siglo de Oro*. Barcelona: Ediciones Destino, 2005. Print.

———. *The Spanish Picaresque Novel and the Point of View*. Trans. Charles Davis with Harry Sieber. Cambridge, UK: Cambridge University Press, 1969. Print.

Riley, E. C. *Cervantes's Theory of the Novel*. Oxford: Clarendon Press, 1962. Print.

Riley, Patrick. "The General Will Before Rousseau." *Political Theory* 6, no. 4 (1978): 485–516. Print.

Riquer, Martín de. *Cervantes, Passamonte y Avellaneda*. Barcelona: Sirmio, 1988. Print.

Rivers, Elias L. *Talking and Text: Essays on the Literature of Golden Age Spain*. Madrid: Juan de la Cuesta, 2009. Print.

Rodríguez, Juan Carlos. *Teoría e historia de la producción ideológica: Las primeras literaturas burguesas*. Madrid: Akal Universitaria, 1990. Print.

Rodríguez de Montalvo, Garci. *Amadís de Gaula*. Edited and annotated by Edwin B. Place. Madrid: Consejo Superior de Investigaciones Científicas, Instituto "Miguel de Cervantes," 1959–69. Print.

Rodríguez Salgado, M. J. "Christians, Civilized and Spanish: Multiple Identities in Sixteenth-Century Spain." *Transactions of the Royal Historical Society*. Vol. 8. Cambridge, UK: Cambridge University Press, 1998, 233–52. Print.

Rorty, Amélie. "The Psychology of Aristotelian Tragedy." In *Essays on Aristotle's Poetics*. Ed. Amélie Oksenberg Rorty. Princeton, NJ: Princeton University Press, 1992), 1–22. Print.

Rowland, Ingrid D. *Giordano Bruno: Philosopher/Heretic*. New York: Farrar, Straus and Giroux, 2008. Print.

Rupp, Stephen. *Heroic Forms: Cervantes and the Literature of War*. Toronto: University of Toronto Press, 2014. Print.

Russell, P. E. *Cervantes*. Oxford: Oxford University Press, 1985. Print.

Schlegel, Friedrich von. *Kritische Schriften*. Ed. Wolfdietrich Raschm. Munich: Carl Hansen Verlag, 1964. Print.

———. *Lectures on the History of Literature, Ancient and Modern*. Vols. 1 and 2. Philadelphia: Dobson and Son, 1818. Print.

Schmidt, Rachel. *Forms of Modernity*: Don Quixote *and Modern Theories of the Novel*. Toronto: University of Toronto Press, 2011. Print.

Schramm, Percy. *Las insignias de realeza en la Edad Media española*. Madrid: Instituto de Estudios Políticos, 1960. Print.

Sevilla Arroyo, Florencio, and A. Rey Hazas. "Introducción." In *Los baños de Argel*. In Cervantes, *Obra completa*, vol. 14. Madrid: Alianza Editorial, 1998. Print.

Shakespeare, William. *The Arden Shakespeare Complete Works*. Ed. Richard Proudfoot, Ann Thompson, and David Scott Kastan. Walton-on-Thames, UK: Thomas Nelson, 1998. Print.

Sieber, Harry. *The Picaresque*. London: Methuen, 1977. Print.

———. "The Romance of Chivalry in Spain." In *Romance: Generic Transformation from Chrétien de Troyes to Cervantes*. Ed. Kevin Brownlee. Hanover: Published for Dartmouth College by University Press of New England, 1985, 203–19. Print.

Sosa, Antonio de. *An Early Modern Dialogue with Islam: Antonio de Sosa's Topography of Algiers (1612)*. Ed. María Antonia Garcés. Trans. Diana de Armas Wilson. Notre Dame, IN: University of Notre Dame Press, 2011. Print.

Spadaccini, Nicholas. "Cervantes and the Question of Metafiction." *Vanderbilt e-Journal of Luso-Hispanic Studies* 2 (2005): n.p. Accessed Mar. 15, 2013, http://ejournals.library.vanderbilt.edu/ojs/index.php/lusohispanic/article/view/3176/1359.

———. "Writing for Reading." In El Saffar, Ruth S. *Critical Essays on Cervantes*. Boston, MA: G. K. Hall, 1986, 162–76. Print.

Spadaccini, Nicholas, and Jenaro Talens. *Through the Shattering Glass: Cervantes and the Self-Made World*. Minneapolis: University of Minnesota Press, 1993. Print.

Standage, Tom. *Writing on the Wall: Social Media, the First 2000 Years*. New York: Bloomsbury, 2013. Print.

Stephens, Walter. *Demon Lovers: Witchcraft, Sex, and the Crisis of Belief*. Chicago, IL: University of Chicago Press, 2002. Print.

Stoichita, Victor I. *The Self-Aware Image: An Insight into Early Modern Meta-painting*. Cambridge: Cambridge University Press, 1997. Print.

Strohschneider-Kohrs, Ingrid. *Die romantische Ironie in Theorie und Gestaltung*. Tübingen: Niemeyer: 1977. Print.

Suárez Figaredo, Enrique. *Cervantes, Figueroa, y el crimen de Avellaneda*. Barcelona: Ediciones Carena, 2004. Print.

Surtz, Ronald. *The Birth of a Theater: Dramatic Convention in the Spanish Theater from Juan del Encina to Lope de Vega*. Madrid: Castalia, 1979. Print.

Suskind, Ron. "Faith, Certainty and the Presidency of George W. Bush." *New York Times Magazine*. Oct. 17, 2004. Accessed June 21, 2013, http://www.nytimes.com/2004/10/17/magazine/17BUSH.html.

Tasso, Torquato. *Jerusalem Delivered*. Trans. and ed. Ralph Nash. Detroit, MI: Wayne State University Press, 1987. Print.

———. *La Gerusalemme liberata*. Ed. H. B. Cotterill. Oxford: Clarendon Press, 1875. Print.

Tomás y Valiente, Francisco. "La monarquía española del siglo XVII: El absolutismo combatido." *Historia de España, Vol XXV*. Madrid: Espasa-Calpe, 1982, 21–82. Print.

Trilling, Lionel. *Sincerity and Authenticity*. Cambridge, MA: Harvard University Press, 1972. Print.

Usunáriz Garayoa, José María. "Mentalidades y cultura." In *Historia de España en la edad moderna*. Ed. Alfredo Floristán. Barcelona: Ariel, 2004, 103–31. Print.

Vega Carpio, Felix Lope de. *Arte nuevo de hacer comedias*. Ed. Enrique García Santo-Tomás. 1st ed. Madrid: Cátedra, 2006. Print.

———. *Comedias*. Barcelona: Iberia, 1965. Print.

Vesely, Dalibor. *Architecture in the Age of Divided Representation: The Question of Creativity in the Shadow of Production*. Cambridge, MA: MIT Press, 2004. Print.

Vilanova, Antonio. *Erasmo y Cervantes*. Barcelona: Lumen, 1989. Print.

Watt, Ian P. *Myths of Modern Individualism: Faust, Don Quixote, Don Juan, Robinson Crusoe*. Cambridge, UK: Cambridge University Press, 1996. Print.

Wesley, Carlos. "The Joy of Reading Don Quixote." *Fidelio* 12, no. 3 (Fall 2003): n.p. Available at the Schiller Institute website, accessed Mar. 19, 2013, at http://www.schillerinstitute.org/fid_02-06/033_cervantes.html.

Wilde, Oscar. *The Artist as Critic: Critical Writings of Oscar Wilde*. Ed. Richard Ellmann. New York: Random House, 1969. Print.

Williams, Bernard Arthur Owen. *Descartes: The Project of Pure Enquiry.* London: Penguin Books, 1990. Print.

Williams, Michael. "Descartes's Transformation of the Skeptical Tradition." In Ed. Richard Bett. *The Cambridge Companion to Ancient Scepticism.* Cambridge, UK: Cambridge University Press, 2010. 288–313. Print.

Wilson, Diana de Armas. *Allegories of Love: Cervantes's* Persiles and Sigismunda. Princeton, NJ: Princeton University Press, 1991. Print.

———. "Uncanonical Narratives: Cervantes's Perversion of Pastoral." In Ruth el Saffar, ed. *Critical Essays on Cervantes.* Boston, MA: G. K. Hall, 1986, 180–210. Print.

Wilson, Gaye. "Spanish Language." In Thomas Jefferson's Monticello (website), Sept. 1998. Accessed Apr. 9, 2013, http://www.monticello.org/site/research-and-collections/spanish-language.

INDEX

NOTE: Page numbers in *italics* indicate a photograph or illustration. Page numbers followed by an *n* indicate a note on that page.

Acevedo, Pedro Pablo de, 41
Acquaviva, Giulio, 44, 51
"Age of the World Picture, The" (Heidegger), 198*n*24
Aikins, Matthieu, 87–88
Alcalá de Henares, Spain, xviii, 38–39
Alemán, Mateo, 142, 147, 155
Alfarache, Guzmán de (character in *Guzmán de Alfarache*), 142
Algiers, 70, 76–77, 96. *See also* Cervantes–captivity in Algiers
Allegory of the Cave (Plato), 176, 209*n*35
Alter, Robert, 204*n*25
Amadís/Beltenebros (character in *Amadis of Gaul*), 132
Amadís of Gaul (de Montalvo), 132
Ambrosio (character in *Don Quixote*), 131
Anselmo (character in *Don Quixote*), 134–35
Antonio (character in *The Diversion*), 111, 113
Arcadia (Sannazaro), 201*n*2
Aristotle, 7–8, 171, 191*n*13, 192*n*17
arts
   overview, xix
   emergence of individual perspectives, 81
   painting, 82, *82*, *83*, 83–84, 197*n*18, 198*n*19–22
   portraiture, 82–83
   See also literature; theater
As You Like It (Shakespeare), xxi

Auerbach, Erich, xiv
Austin, John, 106–7
Avellaneda, Alonso Fernández de, 168–69, 207*n*14
Aznar, José María, 61–62, 196*n*27

Baena, Julio, 205*n*29
Bagnios of Algiers, The (Cervantes), 86, 89
Bakhtin, Mikhail, 17
Barahona de Soto, Luis, 5
Beaumont, Francis, 18
Belica/Isabel (character in *Pedro de Urdemalas*), 114–15
Benjamin, Walter, 160
Berganza (dog in *Dogs' Colloquy*), 157–58
Bernstein, J. M., 209*n*38
Bertuch, Friedrich Justin, 175
Blanco de Paz, Juan, 90, 91
blood purity statute in Spain, 33–34, 35–36, 40, 193*n*19, 194*n*24
Bloom, Harold, xxiii, 163–64
Boccaccio, Giovanni, 12–13, 192*n*31, 192*n*33
books. *See* literature
Borges, Jorge Luis, 10
Botero, Giovanni, 62, 68, 196*n*28
Bragadino, Marcantonio, 53
Brunelleschi, Filippo, 81
Business of Algiers, The (Cervantes), 78, 79, 85–86, 89, 93, 98
Byrne, Susan, 195*n*21, 196*n*31

Cádiz, Spain, 139
Calderón de la Barca, Pedro, 36, 105
Camila (character in *Don Quixote*),
    134–35
Campuzano (character in *The Deceitful
    Marriage*), 156–57, 158
Camus, Albert, 21
Canavaggio, Jean, 201*n*38
Cancionero (Laínez), 122
Cancionero (López Maldonado), 31
"Captive's Tale, The" (Cervantes),
    78–79, 85, 88–90
Cardenio (character in *The Diversion*),
    111–13
Cardenio (Shakespeare and Fletcher),
    19
Carriazo, Diego de (character in *The
    Illustrious Kitchen Maid*),
    150–52
Cascardia, Anthony J., 195*n*18, 195*n*24
Castile and Aragon, *38*
Castillo, David, 196*n*27, 206*n* 37, *n*39,
    *n*40–41
Castillo, Moisés, 194*n*24,
Castro, Américo, xxiii, 205*n*32
Castro del Río, Spain, 146, 205*n*32
Celenza, Christopher, 190*n*16
censorship, 6–7, 11, 60, 101, 102–3
Cercas, Javier, 17–18
Cervantes, Andrea de (sister), 19–20, 39,
    135–36, 179
Cervantes, Andrés de (uncle), 39, 41
Cervantes, Constanza de (niece),
    19–20, 152
Cervantes, Juan de (grandfather),
    37–40, 41
Cervantes, Luisa de (sister), 39
Cervantes, Magdalena de (sister),
    19–20, 39, 135–36, 179
Cervantes, Miguel de
    ambivalence for war, 55–60
    and Aristotelian thought, 9
    assignment from Philip II in Northern
        Africa, 95–96

biographical information (*See below*)
and books, xxi, 4, 31, 191*n*21
bravery of, 54
captivity in Algiers (*See below*)
debt repayment program, 94
Erasmus's influence on, 25–26, 27,
    194*n*38
and Europe's political landscape, xviii,
    xix
injury to left hand, 51
letters of recommendation from
    military leaders, 66, 73
letter to Archbishop of Toledo, *4*
and Lope de Vega, 27
in Madrid as a young man, 31
personality/inner beauty, xxi, xxii,
    20–21, 45
petitions for employment, 95, 96–97,
    110, 139
poems for Philip II, 32, 43–44, 155,
    194*n*39
and politics, 42–43
and royal censor, 7
success of, xvi, xxii, 137–38,
    190*n*20
writing as means for dealing with
    personal pain, 84–86
writing style (*See below*)
Cervantes–biographical information
    ancestors and blood purity issues, 36,
        40
    autobiographical poem, 11–12
    childhood, 39, 40–43
    as commissary agent for the Spanish
        government, 145–47, 153
    convalescence, 65–66
    description of, 1–2, *2*
    duel and exile, xx, 44–45, 51
    excommunication, 146
    final years and death of, 179–80, 184,
        210*n*51
    financial and familial woes, 19–20
    jail time in Seville, 144–45, 147, 154–55,
        160–61, 168

malaria, 53–54
marriage of, 116, 122–24, 137, 161
in Naples, 52, 68–69
service in Catholic League, xx
in Urbina's company fighting Turks,
    51–55
Cervantes–captivity in Algiers
capture, 69–70
escape attempts, 72, 73–74, 90
freedom to move about, 72, 88
and Hasan Pasha, 71, 73–74, 79, 88,
    90–91
healing process, post-escape, 84–87,
    88–90, 198n27
and letters of recommendation from
    military leaders, 73, 77
pirates of Algiers, 69–70
ransom amount, 73, 91
rescue plan for Christian captives,
    71–73
return to Spain, 91–92, 93–94
Cervantes–writing style
overview, 183–84
balance of peace and war, 50, 56
characters and readers on same
    emotional plane, 26–27
characters in plays, 108–10
clash between ideals and reality, 57–58
disjunction between conventional roles
    and actual roles, 152, 153
empathy projected into characters, 26,
    80, 189–90n15
hypocrisy and dogma as tools, 27–28
identifying with his characters, 29, 56
intercalated tales, 203n40
irony, 43–44, 155
masks of characters vs. their internal
    feelings and emotions, 13–14
mirror/mirror analogy, 80
moral figures in plays, 100–101
narratives lead reader to question
    intent, 13–14
North African love intrigues, 85–87,
    88–90

perceptions and misperceptions of
    characters, 14–15
playing with boundaries of reality and
    fiction, 7
plays, 85–87, 93, 98–101, 107, 110–15,
    200n30
production of new image of the world
    while in the world as we know
    it, 200–201n37
prologue to Don Quixote, 26–28
reality vs. individual awareness of what
    is, 84
satire of war themes, 48–50, 56–57, 63,
    195n16, 195n18
treatment of history and poetry, 9–10
using characters to discuss plagiarism
    of Don Quixote, 169
Velázquez compared to, 84, 198n23–24
Cervantes, Rodrigo de (brother), 20, 52,
    65, 67, 69–70, 72
Cervantes, Rodrigo de (cousin), 41
Cervantes, Rodrigo de (father), 30–31,
    39–42, 138
Cervantes's Christian Romance
    (Forcione), 204n29
character creation
about, xvii
overview, xvii–xviii, xx–xxii
and catharsis, 8–9
characters and readers on same
    emotional plane, 26–27, 63
dogs in Dogs' Colloquy, 157–58
and experiencing the world from
    within and without, xix, 79–80
in journalism, 87–88
in plays, 108–10
three-dimensional characters, 150–52,
    205n25
transformation through, 89–90
Charles V, emperor of Spain, 23,
    32–36, 34
Chaucer, Geoffrey, 206–7n5
Childers, William, 205n29
chimeras, 178

chivalry novels, 132–39

chivalry, Quixote on, 177

Christians

The Business of Algiers about Christian captive, 79

and expulsion of Moriscos, 158–59

Genesius, in *True Pretense,* 107

Moorish woman's love for a Christian captive, 85, 88–90

Muslims compared to, 75, 76

Cipión (dog in *Dogs' Colloquy*), 157–58

Coleridge, Samuel Taylor, xvi

Colonna, Ascanio, 98

Control of the Imaginary (Costa Lima), 208n17, 208n20

conversos (converted Christians), 35, 37, 194n25

Córdoba, Spain, 37–38

Corral de Comedias, Almagro, Spain, 102

Corral de la Cruz, El, Madrid, 101–2

Corral del Principe, El, Madrid, 101–2

Cortina, Leonor de (mother), 31, 39, 94, 138, 153

Costa Lima, Luiz, 208n17, 208n20

Costanza (character in *The Illustrious Kitchen Maid*), 151–52

Council of the Indies, 96

Coxcomb, The (Fletcher and Beaumont), 18

Cristina (character in *The Diversion*), 111–13

critics of *Persiles,* 153, 205n29

Crooks, Esther, 210n42

Crusades, 47–48

Cuesta, Juan de la, 18

"Curious Impertinent, The" (Cervantes), 134–35

Cyprus, 53

Dalì Mamì, 70, 73

Decameron (Boccaccio), 12–13

Deceitful Marriage, The (Cervantes), 156–58

demon-caused illusions, 177–78, 210n43

Descartes, René, 172, 174, 176–78, 209n38, 209n35–36, 210n44

desengaño (disillusionment or disappointment), xix, xxi

Destruction of Numancia, The (Cervantes), 98, 100

Diana (de Montemayor), 117–18

Díaz Cervantes, María (aunt), 37

Díaz de Cervantes, Rodrigo (great grandfather), 37

Discourse on Method (Descartes), 177, 209n38

Diversion, The (Cervantes), 111–14, 201n38

Dogs' Colloquy, The (Cervantes), 19, 40–41, 125, 156

Don Quixote (Bertuch, trans.), 175

Don Quixote (Cervantes)

overview, 136–37

attempted book burning, 4–5

barber and magical helmet of Mambrino, 172–73

books in, xi, xvii–xviii, 4, 118–19, 132–33, 135

conflict between individual and society, 90, 199n33

criticism of, 160

Decartes's *Meditations* compared to, 176–77

defeat of the "Knight of the Mirrors," 13

exploration of golden age, 128–31

on expulsion of the Moriscos, 159–60, 206n38

galley slaves, 147–49

handmaidens laughing at Quixote, 13–14

as humorous book, 14, 15–16, 56

Maritornes as innkeeper's beautiful daughter, 15

pirated editions, 18

plagiarism, 168–69

on plays, 99

prologue, 26–27
puppet master with soothsaying
    monkey, 107–8, 109–10
success of, xvi, xxii–xxiii, 18–19, 165–66,
    168, 177, 190*n*20, 193*n*44,
    210*n*42
tavern-goers reveling in, xi–xv
test for equinoctial line, 14
"The Captive's Tale," 78–79, 85, 88–90
"The Curious Impertinent," 134–35
treatment of history and poetry, 9–10
See also specific characters
Don Quixote, Volume 2 (Cervantes)
barber's story of a madman, 63
discussion of intercalated tales, 203*n*40
publication of, 179
Quixote's encounter with Dulcinea,
    133–34
on reason of state and ways of
    governing, 59–60, 195*n*24
response to plagiarism, 168–69
and royal censor, 7
Drake, Sir Francis, 139
dualism between what can be doubted
    and what cannot, 174–75,
    176–77, 209*n*35–36
Dulcinea of Toboso (character in *Don
    Quixote*), 15, 132–34, 181–82
Dürer, Albrecht, 82, *82,* 197*n*18, 198*n*19
Dutch humanism, 42

Écija, Spain, 145–46
*Eight Comedies and Eight Interludes Never
    Performed Onstage* (Cervantes),
    42
Elicio (character in *La Galatea*), 120, 121,
    127–28, 202*n*5–121
Elizabeth, queen of England, 139
Elliott, J. H., xix
empathy and characterization, 26, 80,
    189*n*15
Enchiridion (Erasmus), 24
Enlightenment, 199*n*33
epic poems, 48

Erasmus, 23–26, 27, 35, 42, 194*n*38
erroneous attributions, 10–11
Escorial, The, 30
Esquivias, Spain, 116, 122–24, 153
Estefanía (character in *The Deceitful
    Marriage*), 156–57
Estrada, López, 201*n*2
Europe
    political power in, xviii, 62, 104–5,
        190*n*16, 200*n*22
    shift from feudal fiefdoms to nation-
        states, xviii
Exemplary Novellas (Cervantes), 11–12,
    205–6*n*32
expulsion of the Moriscos, 158–60,
    206*n*38
Ezpeleta, Gaspar de, 166–68

Fame (moral figure in *The Destruction of
    Numancia*), 100–101
Faulkner, William, 166
fiction
    and Aristotle's *poeisis* concept, 7–8
    breaking the boundaries set by society,
        84
    Cervantes's influence, 171–72
    clash between ideals and reality, 57–58
    connotations in Cervantes's time, xvi
    defining, xv, xvi, 86, 114–15
    and erroneous attributions, 10–11
    experiencing the world from within
        and without, xix, 79–80, 121–22
    fusing of essential elements, 87
    human experience of, xv–xvi, xvii,
        189*n*13, 189*n*15
    and journalism, 87–88
    liar's paradox, 86–87, 198*n*29
    moral standards, 206–7*n*5
    as natural fantasy, 11–12, 192*n*29
    pastoral novels, 201*n*2
    as picture of how we picture the
        world, 158
    questioning social reality, 131
    sentences that are true and false, 56

transformation of reality, 90
writer's goal, xvi–xvii
See also character creation; pastoral
    novels; truth
Fitzgerald, F. Scott, xv
Flaubert, Gustave, 207*n*10
Fletcher, John, 18
Forcione, Alban K., 192*n*33, 194*n*38,
    204*n*29
Forni, P. M., 192*n*31
Foucault, Michel, 198*n*21, 198*n*23–24,
    204*n*9
Frankfurt, Harry G., 210*n*44
Freud, Sigmund, 16
Friedman, Edward, 200–201*n*37
Frye, Northrop, 8–9

Gaitán, Juana, 122
Galatea (character in *La Galatea*), 120,
    121, 202*n*5–121
Galatea, La (Cervantes)
    overview, 120–21, 126, 202*n*5
    dedication to Colonna, 98
    poetry in, 77, 119–20, 127–28
    publication of, 78, 96, 137–38
    tributes to Silena, 68–69
Gálvez de Montalvo, Luis, 31
Garcés, María Antonia, 196*n*37, 197*n*13
Gardner, John, 189*n*13
Gassett, Ortega y, 211*n*59
Genesius (character in *True Pretense*), 107
Genius of Spain (Giménez Caballero), 160
Gil, Juan, 90–91
Giménez Caballero, Ernesto, 160
Glass Licentiate, The (Cervantes), 63–65,
    110–11, 196*n*37
golden age and lost golden age, 124–26,
    128–31, 202*n*20, 202*n*26
Great Gatsby, The (Fitzgerald), xv
Great Stage of the World, The (Calderón
    de la Barca), 105
Greenblatt, Stephen, 190*n*17
Grossman, Edith, 178
Gumbrecht, Hans Ulrich, 208*n*17

Gutenberg, Johannes, 5
Gutiérrez de Castro, Tomás, 41, 145
Guzmán de Alfarache (Alemán), 142,
    147

hamartia (error in judgment), 8, 191*n*15
Hamete, Cide (character in *Don Quixote*,
    Volume 2), 183, 203*n*40
Hasan Pasha, 71, 73–76, 79, 88, 90–91
Hegel, Georg Wilhelm Friedrich, 175,
    176
Heidegger, Martin, 198*n*24
Hemingway, Ernest, 91–92
Herrera y Tordesillas, Antonio de, 6, 60,
    62
Herrero García, Miguel, 197*n*43
Historia de los Reyes Godos (Castillo), 61
history books
    Aristotle's views on, 7–8, 171
    Cervantes's fun with poetry and, 9–10,
        21
    conveying a personally meaningful
        truth through, 86
    goal of, 17
Homer, 65
honor
    country living vs. city living, 124
    degeneration of, 125–26, 202*n*20
    importance of, in Spain, 36
    meaning of, in Spanish society, 103–4
    and Quixote, 134
    as theme of new theater, 103
    as universal patrimony of the soul,
        105
Horace (Roman), xvi
human experience
    awareness of deception, 120
    constancy, 208*n*20
    emotions related to our experience of
        other people, 80–81
    enchanter or demon-caused illusions,
        177–78, 210*n*43
    experiencing the world from within
        and without, xix, 79–80, 107

exploration of, 120–21
of fiction, xv–xvi, xvii, 189*n*13, 189*n*15
imagination, 165
leaders' use of media, xviii
of love, 126–28, 134–35
masking and revealing emotions, 121,
    164
of meditation, 174
multiple perspectives, xix
paradox of acting/believing a
    statement knowing it's false,
    106–10
playing roles for one another, 111
soul's struggle to know the world, 175
See also reality; truth
hypocrisy and dogma as tools, 27–28

ideals vs. reality, 57–58, 65
Iliad, The (Homer), 65
illusions, demon-caused, 177–78, 210*n*43
Illustrious Kitchen Maid, The (Cervantes),
    150–52, 205*n*25
Index Librorum Prohibitorum
    (Inquisition), 6
*Ingenious Gentleman Don Quixote of La
    Mancha. See Don Quixote*
    (Cervantes)
Inquisition, 6, 35, 144–45
International Day of the Book, 178–79
Islam. *See* Muslims
Italian Renaissance, 42

Jefferson, Thomas, 166
Jerusalem Delivered (Tasso), 48
Jesuit school, Seville, 40–42
Jiménez, Fernando, 33–34
journalism and fiction, 87–88
Journey to Parnassus (Cervantes), 11–12,
    51, 68–69, 98–99, 110
Juan of Austria, 52, 66–67, 73

Keen, Suzanne, 189–90*n*15
Knausgaard, Karl Ove, 84
"Knight of the Mirrors" battle, 13

Laínez, Pedro, 31, 52, 68, 122
Landy, Joshua, 206*n*5
Lauso (character in *La Galatea*), 68–69,
    126–28
Lazarillo de Tormes (author unknown),
    142, 204*n*4
leaders of sixteenth century
    censorship of printed material, 6–7
    Erasmus's beliefs about, 24
    political power in Europe, xviii, 62,
        104–5, 190*n*16, 200*n*22
    use of theater to maintain order, 104–5,
        200*n*22
    See also entries beginning with "Philip"
Leibniz, Gottfried, 165
Lemos, count of, 180
Lepanto, Battle of, 53–55, 57
liar's paradox, 86–87, 198*n*29
Life magazine, xxiii
linear perspective for paintings, 81
Lisandro (character in *La Galatea*), 120,
    202*n*5
literacy rates in Spain, 3–4, 48, 118
literature
    overview, 165
    in Algiers, 77–78
    attempted book burning in *Don
        Quixote*, 4–5
    and Cervantes, xxi, 31, 191*n*21
    country life themes, 124, 128
    International Day of the Book, 178–79
    and literacy rates in Spain, 3–4, 48, 118
    mass market for, 5–6
    and Quixote, xi, xvii–xviii, 4, 118–19,
        132–33, 135
    as reader's opportunity to digest a
        work slowly, 110
    romance novels, 8–9, 120–22, 126–28
    See also history books; picaresque
        books
López de Hoyos, Juan, 31
López Maldonado, Gabriel, 31
Lotario (character in *Don Quixote*),
    134–35

Lucretius, 190n17

Machiavelli, Niccolò, 62
Madrid, Spain, 29–31, 101–2, 154, 168,
        179–80
Malik, Abd al-, 88
Manual of the Christian Knight
        (Erasmus), 23
Maravall, José Antonio, 198n20
Marcela (character in *Don Quixote*),
        130–31
Marcela (character in *The Diversion*), 111,
        112
Marín, Astrana, 194n39
Maritornes (character in *Don Quixote*), 15
Márquez Torres (character in *Don
        Quixote, Volume 2*), 7, 191n11
Márquez Torres, Francisco, 7, 191n11
Martí, Juan, 142
Martín de Córdoba, Don, 95
Martínez Siliceo, Juan, 33–34
Mary, queen of Scotland, 139
Meditations (Descartes), 172, 174,
        176–78, 209n38, 209n35–36,
        210n44
Mediterranean map, 54
Menard, 10
Menard, Pierre, 10
Méndez, Simón, 168
Mendoza, Martín de, 37–38
Meninas, Las (Velázquez), 83, 83–84
Messina, Sicily, 52–53
Montalvo, Rodríguez de, 132
Montemayor, Jorge de, 117–18
Moorish woman's love for a Christian
        captive, 85, 88–90
moral figures in Cervantes's plays,
        100–101
moral given in *The Diversion*, 113
moral standards for fiction, 206–7n5
moral truth, 11
Morato, Agi (character in "The Captive's
        Tale"), 88, 89–90
More, Thomas, 24–25

Moriscos, 9, 36, 122, 158–60, 194n25
Murad, Hajji, 88
Murad, Zahara, 88–89
Muslims
        overview, 75–76
        and Cervantes, 89–90, 96
        invaders of Spain, 61–62
        and Koran, 77–78
        laws governing women, 88
        Moorish woman's love for a Christian
                captive, 85, 88–90
        Moriscos as converted Muslims, 9, 36,
                122, 158–60, 194n25
        Ottoman/Turkish Empire, 51–57,
                66–67, 75–77
        spread of, 67
My Struggle (Knausgaard), 84

Nabokov, Vladimir, 203n40
Naples, Italy, 52, 68–69
Naval Battle, The (Cervantes), 98
*New Art of Writing Plays in Our Time,
        The* (Lope), 99, 103
Nicholas of Cusa, bishop, 24
Nobel Institute, xxiii
North African love intrigues, 85–87
Northern Africa, Cervantes in, 95–96.
        See also Cervantes–captivity in
        Algiers
"Nun's Priest's Tale, The" (Chaucer),
        206–7n5
Nussbaum, Martha, 189–90n15

Ocaña (character in *The Diversion*), 111,
        113
O'Connor, Thomas, 200–201n37
Oedipus the King (Sophocles), 8
Of Learned Ignorance (Nicholas of Cusa),
        24
On Naïve and Sentimental Poetry
        (Schiller), 175
On the Nature of Things (Lucretius),
        190n17
oral tradition for storytelling, 5, 47–48

Ottoman/Turkish Empire, 51–57, 66–67, 75–77

Panofsky, Erwin, 197n18
Panza, Sancho (character in *Don Quixote*)
    acceptance of Quixote's dream, 181–82
    compassion of, xiii–xiv
    effect on perception of Quixote, xiii
    as extension of Cervantes's own struggles, xxii
    and Quixote's narrative of two armies, 48–49
    and Quixote's obsession with Dulcinea, 132–34
    relationship with Quixote, xiv, 14–15, 181–82
    relieving himself in presence of Quixote, 16–17
    on returning home, 181
    on Spaniards' battle cry, 32
Parker, Geoffrey, 55
Pasamonte, Ginés de (character in *Don Quixote*), 148–49
Pascal, Blaise, 209n38
Pasha, Mustafa, 53
pastoral novels
    overview, 117–18, 201n2
    attraction of country life, 124–25, 128
    Diana, 117–18
    golden age and lost golden age, 124–26, 128–31, 202n20, 202n26
    romances, 120–22, 126–28
    See also *Galatea, La*
pastor de Fílida, El (Gálvez de Montalvo), 31
Payne, Mark, 189n14
Pedro de Urdemalas (Cervantes), 114–15
Periandro (character in *The Trials of Persiles and Sigismunda*), 152–53
Persiles and Sigismunda (Cervantes), 152–53, 180
Petronius Arbiter, Gaius, 105
Phenomenology of Spirit (Hegel), 175

Philip II, king of Spain
    and annexation of Portugal, 94–95
    bankruptcies, 55, 67, 196n40
    and blood purity statutes, 35–36
    Cervantes's poems for, 32, 43–44, 155, 194n39
    death of, 155
    eminent power of, 104–5, 200n22
    moving court from Toledo to Madrid, 29–30
    petitioners, including Cervantes, 95
    planning invasion of Britain, 139
    as ruler, 33
    and Turkish Empire, 52, 66
    wife's death in childbirth, 31–32
Philip III, king of Spain, 3, 14, 36, 60, 158, 161
Philip IV, king of Spain, *83*, 83–84
Philosophy of the Novel, The (Bernstein), 209n38
picaresque books (roguery)
    overview, 143
    Cervantes's interpretation of, 155–56, 160, 205–6n32–33
    The Deceitful Marriage, 156–58
    The Dogs' Colloquy, 19, 40–41, 125, 156
    Don Quixote rogue, Ginés, 148–49
    Guzmán de Alfarache, 142
    Illustrious Kitchen Maid, The (Cervantes), 150–52, 205n25
    Lazarillo de Tormes, 142
    Rinconete and Cortadillo (Cervantes), 149–50, 204n21
    The Trials of Persiles and Sigismunda, 152–53, 180
pirated copies of *Don Quixote*, 18
pirates of Algiers, 69–70, 76. *See also* Cervantes–captivity in Algiers
Pius V, Pope, 66
plague, 161
playwrights, 97
Poetics, The (Aristotle), 7–8, 171
poetry

overview, xvi
Aristotle's views on, 7–8, 192n17
Bloom's defense of, 163–64
Cervantes on, 119
Cervantes's fun with history and, 9–10, 21
Cervantes's poems for Philip II, 32, 43–44, 155, 194n39
epic poems, 48
in *La Galatea*, 77, 119–20, 127–28
losing readers to chivalry and pastoral, 119
moral benefits of, 11, 17
pastoral themes, 124–25
political power in Europe, xviii, 62, 104–5, 190n16, 200n22
Ponce Hegenauer, Gabrielle, 199n13
Popkin, Richard H., 209n38
portraiture, 82–83
Portugal, Philip II's annexation of, 94–95
Praise of Folly, The (Erasmus), 24–25
print industry
and censorship, 6–7, 11
and epic poems, 48
invention of the press, 5, 6
and original manuscripts, 3–4
scribes, 5–6, 48
Promontorio (character in *Journey to Parnassus*), 68–69
puppet master with soothsaying monkey, 107–8, 109–10
purity statute in Spain, 33–34, 35–36, 40, 193n19, 194n24

Quiñones (character in *The Diversion*), 111
Quixote (character in *Don Quixote*)
advice to King Philip, 59–60
battle of two great armies, 49–50
and books, xi, xvii–xviii, 4
and boy who is beaten for corroborating Quixote's tale, 136
change wrought by Sancho Panza, xiii–xv
on deathbed, 180, 182–83

as extension of Cervantes's own struggles, xxii
inability to suspend disbelief, 108–10
on mechanization of war, 58
relationship with Sancho Panza, xiv, 14–15, 50, 181–82
on soldier's life, 57
on superiority of arms over letters, 56, 57, 59, 196n31
tavern-goers ridicule of, xv
on theater, 105–6

Rabelais, François, 16
Ramadan Pasha, 73–74
reality
defining, 171–72, 173
desire vs., 180
embrace of illusions with real consequences, 134–35
fiction as questioning social reality, 131
fiction for transformation of, 90
ideals vs., 57–58, 65
imagined realities as if they were true, 87
individual awareness of what is vs., 84
in plays, 106–8, 112–13
psychology of masking and revealing emotions, 121, 164
of war, 68
See also truth
religion
and blood purity statute in Spain, 33–34, 35–36, 40, 193n19, 194n24
Cervantes's excommunication, 146
control of grain, 146
conversos, 35, 37, 194n25
Crusades, 47–48
Erasmus on, 24
Inquisition, 144–45
in Spain, 23
and "world is a stage" concept, 104–5
Renaissance humanism, 42

Revolt of the Comuneros (municipal governments), 35
Rico, Francisco, 204n4
Ricote (character in *Don Quixote*), 159–60
Riley, E. C., 192n29
Rinaldo, Fra (character in *Decameron*), 12–13
Rinconete and Cortadillo (Cervantes), 149–50, 204n21
Robles, Francisco de, 18, 27, 161–62, 168
Rodaja, Tomás (character in *The Glass Licentiate*), 63–65, 196n37
roguery. *See* picaresque literature
rogues, 152
Rojas, Ana Franca de, 115–16, 161
"Romance de Sayavedra, El" (ballad), 78
romance novels, 8–9, 120–22, 126–28.
    See also *Galatea, La*
Rome, Italy, 51, 152–53
Rueda, Lope de, 42
Rupp, Stephen, 195n16

Saavedra (Cervantes's character post-Algiers), 78, 79
Saavedra, Cervantes's personal use of, 3, 78, 85
Saavedra, Isabel de (daughter of Cervantes)
    acrimony toward Cervantes, 180
    birth of, 115–16
    childhood, 138
    dalliances with men, 19–20, 134, 168
    death of mother of, 161
    and Saavedra name, 78, 116
Sainz del Águila, Diego, 168
Salazar, Catalina de (wife), 116, 122–24, 161
Sánchez de Córdoba, Pedro, 31
Sannazaro, Jacopo, 201n2
Sayavedra (Cervantes's character post-Algiers), 74, 78, 79
Sayavedra, Don Fernando (character in *The Valiant Spaniard*), 79

Sayavedra, Juan de, 78
scatological references, 15–17
Schelling, Friedrich, 174, 175–76
Schiller, Friedrich, 124, 175
Schlegel, Friedrich, 174–75
science, sixteenth-century evolution of, xix
Scipio (character in *The Destruction of Numancia*), 100–101
sea battles, 57, 58
Sebastian, king of Portugal, 94
Seville, Spain
    black plague, 161
    Cervantes in, 40–42, 138–39, 160–61
    Cervantes's jail time, 144–45, 147, 154–55, 160–61, 168
    crime in, 143
    Jesuit school, 40–41
Shakespeare, William, xxi, 19, 210n48
Shelton, Thomas, 18
Sieber, Harry, 205–6n32–33
sieges, 57–58
Silena (character in *La Galatea*), 68–69, 126–28
Sir Marvellous Crackjoke: The Wonderful Adventures of Don Quixote and Sancho Panza Adapted for Youthful Readers, v, 167
Soldato, Giannizzero, 75
Sophocles, 8
Sosa, Antonio de, 77
Spadaccini, Nicholas, 200–201n37, 200n30
"Spagnuolo nobile" (Veccellio), 103
Spain
    age of disillusionment, xix
    blood purity statute, 33–34, 35–36, 40, 193n19, 194n24
    Cervantes's love for, 32
    Charles V, 23, 32–36, 34, 35
    conquest of the Americas, 194n24
    contrived history, 60–62, 195n25, 196n27, 196n31
    coup attempt of February 23, 1981, 17

cultural influence Europe, 18
expansion of empire, 32–36
expulsion of the Moriscos, 158–60,
    206*n*38
financial challenges, 55, 67, 101,
    146–47, 196*n*40
Honor concept, 36
humanism in, 42
map of, *170*
Muslim invaders, 61–62
Philip III, 3, 14, 36, 60, 158, 161
Philip IV, *83*, 83–84
and pirates of Algiers, 76, 159
religious dogma, 23
state power, 23, 104–5, 200*n*22
war with Turks, 55–59, 60, 66
worldwide military commitments,
    67
See also Philip II; *specific cities and towns*
Spanish government, Cervantes as
    commissary agent for, 145–47,
    153
Spanish Picaresque, The (Rico), 204*n*4
Spanish society
    and captives returning from
        Algiers, 91
    Cervantes's loss of faith in, 155
    conflict between individual and
        society, 90, 199*n*33
    criminality and traditional justice,
        143, 204*n*7, 204*n*9
    exploring in plays, 112–13
    literacy rates, 3–4, 48, 118
    noble patronage system, 98
    orders or estate divisions, 197*n*8
    and purity ideology, 36, 40, 42
    rise of the modern state, 144–45,
        204*n*10
    state support of powerful and
        privileged, 59
    and theater, 97–98, 101–2
    See also honor
Stephens, Walter, 210*n*43
Sun Also Rises, The (Hemingway), 91–92

Swerve, The (Greenblatt), 190*n*17

Taléns, Jenaro, 200–201*n*37
Tasso, Torquato, 48
tavern goers listening to book readings,
    xi–xv, 118–19
Tears of Angelica, The (Barahona de
    Soto), 5
theater
    overview, 97–98
    applying techniques of perspective,
        81–82
    Cervantes on, in *Don Quixote*,
        105–6
    Cervantes's plays, 85–87, 93, 98–101,
        107, 110–15, 200*n*30
    Cervantes's success, 115–16
    experiencing the world from within
        and without, xix, 100–101,
        107
    monarchy's use of, 104–6, 200*n*22
    regulations and censors, 101, 102–3
    sixteenth century evolution of,
        xviii–xix
    stage within the stage, 106–7
    Lope's effect on, 99, 102–3
    women as actresses, 115
    "world is a stage" concept, 104–5, 111
    three-dimensional characters, 150–52,
        205*n*25
Through the Shattering Glass (Spadaccini
    and Taléns), 200–201*n*37
Tieck, Ludwig, 175
Timbrio (character in *La Galatea*), 128
Titian, 33, *34*
Toledo, Spain, 33–34, 139
Topography and General History of Algiers
    (de Sosa), 77
Torrentes (character in *The Diversion*),
    112
tragedy, Aristotle on, 8, 191*n*13, 192*n*17
Trials of Persiles and Sigismunda, The
    (Cervantes), 152–53, 180
Trilling, Lionel, 164

True Pretense (Lope), 107
Truman Show syndrome, 209*n*37
truth
    as conveyed by fiction, 17–18, 25–26,
        64–65, 86–87, 198*n*29
    direct relation between individuals
        and, 24
    dualism between what can be doubted
        and what cannot, 174–75,
        176–77, 209*n*35–36
    and God, 170, 208*n*17
    history conveying a truth about
        ourselves, 86, 171
    moral truth, 11
    in poetry or fiction, 8, 9–12, 21, 171
    presenting risky truths in fiction, 24,
        27–28, 43–44
    suspending judgment of truth or
        falsity, 170, 208*n*17
    See also reality
Tunis, Tunisia, 66–67
Turkish Empire, 51–57, 66–67, 75–77

Uluç-Ali, 51, 75, 96
UNESCO, 178–79
Urbina, Diego de, 52, 54
Urbina, Juan de, 168
Urdemalas, Pedro de/Nicolás de los
        Ríos (character in *Pedro de
        Urdemalas*), 114–15
Utopia (More), 24

Valdivia, Diego de (character in *The Glass
        Licentiate*), 64
Valiant Spaniard, The (Cervantes), 79
Valladolid, Spain, 1–3, 19, 39–40, 161
Vázquez, Mateo, 95
Vega, Garcilaso de la, 98
Vega Carpio, Félix Lope de, 27, 97,
        99–100, 102–3, 107, 199*n*7

Velasco, Bernardino de, 159–60
Velázquez, Diego, *83*, 83–84,
        198*n*20–22
Venice and Turkish Empire, 51–52
Viedma (character in "The Captive's
        Tale"), 88–90
Vineti, Jean, 210*n*43

war
    Cervantes's satire of, 56–57, 195*n*16,
        195*n*18
    commoners' obligation to billet
        troops, 104
    in Europe, 32, 193*n*18
    in Flanders, 67
    in *The Glass Licentiate,* 63–65
    and honor, 103
    against Muslims, 53–55, 56–59, 60–62,
        67
    and pirates of Algiers, 69–70, 76
    reality of, 68
    and Tunis, 66–67
    with Turks, 95–96
warships, 57, 58
Western Canon, The (Bloom), 163–64
Wilde, Oscar, 163, 164
Williams, Bernard, 209*n*36
women
    as actresses, 115
    ideal image of, 134–35
    and Islam, 88
    literacy rate, 118
    plight of exploitation, 135–36
"Writing for Reading" (Spadaccini),
        200*n*30
writing style. *See* Cervantes–writing
    style

Zoraida (character in "The Captive's
        Tale"), 88–90

A NOTE ON THE AUTHOR

William Egginton is the Andrew W. Mellon Professor in the Humanities at the Johns Hopkins University. He is the author of six highly praised academic books: *In Defense of Religious Moderation, How the World Became a Stage, Perversity and Ethics, A Wrinkle in History, The Philosopher's Desire*, and *The Theater of Truth*. He is also coeditor of *Thinking with Borges* and *The Pragmatic Turn in Philosophy*. Egginton writes for the digital salon *Arcade*, published by Stanford University, and has written for the *New York Times, The European* magazine, and other popular publications. He lives in Baltimore, Maryland, and in Vienna, Austria, with his wife, Bernadette Wegenstein, and their three children.